"Distinct, but Inseparable"

"Distinct, but Inseparable"

Thomas Aquinas and
John Wesley on
Grace and Nature

Jaesung Ryu

Peter Lang

Oxford · Bern · Berlin · Bruxelles · New York · Wien

Bibliographic information published by Die Deutsche Nationalbibliothek.
Die Deutsche Nationalbibliothek lists this publication in the Deutsche
Nationalbibliografie; detailed bibliographic data is available on the Internet at
http://dnb.d-nb.de.

A catalogue record for this book is available from the British Library.

Library of Congress Cataloging-in-Publication Data

Names: Ryu, Jaesung, 1983- author. Title: "Distinct, but inseparable" : Thomas
Aquinas and John Wesley on   grace and nature / Jaesung Ryu. Description:
Oxford ; New York : PeterLang, 2022. | Includes   bibliographical references
and index. Identifiers: LCCN 2022006303 (print) | LCCN 2022006304 (ebook)
| ISBN   9781800798021 (paperback) | ISBN 9781800798038 (ebook) | ISBN
9781800798045 (epub) Subjects: LCSH: Grace (Theology) | Sin, Original. |
Fall of man. | Thomas,   Aquinas, Saint, 1225?-1274 | Wesley, John, 1703-1791
Classification: LCC BT761.3 .R98 2022 (print) | LCC BT761.3 (ebook) | DDC
234--dc23/eng/20220314 LC record available at https://lccn.loc.gov/2022006303
LC ebook record available at https://lccn.loc.gov/2022006304

Cover design by Brian Melville for Peter Lang.

ISBN   978-1-80079-802-1-(print)
ISBN   978-1-80079-803-8-(ePDF)
ISBN   978-1-80079-804-5-(ePUB)

© Peter Lang Group AG 2022

Published by Peter Lang Ltd, International Academic Publishers,
Oxford, United Kingdom
oxford@peterlang.com, www.peterlang.com

This publication has been peer reviewed.

Soar we now where Christ hath led,
Following our exalted Head,
Made like Him, like Him we rise,
Ours the cross, the grave, the skies.
Alleluia!

– Charles Wesley

Contents

CHAPTER 6

Abstract

"Distinct, but Inseparable" explores the ways in which the Christian doctrine of grace and nature is understood and deployed in the works of John Wesley and Thomas Aquinas. Given the extremely broad nature of this topic, we consider principally their mature works on grace and nature: the *Sermons* for Wesley and the *Summa Theologiae Prima Secundae* for Thomas. We then limit the nature and scope of this book to comparing Wesley's and Thomas' accounts of the cooperation between grace and nature in bringing about the salvation of humanity.

Regarding the structure, we divide this book into six chapters. Chapter 1 reads and analyzes Augustine's work, which underlies the formation of Wesley's and Thomas' theology of grace and nature. Chapter 2 turns to Wesley. Here we focus on Wesley's doctrine of nature and see how Wesley critically and constructively integrates Augustine's doctrine of nature into the eighteenth-century English context where Calvinism and Arminianism collide. Chapter 3 considers Wesley's doctrine of grace, with a particular focus on how Wesley associates God's dynamic grace with human 'responseable' nature. Chapter 4 turns to Thomas. Here we focus on Thomas' doctrine of nature, which constitutes a more optimistic model of human nature than Augustine's. Chapter 5 then proceeds to Thomas' doctrine of grace, where we provide an analysis that shows how Thomas connects grace and nature within a dynamic and cooperative framework. Finally, we come to consider Wesley's and Thomas' teachings about grace and nature from a comparative point of view. By way of comparison, Chapter 6 offers an impressive number of parallels between Wesley's and Thomas's teachings about grace and nature.

Our parallel reading of Wesley and Thomas establishes a whole array of theological continuities between their doctrines of grace and nature. This in turn provides a wealth of surprising clues needed to resolve the complex and subtle theological relationship between Wesley and Thomas – and, more specifically, the only problem that Wesleyans and Catholics share little and has gone into their separate ways: the soteriological problem of grace and nature.

Abbreviations

The following abbreviations of primary SOURCES will be used throughout:

Augustine of Hippo[1]

Contra Faustum	(Reply to Faustus the Manichaean)
Contra Julianus	(Against Julian)[2]
Confessiones	(Confessions)
Contra litteras Petiliani	(Answer to the Letters of Petilian, Bishop of Cirta)
Contra mendacium	(Against Lying)
De correptione et gratia	(On Rebuke and Grace)
De dono perseverantiae	(On the Gift of Perseverance)
De gestis Pelagii	(On the Proceedings of Pelagius)
De gratia et libero arbitrio	(On Grace and Free Will)
De libero arbitrio	(On Free Choice of The Will)
De natura et gratia	(On Nature and Grace)
De peccatorum meritis et remissione et de baptismo parvulorum	(On Merits and Remission of Sin, and Infant Baptism)
De perfectione iustitiae hominis	(On Man's Perfection in Righteousness)
De praedestinatione sanctorum	(On the Predestination of the Saints)
De spiritu et littera	(On the Spirit and the Letter)

---

1   All texts (except his *unfinished* writings *Against Julian*) from *Nicene and Post-Nicene Fathers*, Series 1, ed. Philip Schaff (Grand Rapids, MI: Christian Classics Ethereal Library, 2001); available online at the Christian Classics Ethereal Library <https://ccel.org/fathers>.

2   Augustine, *Against Julian*, trans. Matthew A. Schuhmacher (Washington, DC: The Catholic University of America Press, 2004).

De symbolo ad catechumenos   (On the Creed: A Sermon to
                                                Catechumens)
Enchiridion   (Enchiridion)

John Wesley

OT Notes   *Explanatory Notes Upon the Old
                                                Testament*[3]
NT Notes   *Explanatory Notes Upon the New
                                                Testament*[4]
Works   *The Bicentennial Edition of the Works of
                                                John Wesley*[5]
Works (Albany)   *The Works of John Wesley*[6]
Works (Jackson)   *The Works of the Rev. John Wesley, A.M.*[7]

3   John Wesley, *Explanatory Notes on the Old Testament*, 3 vols. (Bristol,
    UK: Pine, 1765).

4   John Wesley, *Explanatory Notes Upon the New Testament*, 3rd edn., 2 vols. (Bristol,
    UK: Graham & Pine, 1760–2). These Notes have been reprinted multiple times,
    but the content is the same.

5   John Wesley, *The Bicentennial Edition of the Works of John Wesley*, 35 vols., gen.
    ed. Frank Baker, Richard P. Heitzenrater, and Randy L. Maddox (Nashville,
    TN: Abingdon Press, 1984–). All future references to *The Bicentennial Edition
    of the Works of John Wesley* will be listed as *Works* followed only by the Volume
    number and section.

6   John Wesley, *The Works of John Wesley*, 3rd edn., 14 vols. (Albany, OR: Ages
    Software, 1997). All future references to *The Works of John Wesley* will be listed as
    Works (Albany) followed only by the Volume number and section.

7   John Wesley, *The Works of the Rev. John Wesley, A.M.*, 3rd edn., 14 vols., ed. Thomas
    Jackson (London: J. Mason, 1829–31). All future references to *The Works of the Rev.
    John Wesley, A.M.* will be listed as *Works* (Jackson) followed only by the Volume
    number and section.

Works (New York)   *The Works of Rev. John Wesley*[8]
Letters (Telford)   *The Letters of the Rev. John Wesley, A.M.*[9]

Thomas Aquinas

QDM   *Disputed Questions on Evil [De Malo]*[10]
DV   *Disputed Questions on Truth [De Veritate]*[11]
SCG   *Summa Contra Gentiles*[12]
Scriptum   *Scriptum Super Sententiis*[13]
ST   *Summa Theologiae*[14]
ES   *Emitte Spiritum*[15]

---

8   John Wesley, *The Works of Rev. John Wesley: Containing Tracts and Letters on Various Subjects*, 10 vols. (New York: J. & J. Harper, 1827). All future references to *The Works of Rev. John Wesley: Containing Tracts and Letters on Various Subjects* will be listed as *Works* (New York) followed only by the Volume number and section.

9   John Wesley, *The Letters of the Rev. John Wesley, A.M.*, 8 vols., ed. John Telford (London: Epworth, 1931). All future references to *The Letters of the Rev. John Wesley, A.M.* will be listed as *Works* (Telford) followed only by the Volume number and section.

10 Thomas Aquinas, *Disputed Questions on Evil [De Malo]*, ed. Brian Davies, trans. Richard J. Regan (Oxford: Oxford University Press, 2003).

11 Thomas Aquinas, *Disputed Questions on Truth [De Veritate]*, 3 vols., trans. Robert W. Mulligan, James V. McGlynn, and Robert W. Schmidt (Chicago: Henry Regnery Company, 1952–4).

12 Thomas Aquinas, *Summa Contra Gentiles*, 5 vols., ed. and trans. Anton C. Pegis, James F. Anderson, Vernon J. Bourke, and Charles J. O'Neil (Garden City, NY: Image Books, 1955–7).

13 Thomas Aquinas, *Scriptum Super Sententiis: An Index of Authorities Cited*, ed. Charles H. Lohr (Avebury, NY: Fordham University Press, 1980).

14 Thomas Aquinas, *Summa Theologiae*, 5 vols., trans. The Fathers of the English Dominican Province (New York: Benziger Brothers, 1947).

15 Thomas Aquinas, "Emitte Spiritum," *Faith and Reason* 30, nos. 1–2 (2005): 108–39.

Introduction

"All have sinned and fall short of the glory of God, and all are justified freely by his grace through the redemption that came by Christ Jesus" (Rom. 3:23–4). This book investigates the ways in which this Christian doctrine of grace and nature is understood and deployed in the works of John Wesley and Thomas Aquinas. What kind of beings are humans? In what state of nature was the first humanity? And what effect did original sin have on it? How does the grace from God relate to that fallen nature? What does it mean for human beings to live a life of grace? These are the central questions *"Distinct, but Inseparable"* brings to its reading of Wesley and Thomas.

Why Wesley and Thomas? First, while each of them is a great theologian in his own right, they are more than simply individual theologians. In both cases, their theological achievements sparked a whole tradition of theological reflection, and in each of these traditions (and in the ecclesial communions they are embedded in), Wesley and Thomas are considered *authorities*. One might, of course, be tempted to assume that the authoritative theologians of separate religious traditions must inevitably be opposed to each other. A reading, sensitive to the similarities or theological contacts between thinkers, can overturn this assumption, and it is my conviction that a careful, non-oppositional reading of Wesley and Thomas as *theologians* can help us overcome this presumption and lay the foundation for ecumenical dialogue.

Another reason for a parallel reading Wesley and Thomas is that their writings are surprisingly compatible. Both were faithful commentators of Scripture, wrestling with God's words concerning grace and nature.[16]

16 One will be able to see what Wesley refers to in Chapters 2 and 3, and what Thomas refers to in Chapters 4 and 5. But one can also confirm Wesley as a biblical commentator from his *Explanatory Notes upon the Old and the New Testaments* – and from Scott J. Jones, *John Wesley's Conception and Use of Scripture* (Nashville, TN: Kingswood Books, 1995). For Thomas as a biblical commentator, see Thomas

Both also wrote theological synthesis, driven by a desire to overcome any simple bifurcation of grace and nature. These parallels mean that even if they deal with the root cause of the problem differently and employ different conceptual tools to solve it – as will become clear in the following chapters – there are points of contact between the two: Wesley's positive assessment of human nature can be instantly compared with that of Thomas, and the place and function of a particular doctrine in Wesley's *Sermons*, for example, can be compared with that of the same doctrine in Thomas' *Summa Theologiae*.

Finally, there is the paradoxical value of Wesley's unfamiliarity with medieval scholasticism. Wesley was convinced that early Methodists could have an ecumenical friendship with Catholics and Protestants, and therefore pleaded in his "Letter to a Roman Catholic":

> If we cannot as yet think alike in all things, at least we may love alike ... Let us resolve, first, not to hurt one another ... secondly ... to speak nothing harsh or unkind of each other ... thirdly ... to harbor no unkindly thought, no unfriendly temper ... fourthly, endeavor to help each other on in whatever we are agreed leads to the Kingdom. So far as we can, let us always rejoice to strengthen each other's hands in God.[17]

Weinandy, Daniel Keating, and John Yocum, eds., *Aquinas on Scripture: An Introduction to His Biblical Commentaries* (London: T&T Clark, 2005).

17   Wesley, "Letter to a Roman Catholic," in *Works* (Jackson) 10, §16–7; quoted from Randy L. Maddox, ed., *Rethinking Wesley's Theology for Contemporary Methodism* (Nashville, TN: Kingswood Books, 1998), 140–1. The same sentiment was echoed in his sermon "On Schism," though this time the tone was somewhat admonitory: "It is evil in itself. To separate ourselves from a body of living Christian, with whom we were before united, is a grievous breach of *the law of love*. It is the nature of love to unite us together; and the greater the love, the stricter the union. And while this continues in its strength, nothing can divide those whom love has united. It is only when our love grows could, that we can think of separating from our brethren. And this is certainly the case with any who willingly separate from their Christian brethren. The pretenses for separation may be innumerable, but want of love is always the real cause; otherwise they would still hold the unity of the Spirit in the bound of peace. It is therefore contrary to *all those commands of God*, wherein brotherly love is enjoined: To that of St. Paul, 'Let brotherly love continue:' – that of St. John, 'My beloved children, love one another;' – and especially to that of our blessed Master, '*This is my commandment, That ye love on another, as I have loved you*' Yea, 'By this,' saith he, 'shall all men know that ye are my disciples, if ye love

He did show some signs of familiarity with late medieval theology in his two masterpieces, *A Father Appeal to Men of Reason and Religion, Part I–III* and the 50 volumes of *The Christian Library*.[18] It is true, however, that Wesley was largely ignorant of its finer details. Moreover, he was not without prejudice against scholastic theology,[19] but his distance from the details of scholastic theology means that he is capable, perhaps without realizing, of affirming the theses of Catholic theology and even replicating its scholastic logic. So Wesley is described at times (and without too much exaggeration) as a carefully nuanced Catholic theologian.[20] Part of the reason for this is, of course, the fact that Wesley continued to rely on the same biblical and patristic sources that nourished high scholastic theologians: principally the Apostle Paul and the fourth-century Latin Father Augustine of Hippo (354–430 CE). Wesley and Thomas are therefore far from the growing prejudice of today that separates Catholicism and Protestantism, and close enough to each other with respect to their sources, for an ecumenical exchange to take place between them.[21]

one another.'" Clearly, as confirmed in these two documents, Wesley enunciated an important ecumenical principle, that we are characterized to practice love for our religious others. Albert C. Outler, ed., *The Works of John Wesley*, Vol. 3 (Nashville, TN: Abingdon Press, 1984), 64.

18 In these two masterpieces, one can see that Wesley immersed himself not only in the early Church Fathers but also in the works of five French and three Spanish Roman Catholic mystics, namely, Pascal, Brother Lawrence, Fenelon, Mme Guyon, Mme Bourignon, John of Avila, Lopez, and Molinos. See also Frank Whaling, ed., *John and Charles Wesley: Selected Prayers, Hymns, Journal Notes, Sermons, Letters, and Treatises*, Classics in American Spirituality (New York: Paulist Press, 1981), 8–12.

19 In his "To the Reader" (from the first volume of *The Arminian Magazine*) Wesley names Thomas Aquinas, but in a negative tone – as one of the "patrons of particular redemption" (§9). It would seem that, had Wesley spent more time with Thomas, he would not have been so rash in his appraisal. An excellent example of how Wesley resonates with Arminius' theological anthropology (and thus potentially with that of scholastic theology) is Vern A. Hannah, "Original Sin and Sanctification: A Problem for Wesleyans," in *Wesleyan Theological Journal* 18, no. 2 (Fall 1983): See 47–53.

20 See Daniel Castelo, *Embodying Wesley's Catholic Spirit* (Eugene, OR: Pickwick, 2017).

21 In this respect, it would not be surprising that later Wesley founded a monthly magazine called the *Arminian Magazine* and further separated his theological view

Why, then, the doctrine of grace and nature? Why was it chosen as a topic for comparison? The topic was chosen because in the doctrine of grace and nature more than anywhere else the essence of Christian theology is encapsulated. However, since a great many of the mysteries of the Christian faith are considered under the category of grace and nature, it has a fairly extensive scope, which in turn enables us to limit the scope of our research – we are not comparing the entirety of Wesley's doctrine of God and *imago Dei* with that of Thomas. But it enables us also to touch on an ambitiously wide range of *theo*-logical and *anthropo*-logical *loci*.

The next reason for choosing this particular topic is that recent research on Wesley and Thomas has brought new insights into their treatment of grace and nature. For the last half century, Wesleyan theology has been trying to find a real Wesley, an "unaccommodated" Wesley who refuses on principle to align himself with any current systems.[22] In this process, many Wesleyans have identified that Wesley had disrupted denominational boundaries.[23] They also have experienced an eirenic exchange of Wesley's theology with that of Eastern Christianity and, more recently, with that of Western Catholicism by a rediscovery of the dynamic relationship between grace and nature in Wesley.[24] Similarly, recent work on Thomas have

of grace and nature from that of Calvinist pastors in the early Methodist circles and then tied it to a non-Calvinist system sympathetic to Roman Catholics in general and Arminius (or Thomas) in particular. One is encouraged to confirm this theological shift of Wesley from Leon O. Hynson, "Original Sin as Privation: An Inquiry into a Theology of Sin and Sanctification," *Wesleyan Theological Journal* 22, no. 2 (Fall 1987): 65–83.

22   Fred Sanders, *Wesley on the Christian Life: The Heart Renewed in Love* (Wheaton, IL: Crossway, 2013), 17.

23   For a more detailed discussion of his intellectual diversity across various Christian traditions, see Sarah H. Lancaster, "Current Debates over Wesley's Legacy among His Progeny," in Randy L. Maddox and Jason E. Vickers, eds., *The Cambridge Companion to John Wesley* (New York: Cambridge University Press, 2010).

24   "Recent Dissertations in Wesley Studies: Randy L. Maddox [Last Updated: January 19, 2018] – PDF," accessed January 19, 2018, <http://religiondocbox.com/Christianity/70251723-Recent-dissertations-in-wesley-studies-randy-l-maddox-last-updated-january-19-2018.html>. Another note worth mentioning here is that there are national/regional dialogues between Wesleyans and Catholics. These remarkable conversations have been held so far in England, the United States, New

reaffirmed the participational-metaphysical link between divine and human actions in his writings, thereby making the case for a discovery which has cast a new light, an ecumenically styled virtue into his doctrine of grace and nature.[25] In light of these reassessments of Wesley and Thomas, a new comparative reading seems timely.

Such attempts at a joint reading of Wesley and Thomas are, in fact, relatively rare. In this regard, the WMC-Catholic dialogue has raised the need for a comparative study focusing on grace and nature.[26] In recent

Zealand, and Australia. They have produced a number of convergence statements regarding grace and nature. Of particular note are *Mary: Mother of the Lord* (Great Britain, 1995) and *Through Divine Love: The Church in Each Place and All Places* (USA, 2006), both of which share a common interest in comparing and converging Wesleyan and Catholic understandings of Marian doctrine and devotion – whose content and future prospects seem quite radical and even provocative in consideration of the Protestant position (including Wesleyans of all shades) on prayers to the Virgin Mary and of saints. Other notable examples include *Interchurch Marriages* (Australia, 1999) and *The Mission of the Church* (Australia, 2008), which deal in depth with their common beliefs and pastoral concerns about true and apostolic ministries and sacramental means of grace. W. Gibson, P. S. Forsaith and M. Wellings, eds., *The Ashgate Research Companion to World Methodism* (UK: Ashgate, 2013), 129.

25 D. Stephen Long compares Thomas to Wesley through this dynamically relational understanding of grace and nature in *John Wesley's Moral Theology: The Quest for God and Goodness* (Nashville, TN: Kingswood Books, 2005), especially 174–202. See also Edgardo Colón-Emeric, who has proposed a dialogue with a focus on the theme of perfection in *Wesley, Aquinas, and Christian Perfection: An Ecumenical Dialogue* (Waco, TX: Baylor University Press, 2009).

26 The WMC-Catholic dialogue took place in 1967 after World War II. The ecumenical dialogue, which marks its 53rd anniversary in 2020 this year, has set up a joint agenda every five years and conducted a series of comparative studies on it. The cumulative effect of this study is to document a set of differentiated convergences drawn by both parties on the agenda in the form of a report. For the past 53 years, the WMC-Catholic dialogue has documented a total of 10 reports: (1) Denver Report (1971); (2) Dublin Report (1976); (3) Honolulu Report (1981); (4) Nairobi Report (1986); (5) Singapore Report (1991); (6) Rio Report (1996); (7) Brighton Report (2001); (8) Seoul Report (2006); (9) Durban Report (2011); and (10) Houston Report (2016). Of these 10 reports, the sixth report (Rio Report) deals with matters of revelation and faith. But since the question of revelation and faith is fundamentally a matter of the relationship between grace and nature, between

decades, perhaps thanks in part to the works of D. Stephen Long and Edgardo Colón-Emeric, such needs have been addressed to some extent[27]; and both sides have seen that the Houston Report produces a preliminary consensus that Wesleyans and Catholics can reach a mutual agreement on the supernatural nature of grace and the humanity's ability to respond to it.[28] My purpose is to contribute to this conversation, setting out to uncover the deeper theological compatibility between Wesley's and Thomas' doctrines of grace and nature.

Since both Wesley and Thomas are extraordinarily prolific, it will be necessary to limit the focus of this book to some of their writings. We will therefore consider principally their mature works on grace and nature: the *Sermons* for Wesley and the *Summa Theologiae Prima Secundae* for Thomas. However, as it becomes necessary to further clarify or complement what is found in those mature works, we will make additional references to other books as well, specifically Wesley's *Letters* and *Explanatory Notes upon the Old and the New Testaments* and Thomas' *De Veritate* and *Summa Contra Gentiles*.

Finally, given the extremely broad nature of this topic, it may be useful to mention which aspects of this theme will actually not be explored in this project. Both Wesley and Thomas, for example, entered into disputed questions concerning pure nature and were open to consider the possibility of nature existing with merely a partial element of grace.[29] For this

God's initiative self-manifestation in history through the means of grace and (hu) man's graced response to that divine initiative, the report appeals to the undertaking of a joint study on the doctrine of grace and nature. "The Word of Life: A Statement on Revelation and Faith – PDF," accessed December 10, 2019, <http://www.vatican.va/roman_curia/pontifical_councils/chrstuni/meth-council-docs/rc_pc_chrstuni_doc_19951115_word-life-rio_en.html>.

27   Cf. fn. 10.

28   "The Call to Holiness: From Glory to Glory – PDF," accessed December 20, 2019, <http://worldmethodistconference.com/wp-content/uploads/2016/01/The-Call-to-Holiness-Final-copy-28062016.pdf>.

29   Wesley, "On Working Out Our Own Salvation," in *Works* 3, III.4: "Everyone has some measure of that light [i.e., prevenient grace], some faint glimmering ray, which sooner or later, more or less, enlightens every man that cometh into the world." And again in this same sermon, he adds: "No man [and woman] living is entirely destitute of … natural conscience," a gift of God's supernatural grace. Thomas, *De*

book, however, we set this question aside and limit ourselves to comparing Wesley's and Thomas' accounts of the cooperation between grace and nature in bringing about the salvation of humanity.

With all these limiting factors in mind, we proceed to an outline of this book. Since both Wesley and Thomas have retrieved (if not literally) many themes of Augustinian theology, our first chapter will seek to carefully read Augustine's writings on grace and nature. However, such a task is particularly challenging, given the fact that Augustine's views on the subject develop and even change over the course of his life. For this chapter we will not therefore consider the whole of Augustine's work, but only those from 398 CE onwards.[30] The reason for this, of course, is that we can receive from these later works a hermeneutic lens suitable to articulate and present the discussion of grace and nature in the following chapters.

Having established a common theological foundation, we turn to Part I, "Wesleyan Tradition: John Wesley and His View of Grace and Nature." Our first part is divided into two chapters, "John Wesley on Sin and Nature" and "John Wesley on Grace." First in the former chapter we will explore how Wesley is approaching the doctrine of sin and nature. As Wesley failed to organize his thoughts about sin and nature in a systematic way, our goal in this chapter is to establish a systematic framework for our topic. Then in the latter chapter we turn our attention to Wesley's

Malo, q.5, a.15, ad.1 and *De Veritate*, q.27, a.2. And see also *ST* I, q.23, a.1: "The end towards which created things are directed by God is twofold. One end exceeds all proportion and faculty of created nature, and this end is life eternal, which consists in seeing God, which is above the nature of every creature, as shown above (I:12:4). The other end, however, is proportionate to created nature, and to this created being can attain according to the power of its nature." For a brief synthesis of Wesley's teaching on this notion of pure nature, see Umphrey Lee, *John Wesley and Modern Religion* (Nashville, TN: Cokesbury Press, 1936), 124–5; and of Thomas', see Andrew Dean Swafford, *Nature and Grace: A New Approach to Thomistic Ressourcement* (Eugene, OR: Pickwick Publications, 2015), 37–41.

30 From this point on, Augustine shifts his main target from the fatalist Manicheans to the Pelagians (e.g., Pelagius, Caelestius, and Julian of Eclanum), and in earnest he refines and develops his doctrine of grace and nature. Susan Ashbrook Harvey and David G. Hunter, eds., *The Oxford Handbook of Early Christian Studies* (Oxford: Oxford University Press, 2008), 263.

doctrine of grace, specifically to what Wesley relied on as a viable alternative to divine predestination and human self-determination. The purpose here is to read and present how Wesley maintains our God-imaged liberty alongside the efficacy of grace.

In Part II, "Catholic Tradition: Thomas Aquinas and His View of Grace and Nature," we turn our attention to Thomas Aquinas. Divided into "Thomas Aquinas on Sin and Nature" and "Thomas Aquinas on Grace," this second part begins with an investigation into Thomas' understanding of sin and nature. His view of sin and nature, like Wesley's, emphasizes human dignity, authentic human autonomy, and moral responsibility. Our goal in this chapter is to provide a clear glimpse of Thomas' original thinking on sin and nature. Next we move on to "Thomas Aquinas on Grace." In this latter chapter we explore how Thomas came to understand the general nature of grace. Then we go through a sequence of four groups that Thomas considered in his treatise on grace: (1) the necessity of grace, (2) the essence of grace, (3) the division of grace, and (4) the cause and effects of grace. The purpose here is to carefully read Thomas' mature theology of grace and then organize/provide it into an easy-to-understand framework.

Finally, we turn to concluding our work. In this finale, we reaffirm the points of each chapter in turn and organize what is compatible between Wesley's and Thomas' teachings on grace and nature. Our comparison of Wesley and Thomas then shows that none of them fall into either divine predestination or human self-determination but makes the case for an ever-present dialectic of cooperation. The role of human nature is no inversely proportional to grace; rather, the greater the presence of divine grace, the greater human freedom and response.

My study, therefore, is ultimately a comparative study investigating how Wesley and Thomas develop a distinctive understanding of the relationship between grace and nature. But I need to elaborate this brief explanation to help understand the significance of this comparative study, and for this, I need to start the explanation with reference to the Second Vatican Council.

Generally speaking, major changes and contradictions have occurred in modern Catholic theology before and after the Second Vatican Council. The biggest contributors to this change and contradiction were Henry de Lubac, Karl Rahner, Yves Congar, and Hans Urs von Balthasar. De Lubac,

Rahner, Congar, and Balthasar are often regarded as *nouvelle* theologians, and one of the significant contributions they have made to Catholicism is the greater participation of Catholic theology in the ecumenical movement.

Indeed, it was after the Second Vatican Council that the ecumenical exchange of Catholic traditions with non-Catholic traditions became prominent. The Wesleyan tradition I belong to was no exception from here. For it was at this juncture that many Wesleyans have begun to pursue ecumenical dialogue with non-Methodist traditions under the auspices of the WMC. Therefore, it can be said that it was only after the Second Vatican Council that our (Wesleyan) efforts to communicate with Catholics, and vice versa, have come to fruition.

In the last five decades, Christian scholars from both traditions have attempted various theological studies on a variety of topics to achieve an ecumenical unity in faith, mission, and sacramental life: pneumatology, ecclesiology, apostolic tradition, revelation and faith, episcopal/pastoral order and authority, and theological anthropology.[31] However, according to my review, these attempts have not yet been deep enough to fully address the issues of grace and nature. In other words, these two church traditions have not yet been shared enough to realize the formation of a deeper understanding of the other and the constructive suggestion of a new understanding of one's own tradition in relation to the other.

To fill this inadequacy, I adopt Wesley, whose life and teachings become the norm and standard of Wesleyan theology, and develop (especially in the last chapter) a conversation between his theological ideas and those of Thomas who represents one of the important theological pillars of the Catholic tradition. In this conversation, my focus is on the grace-nature debate that Wesleyans and Catholics have failed to dig deeper in their recent ecumenical dialogue/research. In other words, I aim to reprocess the doctrine of grace and nature in the process of de-abstraction (i.e., reading, analysis, and synthesis), to the extent that my parallel reading of Wesley and Thomas could possibly help both Wesleyans and Catholics to see farther, embrace more, and exchange deeper of what they have already shared

---

31   See *Synthesis: Together in Holiness – 40 Years of Methodist and Roman Catholic Dialogue* (Lake Junaluska, NC: The World Methodist Council, 2010).

with each other on the issue of grace and nature. The significance of my study, therefore, lies in putting this "further" treatment in academia for the first time. More specifically, this book hopes to recast the Wesleyan and Catholic grace-nature conceptions into an ecumenically styled and mutually complementary framework.

CHAPTER I

St. Augustine and the Pelagian Controversy

The scriptural basis for grace and nature includes the story of Adam and Eve in Genesis and the teachings of Jesus or the Apostle Paul, who commented on the creation accounts in Genesis in the New Testament. Not only that, but it can also be traced from *either* some extracanonical Jewish writings,[1] some later books of the Old Testament,[2] *or* some early Christian writings that describe the Fall in metaphysical terms.[3] But a more systematic form of this teaching on grace and nature finds its historical origin in the fourth-century Latin Father Augustine of Hippo (354–430 CE). Augustine is a very important figure in Western theology, and his writings on the grace-nature debate play a significant role in Western Christian tradition as they have become a theological norm or interpretive criterion.

This chapter seeks to present Augustine's theology as a hermeneutic lens to articulate and present discussion of grace and nature in subsequent chapters. Such a task is particularly challenging, given the fact that Augustine's views on the subject develop and even change over the course of his life. In light of the teachings that Augustine seeks to refute,

---

1   "O Adam, what have you done?" Ezra asks, "For though it was you who sinned, the fall was not yours alone, but ours also who are your descendants (4 Ezra 7:118)." In Ezra, along with other extracanonical Jewish writings like the Book of Jubilees, 2 Enoch, and 2 Baruch, one can see that the story of Adam and Eve is interpreted as referring to a historical rupture that occurred in the distant past of humanity.

2   "From a woman sin had its beginning, and because of her we all die" (Sir. 25:24), says Sirach. Likewise, the Book of Wisdom gives some complementary readings of Genesis by claiming that God created humans for incorruption, "but through the devil's envy death entered the world" (Wis. 2:24).

3   For further introduction to the teachings of early Christian fathers on grace and nature, see Matthew Knell, *Sin, Grace, and Free Will, Vol. 1: A Historical Survey of Christian Thought* (Cambridge: James Clarke, 2017).

one can distinguish an early Augustine and a late Augustine. In his early teaching about grace and nature, as represented in such writings as the *Contra Faustum* or *De libero arbitrio*, Augustine gives a fairly positive assessment of humanity against the Manichean fatalist (or dualist) idea.[4] But this is overturned in his later writings, as if something modified his entire position. The main culprit behind this change in Augustine was Pelagius, who developed a strongly optimistic view of humanity by references to characters like Enoch in the Bible.[5] For this early English (Anglo-Saxon,

4 In 22.22 of *Contra Faustum*, Augustine engages with a Manichean view of sin that removes responsibility from humanity by creating being of evil that is the root of all sin. This is not quoted here due to issues of space, but it is worth reading, so the reader is encouraged to go back to the original text and read this topic more deeply. Another text that shows Augustine's positive assessment of humanity against Manicheanism is *De libero arbitrio*. In that text, Augustine makes a statement that expresses how optimistic an opinion of human will that he has: "Therefore you see that, as it seems, it is in the constitution of our will that we are able to enjoy or to be lacking in so great and such a true good. For what is so much in the will as that will itself? Indeed, whoever has a good will, that which he has is preferred more than all rule in the world and all desires of the flesh. But whoever does not have it is certainly lacking in that thing which is more excellent than all the goods that are not in our power, which the will alone can give through itself." Augustine, *De libero arbitrio*, 1.12.

5 "It is certain," says Pelagius, "that in the earliest age Adam and Eve, and Cain and Abel their sons, are mentioned as being the only four persons then in being. Eve sinned – the Scripture distinctly says so much; Adam also transgressed, as the same Scripture does not fail to inform us; while it affords us an equally clear testimony that Cain also sinned: and of all these it not only mentions the sins, but also indicates the character of their sins. Now if Abel had likewise sinned, Scripture would without doubt have said so. But it has not said so, therefore he committed no sin; nay, it even shows him to have been righteous. What we read, therefore, let us believe; and what we do not read, let us deem it wicked to add." Augustine, *De natura et gratia*, 44. To further solidify his positive sketch of Christian anthropology while supporting the possibility of a person's sinless life, Pelagius also enumerates those men "who not only lived without sin, but are described as having led holy lives – Abel, Enoch, Melchizedek, Abraham, Isaac, Jacob, Joshua the Son of Nun, Phinehas, Samuel, Nathan, Elijah, Joseph, Elisha, Micaiah, Daniel, Hananiah, Azariah, Mishael, Mordecai, Simeon, Joseph to whom the Virgin Mary was espoused, John." And he adds the names of some women – "Deborah, Anna the mother of Samuel, Judith, Esther, the other Anna, daughter of Phanuel, Elisabeth,

perhaps) Christian ascetic, divine grace is an external aid to human nature, since this allows responsibility for sin and the response to God's salvation to be placed with humans against any sense of Manichean determinism. It is in this changing context, against Pelagius, that Augustine wrote his later writings on grace and nature: *Enchiridion, De spiritu et littera, De natura et gratia, De gratia et libero arbitrio, De correptione et gratia, De praedestinatione sanctorum*, and *De dono perseverantiae*. There is therefore a considerable shift in emphasis between the two stages.[6] With this shift in mind, and in order to carry out its specific task, which will later be used as a taxonomy of this book, this first chapter will look at his work from 398 CE onwards – instead of the one up to the point when Augustine sent a letter to Simplicianus in 397 CE, indicating that his primary target was shifted from the fatalist Manicheans to the Pelagians (e.g., Pelagius, Caelestius, and Julian of Eclanum).[7] And the discussion will proceed as follows: It will first explore, as Augustine did, the nature and effects of sin and evil in nature. It will then move to grace and free will, recognizing that Augustine sees divine grace as dialectically opposed to free will, instead of dynamically penetrating into – and thus cooperating with – it.[8]

and also the mother of our Lord and Saviour, for of her," he says, "we must needs allow that her piety had no sin in it." Augustine, *De natura et gratia*, 42.

6   According to Burn, there is considerable change and even development in orientation after *To Simplicianus*. And he claims that the change does not express a harmonious development of previous principles, but a fundamental replacement by their contraries. J. Patout Burns, *The Development of Augustine's Doctrine of Operative Grace* (Paris: Études Augustiniennes, 1980), 8–9; 183–8. Just like Burns, James Wetzel also insists that Augustine's later doctrines of grace and predestination call into question his early view of humanity. According to Wetzel, Augustine's early commitment to "voluntary willing" is incongruent with his later allowance for "involuntary sin." James Wetzel, *Augustine and the Limits of Virtue* (Cambridge: Cambridge University Press, 1992), 97.

7   Susan Ashbrook Harvey and David G. Hunter, eds., *The Oxford Handbook of Early Christian Studies* (Oxford: Oxford University Press, 2008), 263.

8   This can only provide an indicative, rather than an exhaustive, presentation of Augustine's work in this particular subject – so the reader is, as always, encouraged to go back to the original texts for a fuller examination of Augustine's developing thought. But the presentation here will not be illegit in serving the purpose of this

The Nature and Effects of Sin and Evil in Nature

The clearest definition of sin and evil can be found in *Enchiridion*. In Chapter 11 of his *Enchiridion*, Augustine uses medicine as an analogy and sets out to make a case that evil is the opposite, a privation of all that God has created:

> For what is that which we call evil but the absence of good? In the bodies of animals, disease and wounds mean nothing but the absence of health; for when a cure is effected, that does not mean that the evils which were present – namely, the diseases and wounds – go away from the body and dwell elsewhere: they altogether cease to exist; for the wound or disease is not a substance, but a defect in the fleshly substance – the flesh itself being a substance, and therefore something good, of which those evils – that is, privations of the good which we call health – are accidents. Just in the same way, what are called vices in the soul are nothing but the privations of natural good.[9]

This argument continues a few chapters later in the same book, where Augustine states that all being is good, and therefore all evil is a defect, a detraction from being: "Every being, even if it be a defective one, in so far as it is a being is good, and in so far as it is defective is evil."[10] As these two quotes show, sin is not a substance for Augustine.[11] It is something like a desire or "concupiscence" (in Augustine's words).[12] He separates it

very first chapter, that is, in providing a means whereby the subsequent chapters of this book can readily categorize their subject matters.

9   Augustine, *Enchiridion*, 11.
10   Ibid., 13.
11   See also a passage from the *Confessiones* that answers the question Augustine asks himself about what sin is: "And I inquired what iniquity was, and ascertained it not to be a substance, but a perversion of the will, bent aside from Thee [God]." Augustine, *Confessiones*, 7.16.22.
12   For Augustine, sin is "concupiscence," which means in its root Latin form a desire. He sees that human nature has been corrupted since the Fall of Adam and Eve, and that the innate condition of humanity has been chained to sinful tendencies: "Concupiscence, ... which remains in the members of this body of death, is born with infants ... [and it] is left for the struggle [of their lives]." Augustine, *De peccatorum meritis et remissione et de baptismo parvulorum*, 2.4.

from all that God has created and renders it something by which one comes into play a culpable misrelation to God and the things that God has made. The same point is made in his other works. In Chapter 22 of *De natura et gratia*, Augustine writes:

> Since, then, we have already learned that sin is not a substance, do we not consider, not to mention any other example, that not to eat is also not a substance? Because such abstinence is withdrawal from a substance, inasmuch as food is a substance. To abstain, then, from food is not a substance; and yet the substance of our body, if it does altogether abstain from food, so languishes, is so impaired by broken health, is so exhausted of strength, so weakened and broken with very weariness, that even if it be in any way able to continue alive, it is hardly capable of being restored to the use of that food, by abstaining from which it became so corrupted and injured. In the same way sin is not a substance; but God is a substance, yea the height of substance and only true sustenance of the reasonable creature.[13]

In Chapter 16 of the Book 7 of *Confessiones*, Augustine continues to make the same point:

> And I inquired what iniquity was, and ascertained it not to be a substance, but a perversion of the will, bent aside from Thee, O God, the Supreme Substance, towards these lower things, and casting out its bowels, and swelling outwardly.[14]

In opposition to the Manichean view, which holds that there are two opposing, eternal, and self-existent principles of good and evil, Augustine introduces his definition of sin and evil, which claims that evil is the opposite of the good that comes from God. It is in essence a privation. It does not have any substance or final reality of its own. Thus, in light of these two quotes, along with those that come from *Enchiridion*, one can make a conclusion that the Augustinian definition of sin and evil is primarily, if not exhaustively, viewed as a distortion of what is true, as a perversion of something positive: "I knew not that evil was naught but a privation of good, until in the end it ceases altogether to be."[15]

---

13   Augustine, *De natura et gratia*, 22.
14   Augustine, *Confessiones*, 7.16.22.
15   Ibid., 3.7.12.

This then leads us to a bundle of questions concerning what constitutes a sin. Augustine contrasts sins with errors. The sin he seeks to grasp
is not a mistake one makes involuntarily when he or she does not sense
the truth.[16] It is something more complicated, subtle, and willful in nature
than that which one might be unknowingly doing (e.g., calling a "smooth"
object "rough" by mistake). To clarify *what* constitutes a sin, Augustine
looks further at "ignorance" in Chapter 81 of his *Enchiridion*:

> There are two causes that lead to sin: either we do not yet know our duty, or we do
> not perform the duty that we know. The former is the sin of ignorance, the latter
> of weakness. Now against these it is our duty to struggle; but we shall certainly be
> beaten in the fight, unless we are helped by God, not only to see our duty, but also,
> when we clearly see it, to make the love of righteousness stronger in us than the love
> of earthly things, the eager longing after which, or the fear of losing which, leads
> us with our eyes open into known sin. In the latter case we are not only sinners, for
> we are so even when we err through ignorance, but we are also transgressors of the
> law; for we leave undone what we know we ought to do, and we do what we know
> we ought not to do.[17]

This perspective is evident in his other work, *De gratia et libero arbitrio*.
Augustine repeats:

> It is one thing to be ignorant, and another thing to be unwilling to know ... But
> even the ignorance, which is not theirs who refuse to know, but theirs who are, as
> it were, simply ignorant, does not so far excuse any one as to exempt him from the
> punishment of eternal fire, though his failure to believe has been the result of his
> not having at all heard what he should believe; but probably only so far as to miti-
> gate his punishment.[18]

On the question of whether the act committed in ignorance is a sin, the
two quotes above show that Augustine sees it as sin. One thing to note,
however, is that there is some slight mitigation in comparison with sins of
ignorance and weakness. The point at which such mitigation is surfaced
to the fore is the presence of will. In other words, sin is a problem of the

16   Augustine, *Enchiridion*, 20–1.
17   Ibid., 81.
18   Augustine, *De gratia et libero arbitrio*, 5.

will: "[Our] free will is the cause of our doing evil, and Thy Righteous judgement of our suffering it."[19] And there is no sin if one does not sin by his or her own will. This principle is the key to understanding Augustine's concept of sin, and it is fairly congruent with a view he has in his early stage as opposed to Manicheanism.[20]

One can also find another reference in Augustine's work *De correptione et gratia* that reveals sin as a problem of will. This work was written by Augustine to address the "agent" problem arising as some Hadrumetum monks weakened the role of human will and overemphasized the grace of God as the only agent in and for all practical purposes.[21] The whole dispute began in 425 when a monk named Florus from Hadrumetum went on a journey of charity to his native town of Uzalis. During his stay at the town, Florus visited a library in the monastery of Bishop Evodius, where he found a copy of Augustine's letter to Sixtus. In this letter, Augustine set forth for the Church of Rome the Catholic doctrine of grace in opposition to the Pelagians. Florus was so impressed with the letter that he made a copy and had his fellow monk Felix take it back to Hadrumetum. The problem was, however, that the letter was circulated in the monastery without the knowledge of Valentine, the abbot of Hadrumetum. Some of the "less educated" monks at Hadrumetum thus found the Augustinian doctrine of grace to be destructive of free will and to "eliminate the merit of good or bad works according to which each person is going to be rewarded or punished at the judgement."[22] In an attempt to resolve this issue, Valentine sent two monks, Cresconius and Felix, to Hippo with the copy of the troubling letter of Augustine to Sixtus. Augustine responded promptly with his letter to Valentine. He then returned the two monks

19   Augustine, *Confessiones*, 7.3.5.

20   *C. Fort.* 21: *ego dico peccatum non esse, si non propria uoluntate peccatur.* See also Han-luen Kantzer Komline, *Augustine on the Will: A Theological Account* (Oxford: Oxford University Press, 2019), 82.

21   Rebecca Harden Weaver, *Divine Grace and Human Agency: A Study of the Semi-Pelagian Controversy* (Macon, GA: Mercer University Press, 1996), 23–4.

22   Roland J. Teske, "The Trouble at Hadrumetum," in *Answer to the Pelagians, IV: To the Monks of Hadrumetum and Providence* (Hyde Park, NY: New City Press, 2003), 12–3.

to Hadrumetum with his principal documents on the Pelagian controversy. Here in these documents (especially in the *De correptione et gratia*),
Augustine taught that not only should one plead with the grace of God,
the supreme Physician, for *donum perseverantiae*, but he or she has always
been shepherded by spiritual physicians who use tools of correction and
rebuke to turn sinful Christians from evil to good.[23] For his or her sinning,
in Augustine's teaching, is the result of a will without reins, of a voluntary
action that does not do "things praiseworthy and gladdening" but "things
which are shameful and mortifying."[24]

Where then does this nature of sin find its origin? At what point or
from what event does Augustine infer the origin of evil? Like other patristic
authors, such as Justin Martyr, Tatian, Theophilus, Irenaeus, Tertullian, and
Cyril, Augustine attempts to infer the origin of sin from speculation about
the Fall.[25] But he develops it differently: "Cyril, for instance, conceived of
it as a condition, a disease contracted by Adam and transmitted to every
one of Adam's descendants, whereas Augustine treated it as a condition,
an existential guilt that asks each human hypostasis to bear responsibility
for Adam's fault."[26] In his treatise *To Simplicianus, on Various Questions*,

23   Augustine, *De correptione et gratia*, 2.

24   Ibid., 7.

25   Nicholas E. Lombardo O.P., "Evil, Suffering, and Original Sin," in *The Oxford
      Handbook of Catholic Theology* (Oxford: Oxford University Press, 2019), 140.

26   John Meyendorff, *Christ in Eastern Christian Thought* (St Vladimir's Seminary
      Press, 1975), 116–7. Cyril's teaching of sin can also be explained more systematically
      by the *logos-tropos* dynamics which Maximus the Confessor develops in *Ambiguum*
      42: "The principle [*logos*] of human nature is to exist in soul and body as one nature
      constituted of rational soul and a body, but its mode [*tropos*] … can frequently
      change and undergo alteration without changing at all the nature along with it."
      Like Cyril (and Irenaeus), Maximus sees image and likeness as distinct: the image
      of God in man refers to "being and eternal being" as a God-given and stable reality,
      whereas likeness entails change and free movement. He then depicts the image
      as the *logos* of man at creation while the likeness as sharing and interacting with
      divine attributes through the *tropos* (*The Four Hundred Chapters on Love*, 3.25).
      For him what explains the fall is the variability in the *tropos*. Thus sin in Maximus'
      thought does no essential harm to the image of God in man. It is simply a disorder
      that limits freedom by rendering the *tropoi* of man play at variance with his *logos*.
      Maximus the Confessor, *On the Cosmic Mystery of Jesus Christ: Selected Writings*

Augustine coins the term *peccatum originale* (original sin) and lays the groundwork for a new, different theological synthesis. The most noticeable difference is perhaps that Augustine places emphasis not just on the event of sin but on the cause and ontological consequences of that event. For Augustine, "pride" was the central cause of the Fall of Adam and Eve:

> Our first parents fell into open disobedience because already they were secretly corrupted; for the evil act had never been done had not an evil will preceded it. And what is the origin of our evil will but pride? For "pride is the beginning of sin." And what is pride but the craving for undue exaltation? And this is undue exaltation, when the soul abandons Him to whom it ought to cleave as its end, and becomes a kind of end to itself. This happens when it becomes its own satisfaction ... The devil, then, would not have ensnared man in the open and manifest sin of doing what God had forbidden, had man not already begun to live for himself. It was this that made him listen with pleasure to the words, "Ye shall be as gods," which they would much more readily have accomplished by obediently adhering to their supreme and true end than by proudly living to themselves. For created gods are gods not by virtue of what is in themselves, but by a participation of the true God. By craving to be more, man becomes less; and by aspiring to be self-sufficing, he fell away from Him who truly suffices him.[27]

And that which comes from Adam and Eve is passed down from generation to generation in some way through *propagatio* (propagation) – rather than by *imitatio* (imitation). To support this synthesis, Augustine references many biblical passages – for example, Rom. 7 and 9, and 1 Cor 15 – but the most fundamental one is unarguably Rom. 5:12: "Through one man sin entered the world, and through sin death, and thus was passed on to all human beings in whom all have sinned."[28] If he had used the Greek version of Rom. 5:12 as a reference, not the original Latin Vulgate, Augustine would have interpreted it very differently from that which we know now. But unfortunately, that was not the case at the time.

from St. Maximus the Confessor (St. Vladimir's Seminary Press, 2003), 90. See also Maximus the Confesor, "The Four Hundred Chapters on Love," in *Maximus the Confessor: Selected Writings*, trans. George C. Berthold (Mahwah, NJ: Paulist, 1985), 33–98.

27 Augustine, *The City of God*, 14.13.
28 Rom. 5:12.

Thus, unlike the Eastern Father's reading of the Greek in the text – according to which all sinned *because (eph' hôi)* Adam sinned – Augustine read it as follows: "*in quo omnes pecca verunt* (in whom [Adam] all have sinned)."[29] And with this reading he gives an original view of the ontological implication of all humanity in Adam's own sin. For Augustine, sin was more than just a parody. It must come from somewhere deeply rooted in our existence. So, in his reflection of the Fall, any of Adam and Eve's descendants do not simply replicate the sin of their first parents but are born sinful:

> No doubt all they imitate Adam who by disobedience transgress the commandment of God; but he is one thing as an example to those who sin because they choose, and another thing as the progenitor of all who are born with sin.[30]

But this idea is not necessarily or entirely non- or anti-traditional. At least the notion of our sinning in Adam appears even before Augustine[31] in Ambrose,[32]

---

29   Ken Parry, ed., *The Wiley Blackwell Companion to Patristics* (Chichester, UK: Wiley Blackwell, 2019), 366. In the Apostle Paul, however, the Greek text runs: "*καὶ οὕτως εἰς πάντας ἀνθρώπους ὁ θάνατος διῆλθεν, ἐφ᾽ ᾧ πάντες ἥμαρτον*: so death passed to all men in as much as/because (*ἐφ᾽ ᾧ*) all sinned." Unlike Augustine, the Greek fathers (such as Cyril of Alexandria) read the same text in Greek, and they never understood the expression *ἐφ᾽ ᾧ* of Rom. 5:12 in the sense of "in whom"; nor did they ever think that *ἥμαρτον* referred to a sin committed by all men in Adam. They interpreted it as referring to personal sin only (cf., Cyril's *Commentary on Romans* [in Rom. 5:12–4] [PG, 74] cc. 784–5 *passim*). Donato Ogliari, *Gratia Et Certamen: The Relationship between Grace and Free Will in the Discussion of Augustine with the So-called Semipelagians* (Leuven, Belgium: Peeters, 2003), 244.

30   Augustine, *De peccatorum meritis et remissione et de baptismo parvulorum*, 1.10.

31   G. M. Lukken, *Original Sin in the Roman Liturgy: Research into the Theology of Original Sin in the Roman Sacramentaria and the Early Baptismal Liturgy* (Leiden: Brill, 1973), 268–77.

32   Ambrosius, *Apol. David*, 1. 11. 57: "*in quo (sc. Christo) solo et conceptus virginalis et partus sine ullo fuit mortalis originis inquinamento ... nullum sentiret generationis naturale contagium. Merito ergo David flebiliter in se deploravit ipsa inquinamenta naturae, quod prius inciperet in homine macula quam vita (CSEL 32, 2, 338–3)*." Quoted from Lukken, *Original Sin in the Roman Liturgy*, 275.

Cyprian,[33] Origen,[34] and Tertullian.[35] In other words, without any reference to Augustine, one can still support the Augustinian notion of Adam and Eve transmitting their condition to their offspring. Furthermore, some early liturgical texts had already proposed sexual intercourse as the means by which the primal sin was passed on to everyone through generation, partly by reflecting on Christ's virgin birth and inferring that it should have played a central role in preserving Christ's humanity from any taint of sin.[36] Thus everyone would agree that Augustine's notion of a historical rupture, that our sinful tendencies are traced back to the sin of Adam and Eve, echoes the general consensus of early Eastern or Western fathers, except for Cyril of Alexandria or Theodoret of Cyrus.[37]

33 Cyprian, *EP.* 64. 5: "*Porro autem si etiam gravissimis delictoribus et in Deum multum ante peccantibus, cum postea crediderint, remissa peccatorum datur et a baptism atque gratia nemo prohibetur, quanto magis prohiberi non debet infans qui recens natus nihil peccavit, nisi secundum Adam carnaliter natus contagium mortis antiquae prima nativitate contraxit. Qui ad remissam peccatorum accipiendam hoc ipso facilius accredit quod illi remittuntur non propria sed aliena peccata (CSEL 3.2. 720–1).*" Quoted from Lukken, *Original Sin in the Roman Liturgy*, 195.

34 Origen, In *Lev. Hom.*, 12.4: "*Hoc ipsum ergo quod in vulva matris est positus et quod materiam corporis ab orignie paterni seminis sumit, in patre et in matre contaminates dici potest ... Omnis ergo homo in patre et in matre pollutes est, solus vere Jesus ... in hanc generationem mundus ingressus est (GCS 29, 460).*" Quoted from Lukken, *Original Sin in the Roman Liturgy*, 275.

35 Tertullian, *De testim.*, 3: "*per quem (Satanam) homo a primordiis circumventus ... exinde totum genus a suo semine infectum, suae etiam damnationis traducem fecit (PL 1, 613 A).*" Tertullian, *De Anima*, 40: "*Ita omnis anima eousque in Adam censetur, donec in Christo recenseatur ... peccatrix autem, quia immunda, recipiens ignominiam et carnis ex societate (CC 2, 843).*" Quoted from Lukken, *Original Sin in the Roman Liturgy*, 275.

36 Lukken, *Original Sin in the Roman Liturgy*, 277–96.

37 The position of Cyril of Alexandria or Theodoret of Cyrus differs from that of Augustine, who affirms the Adamic origin of sin. Both agreed that the ἐφ' ᾧ of Rom. humans. Thus, Cyril and Theodoret did not see all human beings born guilty of sin. They rather thought that the principle of non-being, or death, was at work in all human beings from the beginning they would sin. For further discussion of Cyril's and Theodoret's understanding of sin and death as opposed to Augustine's, see Boris Bobrinskoy, "The Adamic Heritage According to Fr John Meyendorff," *St Vladimir's Theological Quarterly* 42, no. 1 (1998): 33–44.

However, Augustine is clearly original in his conceptualization of sin. He made a deduction that his Eastern or Western predecessors had resisted. More than anything else, it is this original reasoning that sets his commentary on original sin apart from any that had preceded it. The brilliantly original reasoning is worked thoroughly in his text *The City of God*:

> But as man the parent is, such is man the offspring. In the first man, therefore, there existed the whole human nature, which was to be transmitted by the woman to posterity, when that conjugal union received the divine sentence of its own condemnation; and what man was made, not when created, but when he sinned and was punished, this he propagated, so far as the origin of sin and death are concerned. For neither by sin nor its punishment was he himself reduced to that infantine and helpless infirmity of body and mind which we see in children ... To this infantine imbecility the first man did not fall by his lawless presumption and just sentence; but human nature was in his person vitiated and altered to such an extent, that he suffered in his members the warring of disobedient lust, and became subject to the necessity of dying. And what he himself had become by sin and punishment, such he generated those whom he begot; that is to say, subject to sin and death.[38]

The result of that reasoning is a fundamental flaw in human nature from this primordial time onwards. Without ceding any ground on the natural goodness of creation, Augustine goes further on to opine:

> Man's nature, indeed, was created at first faultless and without any sin; but that nature of man in which every one is born from Adam, now wants the Physician, because it is not sound. All good qualities, no doubt, which it still possesses in its make, life, senses, intellect, it has of the Most High God, its Creator and Maker. But the flaw, which darkens and weakens all those natural goods, so that it has need of illumination and healing, it has not contracted from its blameless Creator – but from that original sin, which it committed by free will. Accordingly, criminal nature has its part in most righteous punishment.[39]

The beginning of sin is not the only reason or the importance of Adam and Eve according to Augustine. More fundamentally important to this doctor of grace is that Adam and Eve in some way distorted what came from God and, by propagation, handed down the curse to their

38   Augustine, *The City of God*, 13.3.
39   Augustine, *De natura et gratia*, 3.

descendants. This idea of human reality brings new insight into the tragic dimension of man, the limits of human freedom, and the absolute dependence of human nature on God's grace. But it, most of all, shows the mark of his originality, for it was not abandoned but extensively developed when Augustine wrestled with a question that plagued his contemporaries (and an objection that the Pelagians would likely raise). The question is: How could a baptized parent, cleansed of original sin, convey its stains to its children?

Unlike those who had avoided such questions, Augustine gets a grip on them in one of those chapters in his *De peccatorum meritis et remissione et de baptismo parvulorum* that begins with an odd phrase "Unbaptized Infants Damned, But Most Lightly." This strangely sounding chapter states:

> It may therefore be correctly affirmed, that such infants as quit the body without being baptized will be involved in the mildest condemnation of all. That person, therefore, greatly deceives both himself and others, who teaches that they will not be involved in condemnation.[40]

That all human beings, including infants (unbaptized), are present in the first humans who sinned is once again confirmed in his other work, *The City of God*:

> For God, the author of natures, not of vices, created man upright; but man, being of his own will corrupted, and justly condemned, begot corrupted and condemned children. For we all were in that one man, since we all were that one man, who fell into sin by the woman who was made from him before the sin. For not yet was the particular form created and distributed to us, in which we as individuals were to live, but already the seminal nature was there from which we were to be propagated; and this being vitiated by sin and bound by the chain of death, and justly condemned, man could not be born of man in any other state.[41]

Unlike his Eastern counterparts (e.g., Gregory of Nyssa or Gregory of Nazianzus), who resisted the conclusion that infants who died without

---

40   Augustine, *De peccatorum meritis et remissione et de baptismo parvulorum*, 1.21.
41   Augustine, *The City of God*, 13.14.

baptism were necessarily damned,[42] Augustine teaches that all humans are affected by original sin from conception. So in his view, infants are no exception: "But you who are without envy, why do you not see great evils in infants? ... Whence comes the great evils of men – I do not mean moral evils, but evils in the very wits with which they are born – if human origin is not vitiated and there is no condemned mass?"[43] They also sinned in Adam and shared his misery. If they are guilty and without baptism, they too must be damned. But how can the stain of original sin be transmitted from the baptized to their young descendants? Does Augustine take lightly the grace of baptism? More specifically, his theology of sacraments implies that the union with Christ, established in baptism, cleanses original sin and brings salvation to all baptized. According to Augustine, the grace of baptism overcomes the guilt that is transmitted from parents to infants:

> You must not be surprised at what I have said, that although the law of sin remains with its concupiscence [i.e., original sin], the guilt thereof is done away through the grace of the sacrament. For as wicked deeds, and words, and thoughts have already passed away, and cease to exist, so far as regards the mere movements of the mind and the body, and yet their guilt remains after they have passed away and no longer exist, unless it be done away by the remission of sins; so contrariwise, in this law of concupiscence, which is not yet done away but still remains, its guilt is done away, and continues no longer, since in baptism there takes place a full forgiveness of sins. Indeed, if a man were to quit this present life immediately after his baptism, there would be nothing at all left to hold him liable, inasmuch as all which held him is released.[44]

If so, what is Augustine's position on this matter? Is it that baptized parents can give birth to sinless infants? Or is it that all infants, regardless

---

42   In a short treatise by Gregory of Nyssa called *On Infants' Early Deaths*, Gregory said that children who died early in life would not necessarily be damned but receive new life because of the grace of God. In a similar sense, Gregory of Nazianzus assured his readers that infants who died "unsealed" by baptism, but not wicked, would be neither glorified nor punished. Gerard S. Sloyan, *Religions of the Book* (Lanham, MD: University Press of America, 1996), 108.

43   Augustine, *Against Julian*, trans. Matthew A. Schuhmacher (Washington, DC: The Catholic University of America Press, 2004), 308.

44   Augustine, *De peccatorum meritis et remissione et de baptismo parvulorum*, 2.46.

of whether their parents are baptized, are born into the world with a nature that has been corrupted by the sin of Adam and Eve? If it is the former, Augustine will eventually fall into the Pelagian error, according to which a sinless life is theoretically possible. Even if it is the latter, however, there remains some serious problem that besets sacramental grace and its saving activity in the lives of those baptized in the name of the Triune God. So in either case, these two problems can be addressed only by treating it with an "either-or" logic that *either* compromises the baptismal grace *or* emphasizes the persistent power and effects of sin on human nature. Augustine's choice here was to uphold the latter, that is, the logic of a human nature acting from a damaged state.

To understand this logic more concretely, one needs to be introduced to Augustine's idea of various degrees of sins. In addition to the sins of ignorance and weakness, Augustine identifies and distinguishes between different forms or aspects of sin. Of particular note are venial (or trivial) sins and mortal (or heinous) sins. According to Augustine, the former refers to those that "do not hinder the righteous man from the attainment of eternal life, and ... [that] are unavoidable in this life,"[45] while the latter indicates those that separate a person from Christ's body.[46] For Augustine, it is this latter form of sin that the baptismal water takes away from sinners.[47] But this sacramental washing does not mean that those who are baptized no

---

45   Augustine, *De spiritu et littera*, 48.

46   Augustine, *De symbolo ad catechumenos*, 15: "Do not commit those things for which ye must needs be separated from Christ's body."

47   For Augustine, the presence of what is termed original sin (or sometimes "concupiscence," which implies a desire in its Latin root) is overcome in the baptismal waters. Because of this belief in the cleansing activity of baptismal grace, Augustine expressed disappointment in his *Confessiones* that he was not baptized in childhood because his mother could not persuade his father to allow it: "How much better, then, had it been for me to have been cured at once; and then, by my own and my friends' diligence, my soul's restored health had been kept safe in Thy keeping, who gravest it! Better, in truth. But how numerous and great waves of temptation appeared to hang over me after my childhood! These were foreseen by my mother; and she preferred that the unformed clay should be exposed to them rather than the image itself." Augustine, *Confessiones*, 1.11.18.

longer sin. In any case, a Pelagian claim to perfection is unacceptable, and above all, it directly contradicts what he finds in the Bible:

> He, moreover, who says that any man, after he has received remission of sins, has ever lived in this body, or still is living, so righteously as to have no sin at all, he contradicts the Apostle John, who declares that "If we say we have no sin, we deceive ourselves, and the truth is not in us"[48]

So that the power of original sin has been broken by baptism can only mean in Augustine's view that "mortal" sins, which separate us from the attainment of eternal life, can and should be avoided. But even now, "venial" sins remain a stumbling block, or an occasion to fall away from one's spiritual life after regeneration.[49] Thus, in some sense, the baptized have not entirely broken free from the gravity of original sin. Or to put it differently, these Christians have not yet been unchained from the post-lapsarian situation of creation, a reality that has been changed (or corrupted) into one under judgment since the Fall. Since this pessimistic reality is a logical consequence for Augustine, it was virtually inevitable for him to produce an original doctrine of sin, that with or without baptism, all of us *will*, *operate*, and *act* with a substantially twisted (or broken) nature. Not only that, but it was also equally unavoidable for him to change and complicate the resulting doctrines of grace and free will, as we will now see.

Grace and Free Will

The dominant teaching on grace by Augustine unfolds in his later writings on salvation, primarily in opposition to the teachings of the Pelagians who claim that the will is always free and grace is external to human

---

48   Augustine, *De perfectione iustitiae hominis*, 21.
49   Augustine, *Contra mendacium*, 23: "But in all our doings, even good men are very greatly embarrassed in the matter of compensative [or venial] sins."

existence.[50] The following discussion of his later writings will not only advance what this chapter has already discussed about the fallen situation of humanity, but it will also help explain how grace and nature relate to each other in the Augustinian theological framework.

Unlike the Pelagians, Augustine sees that the key is grace, not the will of a person to act in a damaged state. In commenting on the *De gestis Pelagii* for heresy, he makes this point very clear: "Now it is by this Spirit, and not by the strength of their own will, that they who are God's children are governed and led."[51] But the writing goes in a somewhat unexpected way. His anti-Pelagian view of grace is narrated in this book as if God's action overrides or incapacitates human will:

> [G]race is not dying nature, nor the slaying letter, but the vivifying spirit; for already did he possess nature with freedom of will, because he said: "To will is present with me." Nature, however, in a healthy condition and without a flaw, he did not possess ... Therefore it is not from the liberty of the human will, nor from the precepts of the law, that there comes deliverance from the body of this death; for both of these he had already – the one in his nature, the other in his learning; but all he wanted was the help of the grace of God, through Jesus Christ our Lord.[52]

Elsewhere, similar nuances are given with slightly different emphasis, eliciting an image of a controlling or vanquishing power of divine grace. First, in Chapter 43 of the work *De gratia et libero arbitrio*, Augustine says:

> From these statements of the inspired word, and from similar passages which it would take too long to quote in full, it is, I think, sufficiently clear that God works in the hearts of men to incline their wills wherever He wills, whether to good deeds according to His mercy, or to evil after their own deserts; His own judgment being sometimes manifest, sometimes secret, but always righteous.[53]

---

50 For Pelagius the will is always free, and if the act of will was shorn of any vestige of internal freedom, it is not subject to the person, and thus to moral evaluation (cf. Pelagius, *Epistle to Demetrias*, 16). Keith L. Johnson and David Lauber eds., *T&T Clark Companion to the Doctrine of Sin* (London and New York: Bloomsbury T&T Clark, 2016), 342.

51 Augustine, *De gestis Pelagii*, 6.

52 Ibid., 21.

53 Augustine, *De gratia et libero arbitrio*, 43.

And in Chapter 98 of *Enchiridion* he continues: "And, moreover, who will be so foolish and blasphemous as to say that God cannot change the evil wills of men, whichever, whenever, and wheresoever He chooses, and direct them to what is good?"[54]

Such anti-Pelagian accounts gave rise to some problems about free will. Augustine was, however, well aware of this problem, and for that very reason he was able to clarify his point against errors that his doctrine of grace might fall into: "[W]e do not, when we make mention of these things [Rom. 10:2–3, Jn. 14:6, Phil. 2:12, and Lk. 12:37, all of which implies in Augustine's account that free will is not taken away when grace is preached], take away freedom of will, but we preach the grace of God."[55]

But the point was neither clear enough nor widely distributed enough to silence the grace-nature dispute that took place at some point after 418 among the Hadrumetum monks.[56] Thus he had to send *Letter 214* and *Letter 215* – together with his *De gratia et libero arbitrio* and *De correptione et gratia* – to Abbot Valentine, who asked for help in resolving the dispute in his monastery at Hadrumetum.[57]

In these two letters and treatises, Augustine rejects three errors: (1) the error of relying on free will to the extent that the necessity of grace is denied; (2) the error of relying on grace to the point that the effects of free will on good is denied; and (3) the error of relying on grace to the extent that one's responsibility for evil resulting from his or her free will is denied.[58] And he goes on to urge them to identify and cultivate a balanced view of

---

54 Augustine, *Enchiridion*, 98.

55 Augustine, *De natura et gratia*, 36.

56 Peter Brown, *Augustine of Hippo: A Biography* (Berkeley: University of California Press, 2000), 401.

57 Alexander Y. Hwang, *Intrepid Lover of Perfect Grace: The Life and Thought of Prosper of Aquitaine* (Washington, DC: Catholic University of America Press, 2009), 101–3. To get a concise yet useful summary of the two letters, one can see Guido Stucco, *God's Eternal Gift: A History of the Catholic Doctrine of Predestination from Augustine to the Renaissance* (Bloomington, IN: Xlibris Corporation, 2009), 36–7.

58 Augustine, *Letter 214*, 2, 4, 7; *Letter 215*, 1, 8; *De gratia et libero arbitrio*, 31; and *De correptione et gratia*, 7, 9, 10.

faith between (1) the necessity and priority of grace, (2) the freedom of human will, and (3) the righteous judgment of God.[59]

Did these letters and treatises successfully convey Augustine's thoughts to the monks at Hadrumetum?[60] Or perhaps more importantly, can one locate from them that Augustine is keeping the two extremes of grace and nature together in balance? The answer to this question is still in dispute.[61] The rest of this chapter will be limited to a review of the various attributes of grace shown in his later works.

Three Attributes of Grace

One finds at least three attributes of grace in Augustine's later writings. These attributes are arranged here in chronological order. The first attribute is introduced by Augustine in the text, *De spiritu et littera*. This text, later served as an important hermeneutic for Luther and other Protestant writers, is Augustine's biblical commentary on 2 Corinthians

---

59   Weaver, *Divine Grace and Human Agency*, 14.

60   There is no way to confirm the truth, but Valentin assures Augustine that the letters and treatises have happily achieved the desired result of restoring peace and harmony in the Hadrumetum monastery. Robert P. Russell, "Introduction," in *The Teacher; The Free Choice of the Will; Grace and Free Will* (Washington, DC: Catholic University of America Press, 2010), 247. See also Weaver, *Divine Grace and Human Agency*, 23, 35.

61   Needless to say, not everyone in the fifth-century Latin community was satisfied with Augustine's conclusion. As Rebecca Harden Weaver points out, the monks in South Gaul regarded Augustine with less awe than their North African counterparts did. In addition, they considered Augustine's teaching as a challenge to their ascetic life and efforts for Christian perfection (*theosis*). Perhaps those who appeal more to the Eastern tradition that Gallic monks regarded as authoritative than the ones that Augustine generally appealed to would argue that Augustine provides a window onto the church's ongoing struggle to define the relationship between grace and nature, rather than to end the grace-nature debate. Weaver, *Divine Grace and Human Agency*, 35, 37–69.

and Romans.[62] There Augustine sets out a tone of humility and gratitude for God's grace, explaining two different approaches to divine grace that come under the sub-heading "A Comparison of the Law of Moses and of the New Law":

> Now, amidst this admirable correspondence, there is at least this very consider-able diversity in the cases, in that the people in the earlier instance were deterred by a horrible dread from approaching the place where the law was given; whereas in the other case the Holy Ghost came upon them who were gathered together in expectation of His promised gift. *There* it was on tables of stone that the finger of God operated; here it was on the hearts of men. *There* the law was given outwardly, so that the unrighteous might be terrified; here it was given inwardly, so that they might be justified.[63]

The law of Moses and the new law (the one given on the heart by the Spirit) here represent two different approaches to salvation depicted in the Old and New Testaments. Augustine takes these two covenants as a starting point for his conceptualization of grace. He then describes the divine aspect of *transitioning* from this Old approach to that New approach as a key aspect of grace. But there is one thing to note about the idea of transition. In Augustine's view, the transition is not a change. It is not a movement from one side to the other. It is something that shows substantial continuity with the past. Thus, there is a substantial degree of continuity between those two different approaches. One major aspect of this idea is that the grace of the NT is already *present* in that of the OT: "[I]t is evident that the grace of God was promised to the New Testament even by the prophet, and that this grace was definitively announced to take this shape – God's laws were to be written in men's hearts."[64] Although the presence may not be so clearly explicit or visible to the naked eye of creation, Augustine says:

---

62   Hans J. Hillerbrand and Robert Kolb, *The Encyclopedia of Protestantism: D-K* (New York, London: Routledge, 2004), 283.

63   Augustine, *De spiritu et littera*, 29.

64   Ibid., 49.

This grace hid itself under a veil in the Old Testament, but it has been revealed in the New Testament according to the most perfectly ordered dispensation of the ages, forasmuch as God knew how to dispose all things. And perhaps it is [for this very reason that the apostle says,] "For when … it shall turn to the Lord, the veil shall be taken away."[65]

The old covenant is therefore not evil in itself for Augustine, but that alone is not sufficient to restore one's life, to bring one's life to salvation. Thus, Augustine says that a person requires the new covenant, or more specifically, the life-giving work of the Holy Spirit who is the testifier and the testimony of that which dwells inwardly in one's hearts as and through the new covenant:

Let no Christian then stray from this faith, which alone is the Christian one; nor let any one, when he has been made to feel ashamed to say that we become righteous through our own selves, without the grace of God working this in us – because he sees, when such an allegation is made, how unable pious believers are to endure it – resort to any subterfuge on this point, by affirming that the reason why we cannot become righteous without the operation of God's grace is this, that He gave the law, He instituted its teaching, He commanded its precepts of good. For there is no doubt that, without His assisting grace, the law is the letter which kills; but when the life-giving spirit is present, the law causes that to be loved as written within, which it once caused to be feared as written without.[66]

And he continues two chapters later in the same book:

Christ "came not to destroy, but to fulfill" [the law]. Nevertheless, it is not by that law that the ungodly are made righteous, but by grace; and this change is effected by the life-giving Spirit, without whom the letter kills … The law was therefore given, in order that grace might be sought; grace was given, in order that the law might be fulfilled. Now it was not through any fault of its own that the law was not fulfilled, but by the fault of the carnal mind; and this fault was to be demonstrated by the law, and healed by grace.[67]

---

65   Ibid., 27.
66   Ibid., 32.
67   Ibid., 34.

The result of this dialectical approach to grace, then, is not the separation or removal of a person from the law but a restoration or rehabilitation of nature that is in line with what the law teaches:

> Nor ought it to disturb us that the apostle described them as doing that which is contained in the law by nature, – not by the Spirit of God, not by faith, not by grace. For it is the Spirit of grace that does it, in order to restore in us the image of God, in which we were naturally created. Sin, indeed, is contrary to nature, and it is grace that heals it – on which account the prayer is offered to God, Be merciful unto me: heal my soul; for I have sinned against You. Therefore it is by nature that men do the things which are contained in the law; for they who do not, fail to do so by reason of their sinful defect. In consequence of this sinfulness, the law of God is erased out of their hearts; and therefore, when, the sin being healed, it is written there, the prescriptions of the law are done by nature, – not that by nature grace is denied, but rather by grace nature is repaired.[68]

Since grace cures nature, for Augustine, nature does not become void through grace but is established – that is, redeemed and restored to its original condition – by its divine counterpart. To further strengthen this logic, Augustine goes on to enumerate scriptural passages in a dialectical way. For example, in Chapter 52 of *De spiritu et littera*, he takes OT and NT passages – each of which implies two principles (grace and nature) – and lists them in a dialectical structure similar to the way Aquinas develops arguments in a series of dialectical moves from thesis to antithesis. He then concludes that synthesis, which resolves and constructively connects the ontological tension between the two principles, is one of the major attributes of grace:

> Do we then by grace make void free will? God forbid! Nay, rather we establish free will. For even as the law by faith, so free will by grace, is not made void, but established. For neither is the law fulfilled except by free will; but by the law is the knowledge of sin, by faith the acquisition of grace against sin, by grace the healing of the soul from the disease of sin, by the health of the soul freedom of will, by free will the love of righteousness, by love of righteousness the accomplishment of the law. Accordingly, as the law is not made void, but is established through faith, since faith procures grace whereby the law is fulfilled; so free will is not made void through grace, but is

68   Ibid., 47.

established, since grace cures the will whereby righteousness is freely loved. *Now all the stages which I have here connected together in their successive links, have severally their proper voices in the sacred Scriptures.* The law says: "You shall not covet." Faith says: "Heal my soul, for I have sinned against You." Grace says: "Behold, you are made whole: sin no more, lest a worse thing come unto you." Health says: "O Lord my God, I cried unto You, and You have healed me." Free will says: "I will freely sacrifice unto You." Love of righteousness says: "Transgressors told me pleasant tales, but not according to Your law, O Lord." How is it then that miserable men dare to be proud, either of their free will, before they are freed, or of their own strength, if they have been freed? They do not observe that in the very mention of free will they pronounce the name of liberty. But "where the Spirit of the Lord is, there is liberty." If, therefore, they are the slaves of sin, why do they boast of free will? For by what a man is overcome, to the same is he delivered as a slave. But if they have been freed, why do they vaunt themselves as if it were by their own doing, and boast, as if they had not received? Or are they free in such sort that they do not choose to have Him for their Lord who says to them: "Without me you can do nothing;" and "If the Son shall make you free, you shall be free indeed?"[69]

From this example, and from all the quotes I have stated here and connected together in a successive way, one can infer that for Augustine grace is by nature a therapeutic aid or cure necessary to efficaciously bridge the ontological gap between God and creation.

This first attribute of grace recurs in another text, *De natura et gratia*, written by Augustine at the end of 415 CE, about three years after the publication of *De spiritu et littera*. The text came out when Timasius and Jakobus, once Pelagius' students, sent Augustine the untitled and anonymous work of Pelagius, *De natura*. Essentially, *De natura et gratia* is a rebuttal document, where Augustine rebuts that while Pelagius subtly acknowledges grace,[70] not only does *De natura* reject the doctrine of original sin,[71] but it also raises the possibility of a person's not sinning.[72] From Augustine's point of view, *De natura* does nothing more than put nature in the place of grace. This overly inflated concept of nature – whereby nature is treated as

69   Ibid., 52.
70   Augustine, *De natura et gratia*, 11.
71   Ibid., 21.
72   Ibid., 49.

something other than itself – is not only heretical but also quite contrary
to what the Bible teaches about sin:

> He who has a sound judgment says soundly, that the examples of certain persons,
> of whose sinning we read in Scripture, are not recorded for this purpose, that they
> may encourage despair of not sinning, and seem somehow to afford security in com-
> mitting sin, – but that we may learn the humility of repentance, or else discover that
> even in such falls salvation ought not to be despaired of.[73]

Hence, Augustine contrasts grace and nature, as in his earlier text *De
spiritu et littera*. He then refutes Pelagius' teaching on the capacity of not
sinning (*posse non peccare*) by referring to the writings of Catholic authors
such as Hilary, Ambrose, John of Constantinople, Xystus, and Jerome.[74]
Augustine's magisterial rebuttal to Pelagius does not share any form of
moral optimism, nor does it give leeway to any kind of Pelagian interpretation that humanity is perfect in nature and not limited in the choice
of his or her will. It merely reaffirms the nature of grace as opposed to
human nature, and ultimately concludes with a doxological supplication
that makes it possible to infer what this chapter calls the first attribute of
grace – that grace is a divine aid or assistance to cure and restore human
nature:

> Inchoate love, therefore, is inchoate holiness; advanced love is advanced holiness;
> great love is great holiness; "perfect love is perfect holiness," – but this "love is out
> of a pure heart, and of a good conscience, and of faith unfeigned, which in this life
> is then the greatest, when life itself is contemned in comparison with it." I wonder,
> however, whether it has not a soil in which to grow after it has quitted this mortal
> life! But in what place and at what time soever it shall reach that state of absolute
> perfection, which shall admit of no increase, it is certainly not "shed abroad in our
> hearts" by any energies either of the nature or the volition that are within us, but
> "by the Holy Ghost which is given unto us," and which both helps our infirmity and
> co-operates with our strength. For it is itself indeed the grace of God, through our
> Lord Jesus Christ, to whom, with the Father and the Holy Spirit, appertains eternity,
> and all goodness, for ever and ever. Amen.[75]

---

73   Ibid., 40.
74   Ibid., 73, 75, 76, 77, 78.
75   Ibid., 84.

In Augustine's later work, the discussion of the contradictory relationship between divine grace and sinful nature is one of the recurring themes. For that reason, there are many passages worth referring to on this subject, but here I will extract only two representative passages. (1) Augustine's *De gestis Pelagii*:

> [G]race is not dying nature, nor the slaying letter, but the vivifying spirit; for already did he possess nature with freedom of will, because he said: "To will is present with me." Nature, however, in a healthy condition and without a flaw, he did not possess ... Therefore it is not from the liberty of the human will, nor from the precepts of the law, that there comes deliverance from the body of this death; for both of these he had already – the one in his nature, the other in his learning; but all he wanted was the help of the grace of God, through Jesus Christ our Lord.[76]

And (2) Augustine's De peccatorum meritis et remissione et de baptismo parvulorum:

> While Adam produced sinners from his one sin, Christ has by His grace procured free forgiveness even for the sins which men have of their own accord added by actual transgression to the original sin in which they were born ... still, even that sin alone which was originally derived unto men not only excludes from the kingdom of God, which infants are unable to enter (as they themselves allow), unless they have received the grace of Christ before they die, but also alienates from salvation and everlasting life, which cannot be anything else than the kingdom of God, to which fellowship with Christ alone introduces us.[77]

The second attribute of grace is introduced in *De gratia et libero arbitrio*, one of the documents Augustine sent to Valentine to resolve the grace-nature controversy among Hadrumetum monks. In this early fifth-century document, Augustine teaches that grace is not a knowledge of the law or nature, nor is it simply a pardon of sin.[78] But it is, as can be inferred from the preceding discussion of grace, an efficacious grace (*gratia efficax*)

76 Augustine, *De gestis Pelagii*, 21.
77 Augustine, *De peccatorum meritis et remissione et de baptismo parvulorum*, 1.14–5.
78 Augustine, *De gratia et libero arbitrio*, 26, 27.

that works in us to accomplish the "fulfillment of the law," the "liberation of nature," and the "removal of the dominion of sin."[79]

The concept of *gratia efficax* reflects two important elements identified in this chapter as the second and third attributes of grace, respectively. One is the profound mystery of gratuitous grace (*profunditas gratuitae gratiae*) that does not require any of our merit or human deservings in prolonging our existence to everlasting life, and the other is the accompanying grace of perseverance (*gratia perseverantiae*) that allows us to remain in a state of grace until death. Each of these elements implies the "means" and "end" – or the "initiatory" and "persevering" appellation – of *gratia efficax*, as noted by Francisco Marín-Sola, O.P. in his analysis of two gifts that come from efficacious grace: (1) divine merit for salvation and (2) divine predestination to glory.[80] In other words, in relation to that "means," it explains how grace is given to man, not through human merit but solely through God's own compassion in Christ through the Spirit. And in relation to that "end," it explains how far grace will ultimately take a person out of his or her present life/reality. As we will see later in this chapter, the "means" and "end"

---

79   Ibid., 27. In quoting Ezekiel's teaching, Augustine also stresses that grace is not merely an external aid but an internal efficacy that works in nature and makes it work with its efficacious powers: "It is certain that it is we that act when we act; but it is He who makes us act, by applying efficacious powers to our will, who has said, 'I will make you to walk in my statutes, and to observe my judgments, and to do them.' When he says, 'I will make you … to do them,' what else does He say in fact than, 'I will take away from you your heart of stone,' from which used to arise your inability to act, 'and I will give you a heart of flesh,' in order that you may act? And what does this promise amount to but this: I will remove your hard heart, out of which you did not act, and I will give you an obedient heart, out of which you shall act? It is He who causes us to act, to whom the human suppliant says, 'Set a watch, O Lord, before my mouth.' That is to say: Make or enable me, O Lord, to set a watch before my mouth – a benefit which he had already obtained from God who thus described its influence: 'I set a watch upon my mouth.'" Augustine, *De gratia et libero arbitrio*, 32.

80   Francisco Marin-Sola, O.P., *Do not Resist the Spirit's Call* (Washington, DC: Catholic University of America Press, 2013), 35. Since Augustine does not use this twofold category, "means" and "end," one needs to be informed that such a classification above is not his own, but an interpretive strategy that this book maps out to clarify the nature of grace that Augustine describes in his later writings.

of *gratia efficax* serves to engender a theological criteriology that affirms at one and the same time the absolute prevenience of grace and the absolute irresistibility of grace. This theological criteriology, in turn, opens the way for a logical conclusion that grace and nature work in an inverse, rather than proportional, ratio; to wit, that humans with the efficacious aid of grace would have their nature constrained rather than freed.

Of these two elements, the treatise *De gratia et libero arbitrio* explores the first element, that grace is absolutely gratuitous (*gratuitas gratia*).[81] There the idea of *gratuitas gratia* is consistently linked into the Lord Jesus Christ, who has given us grace in His kindness and love:

> Perhaps you ask whether we ever read in the Sacred Scriptures [about the One in whom we are crowned with grace]. Well you possess the Gospel according to John, which is perfectly clear in its very great light. Here John the Baptist says of Christ: "Of His fullness have we all received, even grace for grace." So that out of His fullness we have received ... grace.[82]

Unsurprisingly, the grace granted in and through the Son contrasts with the one that comes from our human merit. To support this point, Augustine appeals to the example of the Apostle Paul in Chapter 12 of his *De gratia et libero arbitrio*:

> Now there was, no doubt, a decided merit in the Apostle Paul, but it was an evil one, while he persecuted the Church, and he says of it: "I am not meet to be called an apostle, because I persecuted the Church of God." And it was while he had this evil merit that a good one was rendered to him instead of the evil; and, therefore, he went on at once to say, "But by the grace of God I am what I am."[83]

---

81   The second element – that grace is absolutely irresistible to the point that a person who is graced is preserved and kept unto eternal glory, even though he or she may be troubled by many infirmities – will be discussed as this chapter goes on to read Augustine's other works: *De praedestinatione sanctorum*, *De correptione et gratia*, and *De dono perseverantiae*.

82   Augustine, *De gratia et libero arbitrio*, 21. For more descriptions of Christ as the Bestower of grace in the text, see Augustine, *De gratia et libero arbitrio*, 26, 27, 28.

83   Ibid., 12.

Then he continues to do so in Chapter 14 of the same text: "Let us return now to the Apostle Paul, who, as we have found, obtained God's grace, who recompenses good for evil, without any good merits of his own, but rather with many evil merits."[84] Following these examples, in which no causal link can be found between grace and any good or evil merits of our own, Augustine concludes:

> Observe, therefore, what follows: "There is henceforth laid up for me," he [the Apostle Paul] says, "a crown of righteousness, which the Lord, the righteous Judge, shall give me at that day." Now, to whom should the righteous Judge award the crown, except to him on whom the merciful Father had bestowed grace? And how could the crown be one of righteousness, unless the grace had preceded which justifies the ungodly? How, moreover, could these things now be awarded as of debt, unless the other had been before given as a free gift?[85]

For Augustine, grace is not what the Pelagians teach in appealing to Zechariah 1:3, "Turn ye unto me, and I will turn unto you," that "God's grace is given according to our merit."[86] It is a free gift that comes from God. And for that reason, it is given, independently of merits, apart from human deservings. For what is grace if it is bestowed according to a person's deserts; otherwise, grace would be no longer a gift but a reward of debt. It must therefore be given gratuitously, in view of this early anti-Pelagian Latin Father:

> It follows, then, dearly beloved, beyond all doubt, that as your good life is nothing else than God's grace, so also the eternal life which is the recompense of a good life is the grace of God; moreover it is given gratuitously, even as that is given gratuitously to which it is given. But that to which it is given is solely and simply grace; this therefore is also that which is given to it, because it is its reward – grace is for grace, as if remuneration for righteousness; in order that it may be true, because it is true, that God "shall reward every man according to his works."[87]

---

84   Ibid., 14.
85   Ibid.
86   Ibid., 10.
87   Ibid., 20.

One important characteristic of *gratuitam gratiam* for Augustine is that grace is prevenient. Here the word prevenient, rooted in the Latin term *preveniens*, literally means "going ahead or even coming before."[88] In Chapter 44 of his *De gratia et libero arbitrio*, Augustine uses this term to study the case of God's gratuitous grace given to infants who cannot make any choice or merit for good. Such a case study by Augustine further develops his logic of gratuitous grace – and eventually provides a sketch of his ideas on predestination, as can be seen in his other text, *De dono perseverantiae*, where Augustine claims that the case of infants is of force to confirm the truth of predestination:

> Of two infants, equally bound by original sin, why the one is taken and the other left; and of two wicked men of already mature years, why this one should be so called as to follow Him that calls, while that one is either not called at all, or is not called in such a manner – the judgments of God are unsearchable. But of two pious men, why to the one should be given perseverance unto the end, and to the other it should not be given, God's judgments are even more unsearchable. Yet to believers it ought to be a most certain fact that the former is of the predestinated, the latter is not.[89]

To summarize: To affirm the gratuity of grace, one must affirm that grace comes before any merit of ours. If grace comes after our human will, including any choice we make to seek or receive grace, then it will not be designated as unconditional or gratuitous but as conditional or (causally and logically) dependent on antecedent or foreseen merits. Thus, wholly gratuitous grace means that grace takes precedence over nature, and that God's choice to give grace is not a result, but a cause – and a necessary condition – that precedes any of our choices and their merits. If God chooses to give us grace, then we are given it without preceding merits of our own.

But what happens to a person if God has not chosen to give him or her grace? I think that Augustine would, without hesitation, have responded that there can never be a way for the person to receive grace. For grace in Augustine's view operates preparing the person to receive grace,

---

88 Alister E. McGrath, *Christian Theology: An Introduction* (Chichester, UK: Wiley Blackwell, 2011), 356.

89 Augustine, *De dono perseverantiae*, 21.

and without it, the person is incapable of seeking or obtaining grace. The result is that the ungraced person not only fails to obey the law but fails with the liberation of nature and the removal of the dominion of sin; thus by failing in that which only grace can prepare and effect, the person may be said to increase sin and fall far short of the end of those who are graced.

The inevitable problem here is, as might be expected, the ontological gap between those who are graced and those who are not, or in other words: the efficacy of grace that is to make increasingly tenuous any connection between human wills and their outcomes or between the human agent and that agent's own action. In fact, it was because of this problem that Augustine wrote the treatise *De gratia et libero arbitrio* in 426/427 CE, as Augustine himself states in his *Retractationes*: "Because of those persons who, by thinking that free choice is denied when the grace of God is defended, defend free will in such a manner as to deny the grace of God by affirming that it is bestowed according to our merits."[90] In response to this view, Augustine affirmed the necessity of both grace and free will, explicitly stressing the concepts of free choice, good work, and reward – all of which were basic to the biblical commandments and admonitions to the human agent, and to the monastic ideal of training in those things that are pleasing to God. The connection between human actions and their outcomes was therefore firm: "Human agency does affect human action, and the resulting action does affect the destiny of the human agent."[91] But his far greater emphasis on grace caused a permanent rupture between the graced and the ungraced, and the lopsidedness of the relationship between grace and nature began to appear as Augustine disallowed any suggestion of human autonomy at each step of his anti-Pelagian argument in the treatise.[92] So he gave, in the end, a slight twist to what was originally planned, and as it piggybacked on another attribute of grace, which we will now see,

---

90   Augustine, *Retractationes*, 2.92. From here English translations of quotations from the *Retractationes* will be taken from *Saint Augustine: The Retractations*, trans. Sister Mary Inez Bogan, Fathers of the Church 60 (Washington, DC: Catholic University of America Press, 1968).

91   Weaver, *Divine Grace and Human Agency*, 17.

92   Augustine, *De gratia et libero arbitrio*, 6–7. See also Weaver, *Divine Grace and Human Agency*, 18.

that twist was even more complicated – to the extent that the idea that a person under grace can shape his or her life to God with free will is questionable within the logic of Augustine's claim to grace.

The next element of efficacious grace is the accompanying grace of perseverance (*gratiam perseverantiae*), which this chapter calls the third attribute of grace. This notion of *gratiam perseverantiae* is primarily addressed in the treatise *De correptione et gratia*, as Augustine states: "And, indeed, in that treatise of which the title is, *De correptione et gratia*, which could not suffice for all my lovers, I think that I have so established that it is the gift of God also to persevere to the end, as I have either never before or almost never so expressly and evidently maintained this in writing, unless my memory deceives me."[93] But it is also discussed as a major theme in the last two of his later works on the subject of grace, *De praedestinatione sanctorum* and *De dono perseverantiae*, as Augustine writes: "I have now to consider the subject of perseverance with greater care; for in the former book [*De praedestinatione sanctorum*] also I said some things on this subject when I was discussing the beginning of faith."[94] Therefore, I would like to discuss the way this theme is discussed in these works.

According to Augustine, the efficacious grace granted in and through Christ does not only bring a person back to God but keeps him or her for the remainder of his or her life: "[God's grace] begins a man's faith and … enables it to persevere unto the end."[95] Thus it is linked to his ideas on predestination, which Augustine almost equates with grace:

> Further, between grace and predestination there is only this difference, that predestination is the preparation for grace, while grace is the donation itself … Therefore God's predestination of good is, as I have said, the preparation of grace; which grace is the effect of that predestination.[96]

Interestingly, the effects granted in divine predestination do not include that the elect can ever know they endure in Christ to the end. For

---

93   Augustine, *De dono perseverantiae*, 55.
94   Ibid., 1.
95   Ibid., 33.
96   Augustine, *De praedestinatione sanctorum*, 19.

Augustine, there is no doctrine of assurance. Such knowledge, if possible, would create pride:

> From all which it is shown with sufficient clearness that the grace of God, which both begins a man's faith and which enables it to persevere unto the end, is not given according to our merits, but is given according to His own most secret and at the same time most righteous, wise, and beneficent will; since those whom He predestinated, them He also called, with that calling of which it is said, The gifts and calling of God are without repentance. To which calling there is no man that can be said by men with any certainty of affirmation to belong, until he has departed from this world; but in this life of man, which is a state of trial upon the earth, he who seems to stand must take heed lest he fall.[97]

A similar point is made in *De correptione et gratia*:

> Whosoever, then, are made to differ from that original condemnation by such bounty of divine grace, there is no doubt but that for such it is provided that they should hear the gospel, and when they hear they believe, and in the faith which works by love they persevere unto the end; and if, perchance, they deviate from the way, when they are rebuked they are amended and some of them, although they may not be rebuked by men, return into the path which they had left; and some who have received grace in any age whatever are withdrawn from the perils of this life by swiftness of death. For He works all these things in them who made them vessels of mercy, who also elected them in His Son before the foundation of the world by the election of grace: "And if by grace, then is it no more of works, otherwise grace is no more grace." For they were not so called as not to be elected, in respect of which it is said, "For many are called but few are elected;" but because they were called according to the purpose, they are of a certainty also elected by the election, as it is said, of grace, not of any precedent merits of theirs, because to them grace is all merit.[98]

As these two quotes show, Augustine does not link grace to the question of assurance or certainty in life. He portrays the opposite, writing more of an uncertain reality or spiritual struggle that even a person with this grace of perseverance may deviate from the straight path. So instead of

---

97   Augustine, *De dono perseverantiae*, 33.
98   Augustine, *De correptione et gratia*, 13.

having personal assurance, the elect ought to fear and thus seek in prayer to ensure their divine calling.[99]

But such instability is never found on God's side. God never changes. God never fails. God never withdraws from what He has chosen to persevere to the end. Those whom God has ordained to life will not therefore fail in faith: "For when Christ thus ordained them that they should go and bring forth fruit, and that their fruit should remain, who would dare to say, It shall not remain? Who would dare to say, Perchance it will not remain?"[100] By grace, they "cannot help persevering."[101] Of course, there may be some lapses, but these are only temporary. Grace assuredly restores them out of those lapses and enfolds them to the end with its gifting element of persevering. In other words, even negative actions of those who are graced with the gift of perseverance do not affect their destiny, for that destiny is already and forever determined from outside themselves. In fact, either God will cause the elect to die before they lapse,[102] or God will not allow them to die until they are fully restored and given to Christ the Son – in whom one "may not perish, but have eternal life (Mt. 20:16)."[103]

Yet, the case of those outside the grace of perseverance is quite different. In Chapter 20 of his *De correptione et gratia*, Augustine says:

> [T]here are some who are called by us children of God on account of grace received even in temporal things, yet are not so called by God; of whom the same John [i.e., the Evangelist John] says, "They went out from us, but they were not of us, because if they had been of us they would, no doubt, have continued with us." He does not say, "They went out from us, but because they did not abide with us they are no longer now of us;" but he says, "They went out from us, but they were not of us," – that is to say, even when they appeared among us, they were not of us ... [because those] who are truly children are foreknown and predestinated as conformed to the image of His Son, and are called according to His purpose, so as to be elected. For the son of promise does not perish, but the son of perdition.[104]

---

99 Augustine, *De praedestinatione sanctorum*, 19: "Nevertheless, it is good not to be high-minded, but to fear."
100 Augustine, *De correptione et gratia*, 34.
101 Ibid.
102 Ibid., 13.
103 Ibid., 21.
104 Ibid., 20.

As this quote shows, there are those who are baptized and begin to live in faith. Therefore, they seem to be numbered among the elect. But in reality, they fail in perseverance. Since they were not predestined as elect, they lack the necessary grace.

The non-elect converts who "have not received perseverance" are, nonetheless, accountable for their failure to continue in the good.[105] Just as those who "have not heard the gospel of Christ" will be condemned by their lack of faith, so also those who have heard the same gospel of Christ and even received "faith [that] comes by hearing" will be condemned for their failure to persevere in it. They could have heard, they could have kept, and if they had so willed, they could have persevered to the end, but they did not so will: "O man, in that which you had heard and kept, [...] you might persevere if you would."[106] Of course, without the grace of perseverance, a continued will for the good is not possible; yet the failure of the will to good is up to a person who is not so willing to persevere in it, and on that account he or she is worthy of condemnation: "[W]e still rebuke those, and reasonably rebuke them, who, although they were living well, have not persevered therein; because they have of their own will been changed from a good to an evil life, and on that account are worthy of rebuke."[107]

To consider grace in terms of perseverance may call into question the degree to which our human actions are genuinely natural. For these actions are enacted by the human agent only as that agent is acted upon by God. There is no sense in which they are naturally initiated. Moreover, the human reaction to divine grace has the appearance in Augustine of being somewhat mechanical. Whatever God wills or chooses to persevere is accomplished, for the divine will to give salvation is a will which no human will resists: "[N]o [hu]man's will resists when He wills to give salvation."[108] Blatantly stated, God overrules our human will – efficaciously, gratuitously (or preveniently), and perseveringly.

Suggestions of an automaton may arise at this point. Such inferences may not be entirely inappropriate in the context that free will is not a

---

105   Ibid.
106   Ibid., 11.
107   Ibid.
108   Ibid., 43.

neutral condition in which one may will either the good or the bad. But against this view, Augustine encourages his readers toward a stronger view of divine grace as a comfort or reassurance for them in gaining a right will:

> For, unquestionably to be led is something more compulsory than to be ruled. He who is ruled at the same time does something himself – indeed, when ruled by God, it is with the express view that he should also act rightly; whereas the man who is led can hardly be understood to do any thing himself at all. And yet the Saviour's helpful grace is so much better than our own wills and desires, that the apostle does not hesitate to say: "As many as are led by the Spirit of God, they are the sons of God." And our free will can do nothing better for us than to submit itself to be led by Him who can do nothing amiss; and after doing this, not to doubt that it was helped to do it by Him of whom it is said in the psalm, "He is my God, His mercy shall go before me."[109]

Confronting the idea that his doctrine of grace leads to the vanquishing of free will, Augustine also allows at least some measure of creaturely initiative or describes the situation of a beneficiary of grace as one of freedom.[110] Then he eagerly pronounces:

> Do you not see how he does not say that God's grace is necessary to prevent us from sinning, but because we have sinned? ... Now we do not, when we make mention of these things, take away freedom of will, but we preach the grace of God.[111]

And:

> If I were to propose to you the question how God the Father draws men to the Son, when He has left them to themselves in freedom of action, you would perhaps find it difficult of solution. For how does He draw them to Him if He leaves them to themselves, so that each should choose what he pleases? And yet both these facts are true; but this is a truth which few have intellect enough to penetrate. As therefore it is possible that, after leaving men to themselves in free will, the Father should yet draw them to the Son, so is it also possible that those warnings which are given by the correction of the laws do not take away free will ... No one, therefore, takes away from you your free will. But I would urge you diligently to consider which you would

109   Augustine, *De gestis Pelagii*, 5.
110   Weaver, *Divine Grace and Human Agency*, 31–2.
111   Augustine, *De natura et gratia*, 36.

rather choose – whether to live corrected in peace, or, by persevering in malice, to undergo real punishment under the false name of martyrdom.[112]

Nevertheless, it must be noted that with reference to the elect, there is no allowance for self-initiated willing or doing the good. And on this account, one cannot fail to conclude that Augustine had not entirely resolved the grace-nature debate but provided a window onto the church's ongoing struggle to define the relationship between grace and nature.

Conclusion

This chapter provides a brief summary of Augustine's later views on grace and nature. With regard to nature, this chapter shows that Augustine develops an original concept of *originale peccatum* by discussing infant baptism and assessing the Latin version of Roman 5:12: *in quo omnes pecca verunt* (in whom [Adam] all have sinned), and that on the basis of this concept, Augustine claims all of those descendants born in Adam as corrupted in nature. Then with regard to grace, this chapter summarizes the three attributes of grace – efficacy, gratuity (or prevenience), perseverance (or predestination) – that Augustine emphasizes against Pelagius' teachings on grace and nature. This threefold attribute of grace in Augustine confirms that grace is causally or logically superior to nature, dramatically expanding the radius of activity of divine grace – even at the expense of its counterpart, free will. And especially with the third of them, the grace of perseverance, this radius of activity evolves further into an extreme form, that grace not only predetermines humans into two groups, the elect and the non-elect, but also posits an ontological boundary between them.

This extreme form of grace in Augustine was unevenly accepted in and after the Second Synod of Orange (529). Such differences in acceptance soon led to a cycle of theological, doctrinal, and pastoral divisions between Christian traditions, especially between Protestant and Catholic churches.

112   Augustine, *Contra litteras Petiliani*, 2.85.186.

Perhaps the easiest way to identify the division is to look at Martin Luther and the Trent Council, and how these two Christian heirs of Augustine understand the relationship between grace and nature. However, since the particular contour of this book lies in a further promotion of the ecumenical relationship between Wesleyan and Catholic traditions, the following discussion will focus on Wesley's and then Thomas' views on grace and nature.

PART I

Wesleyan Tradition: John Wesley and His View of Grace and Nature

CHAPTER 2

John Wesley on Sin and Nature

Augustine's view of grace and nature is a very important theological norm in the Western Christian theological tradition. But there is a difference between the ways specific theological traditions accept and interpret this view. The difference can be seen not only between Protestantism and Catholicism but also within each communion of these Christian traditions. It is therefore virtually impossible to list all of the receptive diversity between Christian traditions – or between communions of a particular tradition – that embrace Augustine.

This book does not aim to summarize the views of all who have unevenly inherited Augustine's legacy. As already stated in the Introduction, the purpose of this book is to uncover the deeper theological compatibility between Wesley's and Thomas' doctrines of grace and nature. Thus, this book will seek to compare the two who have formed their theological affirmations around Augustine.

Such anchoring is now cumulatively docked from this Part I onwards with a specific goal in mind. Part I is divided into two chapters, "John Wesley on Sin and Nature" and "John Wesley on Grace." The first chapter, "John Wesley on Sin and Nature," begins by introducing unique theological style that Wesley adopts in approaching the subject (sin and nature). Then it proceeds to chronologically detail Wesley's doctrine of sin and nature. His views on sin and nature, like Augustine's, evolved over the time. Moreover, Wesley left us no systematic framework to lean on. In this respect, this study is necessary, and as a response to this want, its focus will be limited to providing a structural framework for Wesley's doctrine of sin and nature.

The second chapter of Part I, called "John Wesley on Grace," begins with a historical overview of the early Protestant approach to grace, which can provide a suitable context for understanding Wesley's unique account of grace. Then it proceeds to a chronological reading and systematic arrangement of Wesley's teachings on prevenient grace and on many other types of grace. The purpose of this chapter is to read and present Wesley's doctrine of grace, which has deep theological compatibility with Thomas.'

Before we advance to the main body, the source of this Part I needs to be mentioned: Both chapters will use what Geoffrey Wainwright – who is an ordained minister of the Methodist Church of Great Britain and co-chair of the WMC-Catholic dialogue since 1986 – identifies as the source of the most commonly recognized doctrinal criteria in the Wesleyan tradition: Wesley's *Sermons*, Wesley's *Explanatory Notes upon the Old and the New Testaments*, and Wesley's edited version of the Anglican Thirty-Nine Articles – also known as Wesley's *Articles of Religion*.[1] While there is some variety in the normativity of these documents in the various churches following the Wesleyan tradition, the theological authority given to Wesley's writings is one of the distinctive marks of Wesleyan or Methodist churches. Thus, these Chapters 2 and 3 will use Wesley's writings as its authoritative reference, and it will try to gain therefrom a legitimate statement of what Wesley has taught about grace and nature throughout his life.

Wesley's Views of Sin and Nature

Wesley retrieves many themes of Augustinian theology. The similarity is clearly visible, especially concerning the problem of original sin. Indeed, his understanding of original sin seems to accept Augustine's literal-historical interpretation of Genesis 2–3 with no qualifications. The following points may provide further warrants to the similarity between these two theologians: (1) Wesley's comment on Romans 5:12 that all sinned *in Adam*, along with a designation of Adam as the common head or legal representative of all humanity[2]; (2) Wesley's recognition and

---

1   Geoffrey Wainwright, "Speaking the Truth in Love," in Michel René Barnes ed., *A Man of the Church: Honoring the Theology, Life, and Witness of Ralph Del Colle* (Eugene, OR: Pickwick, 2012), 91.

2   Wesley, *NT Notes*, Roman 5:12. See also Wesley, "The Doctrine of Original Sin," in *Works* (Albany) 9, Pt.2, especially on page 274.

affirmative acceptance of Augustine's claim that infant baptism is necessary because all humans, even infants, who die without baptism are necessarily damned[3]; (3) Wesley's recasting of Augustine's *venial* sin and *mortal* sin into "*sin improperly so called*" and "*sin properly so called*"[4]; (4) Wesley's monastic belief in the cleansing activity of baptismal grace – that is, its *partial* relation to the latter form of sin (mortal sin)[5]; and (5) Wesley's teaching that human nature can will or do good only when therapeutically healed by divine grace.[6] These five points seem to fuel some Wesleyan claims that the similarity outnumbers several possible differences between Wesley and Augustine.[7]

However, Wesley assumes a unique theological style in developing his ideas of sin and its negative effects on nature. This style is an intellectual legacy of Richard Hooker that Wesley inherited from the Church of England,[8] and it was once again noticed by John Henry Newman – when

---

3   Wesley, "Treatises on Baptism," in *Works* (New York) 9, IV.9. See also Wesley, "The Doctrine of Original Sin," in *Works* (Albany) 9, Pt.6, V.4, especially on page 468.

4   Wesley, "Thoughts on Christian Perfection" (1760), in *Works* 13, q.6. See also Mark K. Olson, "John Wesley's Doctrine of Sin Revisited," *Wesleyan Theological Journal* 47, no. 2 (Fall 2012): 53–71, at 60.

5   To put it bluntly, this partial cleansing of mortal sin is the background behind Wesley's saying that all believers, even the baptized or the most perfect, needs daily forgiveness. Mark K. Olson, *John Wesley's "A Plain Account of Christian Perfection": The Annotated Edition* (Fenwick: Alethea In Heart, 2005), 116. Cf. Albert C. Outler, *John Wesley* (New York: Oxford University Press, 1964), 177.

6   Wesley, "Original Sin," in *Works* 2, III.5.

7   See Moi Kieng Ting, *Augustine's and Wesley's Concepts of Prevenient Grace: A Comparative Study* (Saarbrücken, Germany: LAP Lambert Academic Publishing, 2010). See also Kenneth J. Collins, *The Theology of John Wesley: Holy Love and the Shape of Grace* (Nashville, TN: Abingdon Press, 2007), 72.

8   After the English Restoration (1660), the religious identity of the Anglican Church as a *via media* was first noticed by Richard Hooker and then officially by Bishop Simon Patrick, at the time vicar of St Paul's, Covent Garden, and later appointed Bishop of Chichester and then Ely following the accession of King William III and Queen Mary II in 1689. For Patrick, such a mean was "no longer Aristotelian" but "an openness to the new learning which would allow the Church to keep up with developments in scholarship." Mark Chapman, *Anglican Theology* (London: T&T Clark International, 2012), 162.

early in life Newman defended Anglicanism[9] – and then reconstituted into a *via media philosophy* with more ecumenical nuances at an academic meeting of the Wesleyan Philosophical Society in March 2007.[10]

Via media philosophy is a conceptual technique that risks affirmation, alteration, or rejection of any dominant, often conflicting, truth claim to explore the potential of additional discoveries (or alternative positions) of truth in other religious traditions.[11] Wesley, an ordained Church of England priest, had great esteem for this *via media* philosophy and intended to continue it by practicing "a moderating sensibility, a tendency to avoid one-sided readings,"[12] and "an instinct for getting around the theological gridlock of competing systems."[13]

According to Kenneth J. Collins, it is this Aristotelian bent, this curious feature of his theological profile that makes Wesley shift intellectually: first a Puritan background, next a Greek Patristic reading program (Holy Club), then a thunderbolt from Luther at Aldersgate, and finally inundation from Roman Catholic mystics and Pietist spiritual writers.[14] In his lifetime, this Anglican priest was not afraid to cross lines. Nor was he reluctant to hold a diversity of truths in tension. But ever since Wesley attracted and appealed differently to people with different traditions in his own lifetime,

9   John Henry Newman, *The Via Media of the Anglican Church Illustrated in Lectures, Letters and Tracts Written between 1830 and 1841* (London: Longmans, 1901), 18.

10 This historic meeting of Wesleyan philosophers allows Roman Catholic philosophers to offer essays on key themes of mutually significant thought. The setting itself was an illustration of *via media philosophy*. Wesleyan scholars challenged Catholic scholars, and vice versa. The divergent opinions expressed at this meeting exemplified a way of engaging in philosophy: striving for a middle way unto truth. L. Bryan Williams, "Introduction," in L. Bryan Williams, ed., *Via Media Philosophy – Holiness unto Truth: Intersection between Wesleyan and Roman Catholic Voices* (Newcastle: Cambridge Scholars Publishing, 2009), vii–viii.

11 Randy L. Maddox, "John Wesley and Eastern Orthodoxy: Influences, Convergences and Differences," *The Asbury Theological Journal* 45, no. 2 (1990): 29–53, at 30. For more information about this philosophical pilgrim, see P. H. Hughes, *The Theology of the English Reformers* (London: Hodder and Stoughton, 1965).

12 Collins, *The Theology of John Wesley*, 4.

13 Fred Sanders, *Wesley on the Christian Life: The Heart Renewed in Love* (Wheaton, IL: Crossway, 2013), 16–7.

14 Collins, *The Theology of John Wesley*, 4.

this unique theological style has drawn a great variety of interpretations of Wesley's ideas of sin and nature.

For example, Randy L. Maddox – a Wesleyan theologian who has emphasized several theological points of contact between Wesley and Eastern Orthodox theology – conceptualizes the wayward nuances of Wesley's theological anthropology with a twofold category of theological anthropology in the Eastern Orthodox Church: Image and Likeness.[15] Also, Gregory P. Van Buskirk sets Wesley's view of human nature into a more ecumenical context and suggests the possibility of constructively recasting it into Arminian' metaphysical terminology[16] or Aquinas' affective moral psychology (intellect-will-liberty).[17] But the most concise and overarching example can be seen in the oft-quoted statement by Albert C. Outler that Wesley represents a third alternative to Pelagian optimism on the one hand and Augustinian pessimism on the other: to wit, "a Protestant doctrine of original sin *minus* most of the other elements in classical Protestant

15   Randy L. Maddox, *Responsible Grace: John Wesley's Practical Theology* (Nashville, TN: Abingdon Press, 1994), 65–93.

16   Contrary to the majority view of Wesley as an adherent to total depravity, Gregory P. Van Buskirk makes a notable exception that Wesley was, in fact, a carefully nuanced advocate of James Arminius' theory of *privation*. The main rationale for this argument lies in his analysis of Vern A. Hannah and Leon N. Hynson, who proposed that Wesley was forming the problem of original sin in ethical and relational categories rather than ontological. Gregory P. Van Buskirk, "Icon Dignity: Nature, Grace, and Virtue in the Theologies of John Wesley and Thomas Aquinas," PhD diss. (Boston University School of Theology, 2019), 219–23. For Arminius' own account of sin as privation, see, James Arminius, "Private Disputation XXXI," §10, in *The Works of James Arminius*, Vol. 2, trans. James Nichols (Auburn, NY: Derby & Miller, 1853), 79.

17   Buskirk argues that for Wesley and Thomas, grace does not destroy but enlightens, strengthens, and invigorates nature (especially, our faculties and their intellectual and affective functioning), so it is a moral matter: it pertains to the dynamics of human behavior on a divine plane; or, more specifically, to the moral psychology of graced human acts (in which our growth in grace is possible and providential). Ibid., 113–60.

soteriology, *plus* a Catholic doctrine of perfection *without* its full panoply of priesthood and priestcraft."[18]

None of these examples confirm Wesley's identity as a purely Augustinian theologian. Moreover, as already expected from them as a corollary, there is no universal norm or standard by which one can level and regulatively grasp Wesley's vocabulary on sin and nature. Ambiguity remains. Scholarly subtlety overflows with different nuances. Above all, Wesley is not a systematic theologian. Therefore, finding the real Wesley is difficult – and becomes particularly confusing when one is asked to systematically express what the real Wesley says about sin and nature.

One way to lessen that confusion and to obtain a more nuanced and systematic account of the relationship between sin and nature in Wesley is to phenomenologically *epoché* (bracket) any attempt to quickly reconcile or synthesize the various types of discrepancy present in Wesley's theological anthropology. Thus, instead of a quick generalization or synthesis, this chapter will read and analyze Wesley's changing ideas of sin and nature across the following periods: (1) the Oxford era (1725–37); (2) the Aldersgate era (1738–58); and (3) the Methodist revival and ensuing schism era (1759–91).[19]

18   Albert C. Outler, *Theology in the Wesleyan Spirit* (Nashville, TN: Tidings, 1975), 33. See also Christian T. Collins Winn, ed., *From the Margins: A Celebration of the Theological Work of Donald W. Dayton* (Eugene, OR: Pickwick, 2007), 119.

19   My distinction between these three periods is based on the changing historical context: The first period extends from 1725, when Wesley decided to enter holy orders in Oxford, until 1737, a year before his Aldersgate experience of 1738. The second period spans from 1738, when Wesley received an experience of assurance of his salvation at a group meeting in Aldersgate and started to carefully interact with Lutheran pietists or Reformed preachers, until 1758, a year before 1759 when his idea of entire sanctification was first consolidated into a book *Thoughts on Christian Perfection*. And the third period corresponds to the rest of his life, where he was defending against any attacks on the doctrine of entire sanctification by unfolding his own position in a lay style.

The Oxford Era (1725–1737)

From the 150 sermon manuscripts written by John Wesley and published in the *Bicentennial Edition*, 19 were written prior to the Aldersgate experience of 1738. Six of these 19 sermon manuscripts contain Wesley's early ideas about original sin and fallen human nature. The table below shows the titles, the Bible verses, and the dates of the six sermon manuscripts:

Sermon Title	Bible Verse	Date of Sermon
Death and Deliverance	Job 3:17	1725-10-01
The Promise of Understanding	John 13:7	1730-07-04
The Image of God	Genesis 1:17	1730-11-01
The Circumcision of the Heart	Romans 2:29	1733-01-01
The One Thing Needful	Luke 10:42	1734-05
The Trouble and Rest of Good Man	Job 3:17	1735-09-21

Although they differ in the content or focus of their messages, these six sermon manuscripts all show that the Augustinian heritage of the Church of England has a profound effect on the formation of young Wesley's theological anthropology. So in each of these sermons, one can see that young Wesley did not qualify Augustine's understanding of the present corruption of human nature: since our souls partake of human nature, in Adam, before they enliven our bodies, we sinned when Adam sinned, and our human nature was vitiated when Adam's was vitiated (cf. Aquinas, *Summa Theologica*, I–II. 81.1–4).[20]

---

20   Wesley, "Death and Deliverance," in *Works* 4, §1; "The Promise of Understanding," in *Works* 4, II.1–3; "The Image of God," in *Works* 4, II.1–4; "The Circumcision of the Heart," in *Works* 1, II.1; "The One Thing Needful," in *Works* 4, I.3; and "The Trouble and Rest of Good Man," in *Works* 3, §§1–3.

However, the young Wesley's theological interest was not simply in subscribing to that popular Augustinian image – for it could hardly make clear *how* exactly (or materially) we were in Adam or *how* Adam acted on our behalf.[21] He desired more than a theological explanation of – or justification for – present human corruption. As such, the young Wesley took a great interest in teasing out a possible explanation for *how* original sin is transmitted and then attempted to substantiate his position through a biological explanation of the propagation of moral and spiritual corruption from Adam to his descendants. For instance, in a 1730 sermon "The Image of God," labeled as the third sermon manuscript in the table above, Wesley speculated that the forbidden fruit which Adam and Eve ate had a juice containing a number of infectious particles that cleaved to and clogged their veins – causing them mortal, laying a foundation for numberless physical disorders, and impairing their threefold human faculties (understanding, volition-will, and liberty).[22] The implication was that our first parents passed this corrupting agent on to the flesh of their sons and daughters. This biological (or *creationist*) explanation may not seem to fit within Augustine's *traducian* version of our juridical or existential connection with Adam and Eve. But it comports with the teachings of the Anglican community where young Wesley received holy orders in Oxford in 1725, specifically with the description of corruption as an "infection of nature" or "naturally engendered" in the Thirty-Nine Articles of the Church of England.[23] And it also resonates with imagery in the young Wesley's favored early Greek theologians like Pseudo-Macarius – in whom sin is viewed as an illness, an interior plague that the human race contracts.[24]

---

21   Jesse Couenhoven, *Stricken by Sin, Cured by Christ: Agency, Necessity, and Culpability in Augustinian Theology* (New York: Oxford University Press, 2013), 27.

22   Wesley, "The Image of God," in *Works* 4, II.1–5.

23   Rev. Joseph Miller, B. D., *The Thirty-Nine Articles of the Church of England: The Ninth Article, Hamartiology* (London: Simpkin, Marshall, & Co., 1885), 35–8. See also Maddox, *Responsible Grace*, 78.

24   Although sin has devastating effects on man, Pseudo-Macarius thinks it does not totally destroy the image of God in man; nor does it leave human nature totally depraved and without any natural capacity for virtue and goodness. Pseudo-Macarius views sin as a disease contracted by Adam and transmitted to every one of Adam's descendants. Thus, in his therapeutic language of soteriology, Pseudo-Macarius

Further concerns about his early inclination toward an infectious transmission of original sin were raised by almost all the sermon manuscripts listed in the table above – one exception is the second manuscript, "The Promise of Understanding," where the focus links up with his anti-Manichean theodicy that God is neither the author of sin by his will nor by his power.[25] In the first sermon manuscript, "Death and Deliverance," Wesley writes: "Vice has always been observed to be of a contagious nature, and its progress is the more sure for being unperceived."[26] Elsewhere, similar nuances are given with slightly different emphasis, eliciting that sin is conceived as an illness that requires healing rather than being conceptualized in legalistic or judiciary terms (as an act which either requires punishment or forgiveness). First, in Chapter 5 of the Section I in the "Circumcision of the Heart," Wesley says:

> This is that lowliness of mind, which they have learned of Christ, who follow his example and tread in his steps. And this knowledge of their disease, whereby they are more and more cleansed from one part of it, pride and vanity, disposes them to embrace, with a willing mind, the second thing implied in circumcision of the heart, – that faith which alone is able to make them whole, which is the one medicine given under heaven to heal their sickness.[27]

And in Chapter 4 of the Section I in the "One Thing Needful," he continues:

> Vile affections [of our sin] are not only so many chains, but likewise so many diseases. Our nature is distempered, as well as enslaved; the whole head is faint, and the whole heart sick. Our body, soul, and spirit, are infected, overspread, consumed, with the most fatal leprosy. We are all over, within and without, in the eye of God,

speaks of Christ as the "true Physician, who cures without costs." "[N]o earthly medicines," Pseudo-Macarius continues, "had any power to cure the human race of so great an interior plague." This type of illness can only "be healed by the help of ... medicine ... a cleansing of his heart by the Holy Spirit." Pseudo-Macarius, *The Fifty Spiritual Homilies and The Great Letter*, trans. George A. Maloney (New York, NY: Paulist Press, 1992), 152.

25 Wesley, "The Promise of Understanding," in *Works* 4, II.1.

26 Wesley, "Death and Deliverance," in *Works* 4, §11.

27 Wesley, "The Circumcision of the Hearth," in *Works* 1, I.5.

full of diseases, and wounds, and putrifying sores. Every one of our brutal passions and diabolical tempers, every kind of sensuality, pride, selfishness, is one of those deadly wounds, of those loathsome sores, full of corruption, and of all uncleanness.[28]

Then with a therapeutic model that could explain God's salvation as a process of restoring fallen humanity toward the original dignity of (hu)man in terms of our "perfect holiness" and our "perfect happiness" with God, Wesley repeats in the Preamble of the "Trouble and Rest of Good Man":

> The whole world is, indeed, in its present state, only one great infirmary. All that are therein are sick of sin; and their one business is to be healed. And for this very end, the great Physician of souls is continually present with them; marking all the diseases of every soul, "and giving medicines to heal its sickness."[29]

This passage – along with those that come from Wesley's early sermon manuscripts in the table above – further clarifies the *nuanced* difference between Augustine's and young Wesley's notions of sin. According to Wesley, everyone is a sinner, not by actual or personal sin but by a sin of nature which is transmitted by natural reproduction and present in each individual prior to actual or personal sins. With this subtle difference in mind, one may probably raise the expectation that this early Wesleyan concept of sin as a deadly illness would not simply ask each human hypostasis to bear responsibility for Adam's fault but for its action: "Our nature ... is so defaced by our original *and* actual corruptions."[30] In other words, for Wesley of this early Oxford era, each human hypostasis somehow – or precisely speaking, "through prevenient grace, which restores a small measure of freedom to humans, enabling them to respond to God"[31] – preserves its freedom (though not fully), the essential part of God's image in human nature. Thus, it is not just that metaphysical factor transmitted

28 Wesley, "The One Thing Needful," in *Works* 4, I.4.
29 Wesley, "The Trouble and Rest of Good Man," in *Works* 3, Preamble §1.
30 Wesley, "On Grieving the Holy Spirit," in *Works* (Jackson) 2, III.1.
31 Henry H. Knight III, "Love and Freedom 'by Grace Alone' in Wesley's Soteriology: A Proposal for Evangelicals," *PNEUMA: The Journal of the Society for Pentecostal Studies* 24, no. 1 (Spring 2002): 57–67, at 60.

from Adam, but this voluntary agent in the individual will that causes a person to commit a sin and be responsible for the resulting guilt.

The Aldersgate Era (1738–1758)

Moving on to the Aldersgate era, one can see that Wesley's early concept of original sin as a disease becomes more carefully nuanced. Of course, this change in nuance does not necessarily result in the complete eclipse of Wesley's early concept of sin. In many of his sermons between 1738 and 1758, he still describes sin as a disease and also says that it has corrupted human nature and threefold faculties.[32] Moreover, Wesley still imbibes the Augustinian commentary on Romans 5:12 to explain the origin of original sin and its transmission to Adam's posterity: *in quo omnes peccaverunt* (in whom [Adam] all have sinned). This appears in his *NT Notes* on Romans 5:12[33] and in many of the sermon manuscripts he wrote during this Aldersgate era.[34] Specifically, what Wesley was trying to say in and through these notes and sermons is that Adam is a federal head representing the entire human race:

> As by one man – Adam; who is mentioned, and not Eve, as being the representative of mankind. Sin entered into the world – Actual sin, and its consequence, a sinful nature. And death – With all its attendants. It entered into the world when it entered into being; for till then it did not exist. By sin – Therefore it could not enter before sin. Even so – Namely, by one man. In that – So the word is used also, 2 Corinthians

32 Wesley, "Upon Our Lord's Sermon on the Mount I," in *Works* 1, I.4.
33 In preparing his *NT Notes*, Wesley relied heavily on Johann Bengel's *Gnomon Novi Testamenti*. One particular example of this dependence is Romans 5:12. His comments follow Bengel in preserving the Augustinian claim that all sinned *in Adam*, along with a designation of Adam as representative of humanity. Wesley's *NT Notes*, including the commentary on Romans 5:12, was completed around September 23, 1755, according to Wesley's *Journal* (September 23, 1755), in *Works* 21, especially on page 31.
34 Wesley, "Justification by Faith," in *Works* 1, I.1, 8; and "The Righteousness of Faith," in *Works* 1, II. 6.

5:4. *All sinned – In Adam.* These words assign the reason why death came upon all men; infants themselves not excepted, in that all sinned.[35]

Thus "by one man sin entered into the world, and death by sin. And so death passed upon all men," as being contained in him who was the common father and representative of us all. Thus, "through the offense of one," all are dead, dead to God, dead in sin, dwelling in a corruptible, mortal body, shortly to be dissolved, and under the sentence of death eternal. For as, "by one man's disobedience," all "were made sinners;" so, by that offense of one, "judgment came upon all men to condemnation."[36]

By the sin of the first Adam, who was not only the father, but likewise the representative, of us all, we all fell short of the favor of God; we all became children of wrath; or, as the Apostle expresses it, "judgment came upon all men to condemnation."[37]

His longest treatise, *The Doctrine of Original Sin* (1757), further developed this "metaphysical man" analogy between Adam and his descendants. As the treatise proceeded to underscore both the common Adamic ancestry and the relation between the common nature and its personal affective-dispositional effects, Wesley started to bring out a second, opposite analogy that exists in the relationship between Adam and Christ, and between those who are in Adam and those who are in Christ.[38] Then he came to a soteriological conclusion, referring to the early fathers – for example, Justin Martyr, Irenaeus, Tertullian, Cyprian, Nazianzen, and Augustine – who testified of these two analogies above.[39]

"Christianity lies properly in the knowledge of what concerns Adam and Christ." For, certainly, if we do not know Christ, we know nothing to any purpose; and we cannot know Christ, without some knowledge of what relates to Adam, who was "the figure of Him that was to come."[40]

35   Wesley, *NT Notes* on Roman 5:12.
36   Wesley, "Justification by Faith," in *Works* 1, I.6.
37   Ibid., I.9.
38   Wesley, "The Doctrine of Original Sin," in *Works* (Albany) 9, Pt.6, V, especially on page 456–70.
39   Ibid.
40   Ibid. A similar point is made in his sermon "Justification by Faith": "By the sin of the first Adam, who was not only the father, but likewise the representative, of us all, we all fell short of the favor of God; we all became children of wrath; or, as the Apostle expresses it, "Judgment came upon all men to condemnation." Even so, by the sacrifice for sin made by the Second Adam, as the Representative of us all, God

In short, Wesley's understanding of sin at this later stage of his life is not entirely inconsistent with what he believed during the Oxford era. But, as we shall see now, Wesley's understanding of sin in the Aldersgate era developed, and it became more complex as he provided further clarification of what was lacking in previous versions.

Speaking of the most characteristic change in the middle period, it can be said that Wesley draws a sharper line between voluntary and involuntary sins. As we saw in our discussion of Augustine's response to the Hadrumetum debate, sin must be a volitional act. Without the engagement of our human volition, there can be no agency, no responsible choice in reference thereto, and therefore no sin. Yet, the very notion of original sin as a disease in the mind of young Wesley seemed to involve no free will or voluntary choice.[41] Moreover, a careful review of Wesley's prose writings in the Oxford era shows that, at least in this early period, Wesley failed to develop his early idea of sin and address the problem of voluntary and involuntary sins. It was only after his 1738 new gospel manifesto "Salvation By Faith" that Wesley began to reconceptualize the problem of sin with regard to the problem of *will*, and introduced a more sophisticated and complex category of sin that would shape his doctrine of sin over the two decades. The table below shows the sermon manuscripts of the Aldersgate era that contain this advanced concept of sin in the middle Wesley and the resulting doctrine of human nature:

Sermon Title	Bible Verse	Date of Sermon
Salvation By Faith	Ephesians 2:8	1738-06-11
Christian Perfection	Philippians 3:12	1741

is so far reconciled to all the world, that he hath given them a new covenant; the plain condition whereof being once fulfilled, "there is no more condemnation" for us, but "we are justified freely by his grace, through the redemption that is in Jesus Christ." Wesley, "Justification by Faith," in *Works* 1, I.9.

41   For this reason, the young Wesley could not help but have to add in his letter to Ann Granville on October 3, 1731: "strictly speaking, [sin] is a *voluntary* breach of a known law [i.e., the one given on the heart by the Spirit." Wesley, Letter to Ann Granville, 10/3/31 in *Works* 24, especially on page 318.

The Way to the Kingdom	Mark 1:15	1746
The First Fruits of the Spirit	Romans 8:1	1746
The Spirit of Bondage and of Adoption	Romans 8:15	1746
The Great Privilege of Those that are Born of God	1 John 3:9	1748
The Original, Nature, Properties, and Use of the Law	Romans 7:12	1750
The Law Established through Faith I	Romans 3:31	1750

In the sermon manuscripts presented in the table above, Wesley first states that the essence of sin is *formally* the loss or privation of "original righteousness" (or what he had once called "ancient perfection"[42] in 1727) and grace as its divine support: "Know that corruption of thy inmost nature, whereby thou art very far gone from *original righteousness*, whereby 'the flesh lusteth' always 'contrary to the Spirit,' through that 'carnal mind' which 'is enmity against God,' which 'is not subject to the law of God, neither indeed can be.'"[43] After detaching his notion of sin from a strict

42   Wesley, "On Mourning for the Dead," in *Works* 4, §5: "It was, indeed, of man's own, not of God's creation; who may permit, but never was the author of, evil. The same hour gave birth to grief and sin, as the same moment will deliver us from both. For neither did exist before human nature was corrupted, nor will it continue when that is restored to its *ancient perfection*."

43   Wesley, "The Way to Kingdom," in *Works* 1, II.1. See also Wesley, "The Doctrine of Original Sin," in *Works* (Albany) 9, Pt.7, especially on page 500: "Adam, by his sin, became not only guilty, but; corrupt; and so transmits guilt and corruption to his posterity. By his sin he stripped himself of his original righteousness and corrupted himself. We were in him representatively, as our moral head; we were in him seminally, as our natural head. Hence we fell in him; 'by his disobedience' we 'were made sinners;' his first sin is imputed to us. And we are left without that original righteousness." Commenting on the Ninth Article of the Church of England, Wesley further clarifies: "Original sin - is the fault and corruption of the nature of every man, - whereby man is very far gone from original righteousness, and is of his own nature inclined to evil, so that the flesh lusteth always contrary to the spirit; and

Calvinist version of total depravity (or if you will, this grafting of it onto a more Catholic version of original sin as privation), Wesley categorizes sin with various lexical modifiers to express what that essence is *materially* – for example, guilt, power, outward, inward, habitual, commission (committing), infirmity, voluntary, involuntary, willful, and etc. Although it does not seem to be organized systematically, such lexical diversity is not so sloppy in use that it blurs the middle Wesley's stated focus to drive a wedge between natural weakness and human volition, and between involuntary and voluntary sins.

His clear focus on human volition is particularly evident in the first, second, and fourth sermon manuscripts in the table above: "Salvation By Faith," "Christian Perfection," and "The First Fruits of the Spirit." In the first sermon manuscript, Wesley distinguishes sin into two main categories: the *guilt* of sin and the *power* of sin.[44] While the *guilt* of sin is simply likened to our personal responsibility in regard to sin, the *power* of sin is further subdivided into four types of sin: "habitual sin," "willful sin," "sinful desire," and "sin by infirmities."[45] Interestingly, Wesley's *controversial* views on perfection come into play at this point. Those born of God do not sin *habitually* since to do so literally means that sin still reigns – a definite mark of non-Christian in whom the efficacy of Christ's victory seems imperfect.[46] Neither does the Christian sin *willfully* since the will is now set on living for Christ. Next, the regenerate does not sin by *sinful desire* since the heart has been thoroughly transformed to desire God's holy and perfect will. Wesley then addresses the last type of sin: "sin by infirmities." Since one's natural weakness has no concurrence of his or her will, such deviations – whether in act, word, or thought – are not "properly" sins.[47] Thus, those born of God do not commit sin willingly, having been

therefore in every person born into this world, it deserveth God's wrath and damnation." Wesley, *A Farther Appeal to Men of Reason and Religion*, in *Works* (Albany) 8, Pt.1, II.5, especially on page 56.

44 Wesley, "Salvation By Faith," in *Works* 1, II.2, 3, 5.

45 Ibid., II.6.

46 This controversial appraisal is carefully overcome by Wesley's more advanced view of sin and nature or, more clearly, by the notion of prevenient grace that we shall treat in Chapter 3.

47 Wesley, "Salvation By Faith," in *Works* 1, II.6.

delivered from "all their sins; from original and actual, past and present sin, 'of the flesh and of the spirit.'"[48]

Though quite rudimentary in structure, the middle Wesley's doctrine of sin is now set on a certain trajectory. Central to that trajectory is the concurrence of the will in the commission of sin and the conviction – already present in the Oxford era – that our innate weakness (infirmity) is due to original sin (disease). The theological premise of "Salvation By Faith" is, therefore: (1) Because of Adam's sin, the power of sin rules over Adam's posterity; (2) however, those born of God do not enslave their innate volition to the power of sin (and its four types of sin); (3) it can, therefore, be said that they are saved from the power of sin, and, consequently from the guilt of sin – that is, their moral and personal responsibility does not come from Adam's fault, but from the actualization of that power by either habit, will, or desire.

From the theological premise above, two implications can arise. The new birth restores human volition. With that restored volition, those born of God attain perfection, as promised in "Whosoever is born of God doth not commit sin; for his seed remains in him: and he cannot sin, because he is born of God (1 John 3:9)." Moving to the winter of the following year, one can find a similar distinction made between natural weakness and human volition in Wesley's doctrine of sin. In the preface to an edition of his *Extract of the Life and Death of Mr. Thomas Halyburton*, Wesley writes:

> What do you mean by the word "sin?" those numberless weakness and follies, sometimes (improperly) termed sins of infirmity? If you mean only this, we shall not putt off these but with our bodies. But if you mean, "It does not promise entire freedom from sin, in its proper sense, or from committing sin," this is by no means true, unless the Scripture be false; for thus it is written: "Whosoever is born of God doth not commit sin" (unless he lose the Spirit of adoption, if not finally, yet for a while, as did this child of God;) "for his seed remains in him, and he cannot sin, because he is born of God." He cannot sin so long as "he keeps himself;" for then "that wicked one touches him not" (1 John 3:9; 5:8).[49]

---

48 Ibid., II.2.
49 Wesley, *Preface to An Extract of the Life and Death of Mr. Thomas Halyburton*, in *Works* (Jackson) 14, §5.

Like the 1738 sermon "Salvation By Faith," Wesley here also draws a sharp line of demarcation between natural weakness and human volition. But his conjoining of "entire freedom from sin" with the promises of 1 John 3:9 and 5:18 essentially relegated his view of perfection to the event of new birth. And this led to dire consequences in both his spiritual and theological equilibrium; first, with regard to spiritual dis-equilibrium, it does not fit into his own description of the spiritual struggle that continues in his post-Aldersgate life.[50] Next, with regard to theological dis-equilibrium, it does not articulate the need to "grow in grace" that those born of God are still required in their present life.[51]

His solution to this twofold dire consequence was found later, as Wesley was informed by Moravianism, the Lutheran pietistic movement, of the tension between intellect and heart, and then made a further distinction in human volition: intellectual volition (will) and affective volition (desire).[52] Coupled with the Moravian doctrine of the heart that the pure cleansing of the *heart* that governs *desire* is achieved in a second moment of our new birth (justification),[53] Wesley began to use a new twofold category

---

50 Wesley, "Journal & Diaries" 1/4/39, in *Works* 19, especially on page 29.
51 Wesley, "Christian Perfection," in *Works* 2, I.9.
52 In his later sermon "Of Good Angels," Wesley insinuates this distinction by saying that will and desire (or affection) are structurally under the single category (human volition), but are distinct from each other in operation. Wesley, "Of Good Angels," in *Works* 3, I.1.
53 In the 1739 and early 1740s, Methodist theology under Wesley's leadership was particularly informed by the Lutheran pietistic movement, Moravianism. However, Wesley's ties with the Moravians became gradually tenuous – and thus less engaged with one another – as a result of his meeting with Count Zinzendorf at Gray's Inn Walks on September 3, 1741. The main issue of this meeting came from the criticism of the concept that Wesley had once mistakenly claimed in his 1738 sermon "Salvation By Faith" and his *Preface to An Extract of the Life and Death of Mr. Thomas Halyburton*. At the meeting, Zinzendorf claimed in Latin that those born of God are entirely sanctified (perfection) at the moment of their new birth (justification). Surprisingly, Wesley replied to this claim: "What! Does not every believer, while he increases in love, increase equally in holiness? ... Is not therefore a father in Christ holier than a new-born babe?" Wesley's somewhat unexpected disapproval of Zinzendorf soon went beyond the differences of opinion between them, leading to a theological separation between Methodism and Moravianism. Despite

of sin – *inward* and *outward* – to define the dimension of salvation from sin as a process, rather than a judicial or forensic moment in time. First appearing in his journal on January 25, 1940, these categories *inward* and *outward* in relation to sin inform Wesley's landmark sermon "Christian Perfection."[54] Inward sin lies deep within human nature – or if you will, it *remains* (not *reigns*)[55] in the *hearts* of the children of God – and refers to any sinful temper, passion, or affection[56]; "such as pride, self-will, love of the world in any kind or degree; such as lust, anger, peevishness; any disposition contrary to the mind that was in Christ."[57] Since Augustine's view of sin as concupiscence, mediated to Wesley through the Thirty-Nine Articles, is closely related to an abiding "desire" for sin which human nature has been plunged into by its fall from original righteousness, one may recast this inordinate, intemperate lustful notion of sin into Augustine's term *desiderium peccati*.[58] Outward sin refers to a *deliberate* act or choice that succumbs to – indeed is *voluntarily* dominated by – inward sin and serves as a synonym for committing sin as *habitual*.[59] Whereas before Wesley had placed the twofold category of human volition (will and desire) under the

this separation, however, Wesley maintained a similar view of sanctification with some of the Moravians (Peter Böhler and August spangenberg), that "justified believers, those who are born of God, are not pure in heart, entirely sanctified." This, of course, was the main reason why Wesley broke up with Zinzendorf, but more importantly, it shows that Wesley was in the process of putting aside a notion to which he, himself, had once mistakenly given assent. Kenneth J. Collins, *John Wesley: A Theological Journey* (Nashville, TN: Abingdon Press, 2003), 112–3.

54   Olson, "John Wesley's Doctrine of Sin Revisited," 56.

55   Wesley first learned of the distinction between "sin remaining" and "sin reigning" from the Moravian evangelist Christian David in the summer of 1738, in *Works* 18, especially on page 274.

56   Wesley, "Christian Perfection," in *Works* 2, II.21, 24; and "The Scripture Way of Salvation," in *Works* 2, I.4.

57   Wesley, "On Sin in Believers," in *Works* 1, II.2.

58   Andrew J. Cheatle, *W. E. Sangster: Herald of Holiness – A Critical Analysis of the Doctrines of Sanctification and Perfection in the Thought of W.E. Sangster* (Eugene, OR: Wipf and Stock), 124.

59   Wesley, "Christian Perfection," in *Works* 2, II.4, 7, 20. See also Wesley, "The Great Privilege of Those That Are Born of God," in *Works* 1, II.7, 9.

single category "power of sin,"[60] the two are now carefully distinguished and placed in separate categories: *intellectual* and *affective* volitions. By making a further distinction between will and desire, Wesley raised the expectation that full salvation is attainable in this present life as a *process* involving several states toward entire sanctification (perfection) – rather than a single moment or event of juridical forgiveness or substitutionary atonement (new birth).[61] And from this more delayed, and protracted, language about perfection, Wesley went on to envision a proper solution to the problem arising out of that spiritual or theological dis-equilibrium.

Another important step Wesley took at the time was to move our innate weakness (infirmity) to a completely separate section in the sermon, thereby driving an even sharper wedge between infirmity and volition in his doctrine of sin.[62] Wesley utilized the term of 2 Corinthians 12:7 – "a thorn in the flesh" – to describe what our innate weakness is. Then by appealing to the early fathers – Tertullian, Chrysostom, Jerome, and Cyprian – who describe this term as a "violent headache" or some "grievous torments of the flesh and of the body,"[63] he went on to argue that our innate weakness itself does not prove that "any Christian must commit sin."[64] Last, coupled with his belief that the Apostle could not glory and take pleasure in anything evil or repressive in the name of sin (cf. 2 Corinthians 12:9), Wesley concluded that our natural weakness as a thorn in the flesh cannot belong to either inward or outward sin.[65] Essential to his sermon "Christian Perfection" is,

---

60 Wesley, "Salvation By Faith," in *Works* 1, II.6.
61 In his 1760 sermon "The New Birth," which further developed his discussion of the new birth, the mature Wesley clearly marks that distinction between the new birth and entire sanctification: "The new birth is not the same with sanctification ... This [new birth] is a part of sanctification, not the whole; it is the gate of it, the entrance into it. When we are born again, then our sanctification, our inward and outward holiness, begins. And thenceforward we are gradually to 'grow up in him who is our head.'" Wesley, "The New Birth," in *Works* 2, IV.3. The same idea is evident in his 1784 sermon "On Patience": "[entire sanctification is] the *constant* resignation of ourselves, body and spirit, to God." Wesley, "On Patience," in *Works* 3, §8.
62 Wesley, "Christian Perfection," in *Works* 2, II.15–6.
63 Ibid., II.16.
64 Ibid.
65 Ibid.

therefore, the concurrence of the human will: To wit, that the process by which sin gains dominion over human nature depends *not* on the passive and involuntary act of our natural weaknesses, but on the active and voluntary act of our intellectual and affective volitions.

Five years later, Wesley examined three more categories in his sermon "The First Fruits of the Spirit": "past sins" (guilt),[66] "sins of infirmity" (involuntary failings),[67] and "sins of surprise" (impulsive or reactive response).[68] Although this additional category of sin may help diversity or describe with nuances the subtle and complex relationship of sin to human nature, it does not add a new twist to the focus of his discussion. In that sermon, Wesley is still pivoting on the question of whether or not human volition is involved in sinning:

> We cannot say, either that men are, or that they are not, condemned for sins of surprise in general: But it seems, whenever a believer is by surprise overtaken in a fault, there is more or less condemnation, as there is more or less concurrence of his will. In proportion as a sinful desire, or word, or action, is more or less voluntary, so we may conceive God is more or less displeased, and there is more or less guilt upon the soul.[69]

So central is the engagement of the human volition in the commission of sin that in 1748 Wesley repeated his former definition of sin as an actual, voluntary breach of the law.[70] Then, with a summary of the dynamics between sin and nature in eight bullet points, he went on to reexamine the process of how sin gains dominion over human nature. At the heart this reexamination implies: Sin as desire (inward sin) results in habitual sin by voluntary will or deliberate choice (outward sin).[71]

---

66   Wesley, "The First Fruits of the Spirit," in *Works* 1, II.1.

67   Ibid., II.8.

68   Ibid., II.9.

69   Ibid., II.11.

70   Wesley, "The Great Privilege of Those That Are Born of God," in *Works* 1, II.2: "By sin, I here understand outward sin, according to the plain, common acceptation of the word; an actual, voluntary transgression of the law; of the revealed, written law of God; of any commandment of God, acknowledged to be such at the time that it is transgressed."

71   Ibid., II.9.

Most of Wesley's term for sin is now set in place. While the early Wesley tried to tease out sin mainly within the category of original sin as disease, in the middle period of his life, Wesley diversified and expanded his doctrine of sin by categorizing it with various lexical modifiers. Sin is now regarded as more complex, requiring more nuanced and rich understanding, knowledge, and approaches as a basis.

Notably, this categorical/grammatical construction of sin reflects originality in Wesley's diagnosis of human nature. Of course, the bedrock of his diagnosis is his doctrine of original sin. At this point, however, one can see that Wesley's ideas of fallen humanity may differ from the Reformed interpretation of the doctrine, particularly from Luther's definition of Christian existence as *simul justus et peccator* and the Calvinist doctrine of total depravity. As we already saw, in the Aldergate era Wesley did not hesitate to claim in Augustinian fashion that sin leads to the loss of original righteousness, as well as to the inordinate desire for created things (concupiscence). This distinctive understanding of human nature in Wesley is evident in his Aldersgate sermons: "The First Fruits of the Spirit," "The Spirit of Bondage and of Adoption," "The Great Privilege of Those that are Born of God," "The Original, Nature, Properties, and Use of the Law," and "The Law Established through Faith." Essential to these sermons is that pure nature does not exist,[72] graced nature is not totally

---

72   In his sermon "The Spirit of Bondage and of Adoption," Wesley introduces the threefold state of human existence: the natural, the legal, and the evangelical. The first state implies a state of pure nature, the second state a state of nature illuminated by the law, and the third state a state of nature thoroughly pierced by grace. These three states cannot exist independently of each other but are always dynamically interpermeated. Wesley, "The Spirit of Bondage and of Adoption," in *Works* 1, IV.1–4. Wesley's idea of natural law also supports his opposing view of pure nature. In his two sermons on natural law, "The Original, Nature, Properties, and Use of the Law" and "The Law Established through Faith," Wesley says that natural law is a visible form of divine virtue and wisdom. This form indicates a remnant of God's image in the fallen nature. Often referred to as "conscience" or "preventing grace," it also engraves "a copy of the eternal mind" and "a transcript of the divine nature" in both pre- and postlapsarian human nature, along with "the brightest efflux of His essential wisdom" and "the visible beauty of the Most High." Wesley, "The Original, Nature, Properties, and Use of the Law," in *Works* 2, II.6, III.10; "The

depr*a*ved,[73] and the reality of that graced nature does not conflict with
grace but is in a dynamic relationship with it:

> From what has been said, we may learn ... God's breathing into the soul and the soul's
> breathing back what it first receives from God; a continual action of God upon the
> soul and a reaction of the soul upon God; an unceasing presence of God ... [in our
> hearts] and an unceasing return of ... our hearts ... [as] a holy sacrifice ... unto God
> in Christ Jesus.[74]

Wesley was, in fact, an ardent proponent of free will (or free response-
ability, if you will) with regard to salvation – as he puts it himself, "Men
are as free in believing, or not believing, as if he [God] did not know it
at all."[75] A similar view repeats in his later sermon on theological anthropology, "What is Man?": "And although I have not an absolute power
over my own mind, because of the corruption of my own nature; *yet*,

Law Established through Faith," in *Works* 2, III.5; and "On Working Out Our Own
Salvation," in *Works* 3, III.4: "No man living is entirely destitute of ... *preventing
grace*. Every man has a greater or less measure of this [grace]."

73 Wesley, "The First Fruits of the Spirit," in *Works* 1, II.4. As can be seen from the
work of Leon O. Hynson and Vern A. Hannah, who find within Jacob (or James)
Arminius a theological source sympathetic to Wesley and many Wesleyans,
Wesley's anthropology retains a softened version of the strict Calvinist anthropology that presupposes the total depr*a*vity of man. His idea of prevenient grace
plays a crucial role in the formation of that soften anthropology, while stimulating
the imagination that his doctrine of human nature can be better grasped through
the term depr*i*vation, not depr*a*vation. According to his sermon "On Working Out
Our Own Salvation," prevenient grace does not cancel human depravity; it restores
to our nature the ability to respond positively to God's grace, to God's work of salvation. For a *more detailed* critical interaction with Wesley's doctrine of *grace and
nature, see* Wesley, "On Working Out Our Own Salvation," in *Works* 3; Thomas S.
Schreiner, "Does Scripture Teach Prevenient Grace in the Wesleyan Sense?" in *The
Grace of God, the Bondage of the Will, Vol. 2: Historical and Theological Perspectives
on Calvinism* (Grand Rapids, MI: Baker Pub Group, 1995), 365–83; Vern A.
Hannah, "Original Sin and Sanctification: A Problem for Wesleyans," *Wesleyan
Theological Journal* 18, no. 2 (Fall 1983): 47–53; and Leon O. Hynson, "Original
Sin as Privation: An Inquiry into a Theology of Sin and Sanctification," *Wesleyan
Theological Journal* 22, no. 2 (Fall 1987): 65–83.

74 Wesley, "The Great Privilege of Those That Are Born of God," in *Works* 1, III. 2.

75 Wesley, "On Predestination," in *Works* 2, §5.

through the grace of God assisting me, I have a power to choose and do good, as well as evil."[76] To be clear, this positive stance on human nature does not exclude human volition, though it entails a limitation of the meaning of freedom. For Wesley, human volition is not irredeemably enslaved (as in the teaching of *servum arbitrium*) to sin.[77] Through fellowship with God's grace, it can return to its original state (perfection): "I only assert, that there is a measure of free-will supernaturally restored to every man, together with that supernatural light which "enlightens every man that cometh into the world."[78]

76   Wesley, "What Is Man?," in *Works* 3, §11.

77   The phrase *servum arbitrium* derives from Augustine, though it is not typical of his thought. Luther used this phrase to teach the enslavement of man by sin. In other words, he regarded the *status corruptionis* as falling into a kind of necessary state. This teaching now serves as an important basis for supporting the Reformed doctrine of justification, from which one could be given a clue necessary to explain the difference between Luther's *Ordo Salutis* and Wesley's. For more explanation of *servum arbitrium*, see Alister E. McGrath, *Iustitia Dei: A History of the Christian Doctrine of Justification, Second Edition* (Cambridge: Cambridge University Press, 1998), 205.

78   Wesley, "Predestination Calmly Considered," in *Works* (Albany) 10, §45, especially on page 229–30. As for the charge of Wesley being a Pelagian, who holds a measure of free will back to man without grace, Wesley defends himself from the accusations of Dr. Erskine, saying that "Why Dr. E. should quarrel with me concerning natural free-will, I cannot conceive, unless for quarrelling's sake. For it is certain, on this head, if no other, we are precisely of one mind. I believe that Adam, before his fall, had such freedom of will, that he might choose either good or evil; but that, since the fall, no child of man has a natural power to choose anything that is truly good. Yet I know (and who does not?) That man has still freedom of will in things of an indifferent nature." Wesley, "Some Remarks on a Defense of the Preface to the Edinburgh Edition of Aspasio Vindicated," in *Works* (New York) 8, IV, especially on page 546.

The Methodist Revival and the Ensuing Schism Era (1759–1791)

In light of the Aldersgate understanding of sin, one can perhaps interpret Wesley's doctrine of perfection in a more positive tone and claim that the deliverance from all sin is possible in this life: or to put it more bluntly, Wesley sees no possibility of backsliding, at least in the Aldersgate period. This was actually confirmed by Wesley in his 1739 sermon on God's grace as a free gift.[79] With the ongoing gift of grace being bestowed on us both before and after salvation, Wesley asserted that the saved person's whole heart and mind should and could be so attuned to God the Spirit that their will was eventually obedient to God's will to grow in grace – thus, enabling ongoing perfection (sanctification) in Christ-like thought and deed.[80] A similar view is repeated in the 1741 sermon "Christian Perfection," where Wesley writes: "Christians are saved in this world from all sin, from all unrighteousness; that they are now in such a sense perfect, as not to commit sins and to be freed from evil thoughts and evil tempers."[81]

Clearly, the doctrine of perfection seems to be more than a theoretical possibility for Wesley. But such a positive view of perfection does not necessarily dismiss its contrary. Indeed, one can find in Wesley's later work a series of attempts to carefully balance his rather positive stance on perfection. For example, Wesley writes in his 1781 sermon "The End of Christ's Coming":

> But it may be observed, that the Son of God does not destroy the whole work of the devil in man, as long as he remains in this life. He does not yet destroy bodily weakness, sickness, pain, and a thousand infirmities incident to flesh and blood. He does not destroy all that weakness of understanding, which is the natural consequence of the soul's dwelling in a corruptible body; so that still, *Humanum est errare et nescire.*[82]

79   Wesley, "Free Grace," in *Works* 3, §14.
80   Ibid.
81   Wesley, "Christian Perfection," in *Works* 2, II.28.
82   Wesley, "The End of Christ's Coming," in *Works* 2, III.3. See also Wesley, "Wandering Thoughts," in *Works* 2, IV.5–7.

What Wesley claimed in this post-Aldersgate sermon seems to deny, though not willfully, the full-orbed category of his Aldersgate doctrine of sin. If the sanctified still need Christ in their priestly office, to atone for "their omissions, their shortcomings, their mistakes in judgment and practice, and their defects of various kinds ... all deviations from the perfect law,"[83] then who is free from all sin?[84] Call these deviations "involuntary," or by some other name or disposition arising from natural weakness (infirmity), the consequence remains unchanged: If such deviations need Christ's atonement, then one must confess them as *sin* before God's tribunal. Therefore, regardless of what Wesley had once claimed to the contrary, it seems that at least within that sermon above, Wesley seems to hold that there is no complete sanctification from all sin in this life.

But again, the problem was that Wesley left that negative view unstructured and made it consistently in tension with his other view that the goal of Christian life might be realized in this life – perhaps as a sort of "realized eschatology."[85] So for Wesley, there is both yes and no to entire sanctification from all sin in this life. One of his very latest sermons, "On the Discoveries of Faith," is perhaps a good example of how these two divergent answers to perfection occur together in his post-Aldersgate work:

> But what is the perfection here spoken of [in Heb. 6:1]? It is not only a deliverance from doubts and fears, but from sin, from all inward as well as outward sin; from evil desires, and evil tempers, as well as from evil words and works. Yea, and it is not only a negative blessing, a deliverance from all evil dispositions, implied in that expression, "I will circumcise thy heart [Deut. 10:16; 30:6]," but a positive one likewise, even the planting all good dispositions in their place, clearly implied in that other expression, "To love the Lord your God with all your heart, and with all your soul [Deut. 13:3, etc.]."[86]

83   Wesley, "A Plain Account of Christian Perfection," in *Works* (Albany) 11, §19, especially on page 463.

84   For more discussion of the relationship between Atonement and Perfection, see "Do the Entirely Sanctified Still Need Christ," a subsection of Chapter 6 in Kenneth J. Collins, *The Scripture Way of Salvation: The Heart of John Wesley's Theology* (Nashville, TN: Abingdon Press, 2010).

85   William J. Abraham and James E. Kirby, eds., *The Oxford Handbook of Methodist Studies* (Oxford: Oxford University Press, 2009), 175.

86   Wesley, "On the Discoveries of Faith," in *Works* 4, §16.

Such an ambivalent position first creates an eschatological ambiguity that Wesley never resolved to the end of his life. In other words, entire sanctification is possible in one sense of this earthly sojourn, but not in the other. There always remains the "already" of present salvation and the "not yet" of full salvation, as he somewhat indirectly acknowledged:

> "Being justified by faith, we have peace with God through our Lord Jesus Christ," – that peace which enables us in every state therewith to be content; which delivers us from all perplexing doubts, from all tormenting fears, and, in particular, from that "fear of death whereby we were all our lifetime subject to bondage." At the same time the Son of God strikes at the root of that grand work of the devil ... But it may be observed, that ... "Both ignorance and error [still] belong to humanity ... till the sentence takes place, 'Dust thou art, and unto dust thou shalt return!'"[87]

But it also creates a period of significant controversy within Methodism about the nature of perfection. One can further articulate this controversial period in two historical contexts that took place within the Methodist Church in the 1740s and 1760s. The *first* concerns the conflict that Wesley had with his friend George Whitefield in the 1740s. In one of his letters to Wesley, Whitefield says: "To the best of my knowledge, at present no sin has dominion over me, yet I feel the strugglings of indwelling sin day by day."[88] For Whitefield, perfection in this life was an impossible reality due to the corruption that has been transmitted to our bodies since the fall:

> these depraved natures of ours, must necessarily undergo an universal moral change; our understandings must be enlightened; our wills, reason, and consciences, must be renewed; our affections must be drawn toward, and fixed upon things above; and because flesh and blood cannot inherit the kingdom of heaven, this corruptible must on incorruption, this mortal must put on immortality. And thus old things must literally pass away, and behold all things, even the body as well as the faculties of the soul, must become new.[89]

---

87   Wesley, "The End of Christ's Coming," in *Works* 2, III.1–3.
88   Wesley, Letter from Whitefield, in *Works* 26, especially on page 11.
89   Lee Gatiss, ed., *The Sermons of George Whitefield*, Vol. 1 (Wheaton, IL: Crossway, 2012), 256.

It is only at the moment of our resurrection that we humans shall eventually be delivered from all sin:

> The most perfect Christian, I am persuaded, must agree, according to one of our Articles, "That the corruption of nature remains even in the regenerate; that the flesh lusteth always against the spirit, and the spirit against the flesh." So that believers cannot do things for God with that perfection they desire; this grieves their righteous souls [sic] day by day, and, with the holy apostle, makes them cry out, "who shall deliver us from the body of this death!" I thank God, our Lord Jesus Christ will, but not completely before the day of our dissolution; they will the very being of sin be destroyed, and an eternal stop put to inbred, indwelling corruption.[90]

This cannot help but mean that no human being is entirely sanctified (perfection) in this life. As a result, Whitefield confirmed that he was "no friend" to any form of "sinless perfection."[91] Then he wrote to Wesley expressing his greatest concern that this was in any way possible and his friend (Wesley) seemed "to own a sinless perfection in this life attainable."[92] Accordingly, Whitefield told Wesley: "I am yet persuaded, you greatly err. You have set a mark you will never arrive at, till you come to glory."[93]

Indeed, Wesley, like Whitefield, rejected any concept of sinless perfection. In his "Preface" to *Hymns and Sacred Poems*, Wesley listed 26 Bible passages to refute the charge imposed on him by Whitefield. Then he affirmed that he was also holding onto the doctrine of the Church of England:

> The perfection I hold is so far from being contrary to the doctrine of our [Anglican] Church that it is exactly the same which every clergyman prays every Sunday: "Cleanse the thoughts of our hearts by the inspiration of thy Holy Spirit, that we may *perfectly love thee*, and *worthily magnify* thy holy name." I mean neither more nor less than this.[94]

---

90   Lee Gatiss, ed., *The Sermons of George Whitefield*, Vol. 2 (Wheaton, IL: Crossway, 2012), 224–5.

91   Gatiss, ed., *The Sermons of George Whitefield*, Vol. 1, 199–200.

92   Wesley, Letter from Whitefield, in *Works* 26, especially on page 32.

93   Ibid., especially on page 43.

94   Rupert E. Davies, ed., *The Works of John Wesley, Vol. 9: The Methodist Societies: History, Nature, and Design* (Nashville, TN: Abingdon Press, 1989), 409; see also Gerald B. Cragg, ed., *The Works of John Wesley, Vol. 11: The Appeals to Men of*

However, while Whitefield understood Wesley's "perfection" as sinless perfection, Wesley referred to it as a form of "perfect love," or the
emptying or simplicity of a life-style, "so as to rejoice evermore, to pray
without ceasing, and in everything to give thanks."[95] He was convinced
that the sanctified could achieve this holy – or kenotic form of – love in
a state of grace as a fitting end for perfection.[96] Thus, Wesley used this
term "perfect love" to define perfection in his later work, as John Tyson
has said:

> John Wesley persistently defined Christian perfection in terms of loving God with all
> one's heart, mind, and strength, and loving one's neighbor as oneself (Matt. 22:37–39).
> This purity of intention is a consistent Christian maturity ("perfection," or "whole-
> ness"), which fulfills God's law through love and does not willfully violate a known
> law of God. Intentional sin ceases to dominate and determine our lives as we are
> being filled and transformed by God's love.[97]

Then he carefully shifted his focus to Christians' pursuit of being open to
what is completely filled by God's grace with God's perfect love, not their

---

    Reason and Religion and Certain Related Letters (Nashville, TN: Abingdon Press,
    1987), 108–17.

95   Wesley, Letter to Whitefield, in *Works* (Telford) 4, especially on page 10.

96   Based on the concise explanation of perfection that Wesley gives in his apologetic
    treatise "A Plain Account of Christian Perfection," one may also distil Wesley's view
    of perfection to purity of intention, the imitation of Christ, and love to God and
    neighbor. See Wesley, "A Plain Account of Christian Perfection," in *Works* (Albany)
    11, §27: "In one view, it [perfection] is purity of intention, dedicating all the life
    to God. It is the giving God all our heart; it is one desire and design ruling all
    our tempers. It is the devoting, not a part, but all our soul, body, and substance to
    God. In another view, it is all the mind which was in Christ, enabling us to walk as
    Christ walked. It is the circumcision of the heart from all filthiness, all inward as
    well as outward pollution. It is a renewal of the heart in the whole image of God,
    the full likeness of Him that created it. In yet another, it is the loving God with all
    our heart, and our neighbor as ourselves. Now, take it in which of these views you
    please, (for there is no material differences,) and this is the whole and sole perfec-
    tion, as a train of writings prove to a demonstration, which I have believed and
    taught for these forty years, from the year 1725 to the year 1765."

97   John R. Tyson, *The Way of the Wesleys* (Grand Rapids, MI: William B. Eerdmans,
    2014), 103.

own efforts to become perfect.[98] But it seems that this shift – the effort to capture the doctrine of perfection in terms of divine love – was not appealing enough to prevent the theological division between the two leaders in Methodism.

Another schism came around 1760. From this historical event one can find the final step in the maturation of Wesley's doctrine of sin. According to Rex D. Matthews, at the beginning of the Methodist Revival and Ensuing Schism Era (1759–91), Wesley became convinced that he had been formulating "such a high standard for ... perfection" that Methodists "were being hindered from experiencing its freedom." He began encouraging Methodists "to seek (through God's grace) the immediate experience of ... perfection" while unwittingly easing the restrictions on that deliverance from sin which comes with such perfection.[99] Two leaders of the Methodist community in London, Thomas Maxfield and George Bell, welcomed this change in nuance and took it to an extreme:

> Maxfield and Bell proclaimed a perfection that was instantaneously attained by the simple affirmation, "I believe," forfeiting any role for responsible growth prior to this event. And they portrayed this perfection as "angelic" or absolute, such that there was no need for growth after the event, or for the continuing atoning work of Christ.[100]

Influenced by high antinomianism and "enthusiasm," Maxfield and Bell superficially read Wesley's heightened emphasis on the possibility of present attainment of perfection and then infused the Methodist communities in London with a more immediate expectation or achievement of sinless perfection. And finally, they brought fanaticism into Methodism, predicting the end of the world on February 28, 1763.[101] As a result,

98   Rex D. Matthews, "John Wesley's Idea of Christian Perfection Reconsidered," *Wesleyan Theological Journal* 50, no. 2 (2015): 25–67, at 53.

99   Matthews, "John Wesley's Idea of Christian Perfection Reconsidered," 32. See also Wesley's "Queries to Those Who Deny Perfection Attainable in This Life" in the 1767 tract "Brief Thoughts on Christian Perfection" in *Works* (Albany) 11, §§1–3, especially on page 523–4.

100   Randy L. Maddox, "Be Ye Perfect?" *Christian History* 69 (2001): 32–4, at 34.

101   Walter Wilson, *The History and Antiquities of Dissenting Churches and Meeting Houses, in London, Westminster, and Southwark*, Vol. 3 (London: W. Button & Son, 1808), 418–9.

Wesley's official sanctions for their extreme behavior became inevitable, and Wesley himself had to further refine his doctrine of sin in a couple of ways.

First, in response to these perfectionists, Wesley corrected his 1759 tract *Thoughts on Christian Perfection*, which caused Maxfield's and Bell's errors, in his 1763 tract *Farther Thoughts on Christian Perfection*. In this later tract on the same subject, Wesley put the brakes on the idea of one's present attainment of perfection. In other words, the continuing nature of sin is once again discussed in Wesley's mature thought.

In the tract *Farther Thoughts on Christian Perfection*, Wesley grounds his doctrine of sin on the Reformed ideas of two covenants: old law of works and new law of faith (or love). The idea of old and new covenants gave Wesley two distinguishable criteria by which to define sin in his doctrine of perfection. Wesley taught that the law of works can be properly called the "Adamic law" or the "angelic law." Common to both angels and humans, this old law was "given to Adam in [his] innocence." Having been "created free from any defect, either in his understanding or his affections," Adam's body "was then no clog to the mind; it did not hinder his apprehending all things clearly, judging truly … and reasoning justly." It was simply "proportioned to his original [righteousness]." Adam was therefore expected to "always think, always speak, and always act precisely right, in every point whatever."[102] This concept of humanity's retrieval of original righteousness in the state of perfection remained a constant in Wesley's mature work.[103]

The next step however is crucial. With the coming of Christ, another law superseded the old. Called by Wesley the "law of faith (or love)," this new law essentially replaced the old law given to Adam. And it is given to those who are justified and sanctified by Christ in faith (or love).[104] Wesley taught that the new law is fulfilled only by love, not by one's perfect performance (i.e., works): "Faith working or animated by love is all that God now requires of man. He has substituted love … in the room of angelic

---

102   Wesley, "A Plain Account of Christian Perfection," in *Works* (Albany) 11, §25.
103   Cf. Wesley, "Original Sin," in *Works* 2; and "The Fall of Man," in *Works* 2.
104   Wesley, "A Plain Account of Christian Perfection," in *Works* (Albany) 11, §25.

perfection."[105] Of particular note is how this mature Wesley integrates these two criteria in his doctrine of perfection:

> Q. 13. But if Christ has put an end to that [old] law, what need of any atonement for their transgressing it?
>
> A. Observe in what sense he has put an end to it, and the difficulty vanishes. Were it not for the abiding merit of his death, and his continual intercession for us, that [old] law would condemn us still. These, therefore, we still need for every transgression of it.[106]

What Wesley means is in one sense that the Adamic law is still in full force. The coming of Christ did not abolish this old law. Without the abiding merit of his death and his continual intercession for us, we would probably be condemned. But it is also true that in other sense the Adamic law does not appear to be in full force, as Wesley claims that Christ is the end of the Adamic law; and that no one is expected to perform it since no one is proportioned to his or her original righteousness.[107] "Even God," according to Wesley, "does not require it of any [hu]man." "Nor is any [hu]man living bound to observe the Adamic [law]."[108] Then what does it mean that a person transgresses the Adamic law? Does it simply mean that a person does not perform it? No. It makes no sense to say that one violates what is not required of him or her. One possible answer for Wesley is thus the transgression pertains to the law of faith (or love), and it can thus only be explained in terms of one's un-loving relationship with God instead of one's non-performance of original righteousness. In Question 11, prior to Question 13 above, Wesley also states the nature of Christ's Atonement for those who transgress the law of faith (or love) in a similar way:

> But observe in what sense the persons in question need the atonement of Christ. They do not need him to reconcile them to God afresh; for they are reconciled. They do not need him to restore the favour of God, but to *continue* it.[109]

105　Ibid.
106　Ibid.
107　Ibid.
108　Ibid.
109　Ibid.

Central to his discussion in Question 11 is that it is *not* a failure of our duty or the end of our practice of original righteousness *but* a cessation of our loving relationship with Christ, the fulfillment of all laws, that makes us accountable for the Adamic law. And only through this interpretation can Christ's atonement appear to be consistent with the perfection that Wesley holds anew: "Love rejoicing evermore, praying without ceasing, and in everything giving thanks."[110]

Here we can take a deeper look at some important qualifications that are being made concerning perfection and sin. First with regard to perfection, one can see that it is accountable to both laws, the law of works and the law of faith (or love). "Perfection not attainable in this life (original righteousness)" pertains to the law of works, "perfection attainable in this life (holy love)" to the law of faith (or love). Then with regard to sin, one can see that it is also accountable to them both. Involuntary sin relates to the law of works, voluntary sin to the law of faith (or love).[111] These qualifications first correct the deviations that Maxfield and Bell brought to the Methodist community in London in the early 1760s. Even more importantly, this helps us gain a closer glimpse of Wesley's mature doctrine of sin and nature. We now turn to the effects of involuntary sin in nature.

Wesley consistently referred to those transgressions that are involuntary as our innate weakness (infirmity) rooted in Adam's primal sin.[112] To explain himself a little farther on this head, Wesley writes:

---

110   Ibid.

111   In each of these qualifications, the eschatological tension of "already" and "not yet" rises to the surface again. So, it seems obvious that Wesley believed in two kinds of perfection and two kinds of sin. Indeed, when asked if even a perfect Christian could sin, Wesley replied once: "Explain the term one way, and I say, Yes; another, and I say, No." Wesley, Letter to Samuel Furly, 9/15/62, in *Works* (Telford), especially on page 190.

112   In *Farther Thoughts on Christian Perfection*, Wesley repeats: "But Adam fell; and his incorruptible body became corruptible; and ever since, it is a clog to the soul, and hinders its operations. Hence, at present, no child of man can at all times apprehend clearly, or judge truly ... Therefore, it is as natural for a man to mistake as to breathe ... Consequently, no man is able to perform the service which the Adamic law requires." In other words, the primal sin of Adam brought about a fallen nature, and this fallen nature is the source, the root cause, of those

(1.) Not only sin, properly so called, (that is, a voluntary transgression of a known law,) but sin, improperly so called, (that is, an involuntary transgression of a divine law, known or unknown,) needs the atoning blood. (2.) I believe there is no such perfection in this life as excludes these involuntary transgressions which I apprehend to be naturally consequent on the ignorance and mistakes inseparable from mortality. (3.) Therefore sinless perfection is a phrase I never use, lest I should seem to contradict myself. (4.) I believe, a person filled with the love of God is still liable to these involuntary transgressions. (5.) Such transgressions you may call sins, if you please: I do not, for the reasons above-mentioned.[113]

This gives insight into Wesley's meaning, for the Christian, even the "most perfect" believer, may fall short of the absolute standard of original righteousness (perfection not attainable in this life). These sins of infirmity do not bring guilt; but they expose to divine tribunal, requiring the perpetual intercession of our high priest Jesus Christ. All Christians, writes Wesley, even the entirely sanctified, need to receive the merits of Christ from moment to moment and continuously "'grow in grace,' till 'an entrance be ministered unto you abundantly into the everlasting kingdom of our Lord Jesus Christ.'"[114] Otherwise, everything goes back to unholiness, and nothing but sin remains to them:

> The holiest of men still need Christ, as their Prophet, as "the light of the world." For he does not give them light, but from moment to moment: The instant he withdraws, all is darkness. They still need Christ as their King; for God does not give them a stock of holiness. But unless they receive a supply every moment, nothing but unholiness would remain.[115]

This sounds very much like Wesley is arguing that (1) evil is pervasive and stubborn, and cannot be overcome without the assistance of divine grace; (2) next follows the stage of spiritual struggle, when the person is indwelt simultaneously by both involuntary sin and divine light (or illuminating grace), the one fighting against the other; and (3) finally, there follows the

---

involuntary transgressions. Wesley, "A Plain Account of Christian Perfection," in *Works* (Albany) 11, §25.

113   Wesley, "A Plain Account of Christian Perfection," in *Works* (Albany) 11, §19.
114   Ibid., §25.
115   Ibid.

stage when involuntary sin is cast out from the person at physical death. It seems therefore evident for Wesley that there is hardly inalienable purity or perfection in this present life. Or to put it another way, perfection can perhaps be attainable in this life, but always in conjunction with effort, temptation, and much struggle.

Yet it would be wrong to conclude from this that Wesley is primarily bound up with a radically negative anthropology, for he in fact affirms there is hope with this endless battle through our cooperation in prayer with God:

> God does nothing but in answer to prayer ... Every new victory which a soul gains is the effect of a new prayer. On every occasion of uneasiness, we should retire to prayer, that we may give place to the grace and light of God and then form our resolutions, without being in any pain about what success they may have ... [For] He will again lift up your head, and cause the bones that have been broken to rejoice.[116]

This passage makes it clear that the main reason for hope lies in God's help. But part of the hope that Wesley envisions in this passage emerges also from the affirmation of human's prayerful, doxological power; that is to say, though that hope is given by God, it is also a human reaction and achievement. Thus, Wesley has no hesitation in claiming the supreme dignity of divine status God confers upon His rational creation: "O stand fast in the liberty wherewith Christ hath made you free."[117] Although involuntary sin has some devastating effects on our human nature, it would seem logical to conclude that in *Father Thoughts on Christian Perfection* Wesley thinks it does not totally destroy the image of God in us; nor does it leave our graced human nature totally depraved and without any natural capacity for our voluntary and doxological cooperation with God.[118]

---

116   Ibid.

117   Ibid.

118   Similar to this logical reasoning is found in one of his very latest sermons, "On Divine Providence," in *Works* 2, §15. In this 1786 sermon, Wesley says: "[God] cannot destroy out of the soul of man that image of himself wherein [man] was made" because God "cannot counteract himself, or oppose his own work." Theologically, if God cannot remove God's image from us, we cannot efface God's image ourselves – though it may seem that we can erase it. If we were to obliterate God's image from our human nature, we would be caught in a non sequitur that we use our God-imaged nature to nullify that nature.

In the same year that *Farther Thoughts on Christian Perfection* was published, Wesley wrote his 1763 sermon manuscript *On Sin in Believers*. In this second response to the perfectionists in the London community, Wesley's focus shifts from *involuntary sin and perfection* to *voluntary sin and perfection*. His main point remains to suggest a positive aspect of human nature and its active participatory role in achieving entire sanctification, while at the same time emphasizing a balanced view of perfection.

In the sermon "On Sin in Believers," Wesley further categorized voluntary sin into three basic types: guilt, power, and being. He writes:

> "But believers walk after the Spirit, and the Spirit of God dwells in them; consequently, they are delivered from the guilt, the power, or, in one word, the being of sin." These are coupled together, as if they were the same thing. But they are not the same thing. The *guilt* is one thing, the *power* another, and the *being* yet another. That believers are delivered from the guilt and power of sin we allow; that they are delivered from the being of it we deny.[119]

These three basic types seem to match up to his Aldersgate categories of the guilt of sin,[120] outward sin,[121] and inward sin.[122] However, a careful review of "On Sin in Believers" shows that Wesley is not simply playing a matching game here. By introducing the language of "being" to describe inward sin, Wesley made the link between inward sin (concupiscence) and original sin even more organic and explicit. Of course, that link had always been there, but Wesley now united the two more tightly to correct the perfectionist claim that all sin – guilt, power, outward, inward, and original – is entirely vanquished in the "already" of present salvation. He thus reaffirms that sin no longer reigns, but it does remain as a "φρονημα σαρκος [*phronema sarkos* – Romans 8., carnal mind]" in the nature of every person.[123]

Of particular note is that Wesley lumped the "being" of sin with the Greek term φρονημα σαρκος and then vaulted it onto a carnal principle that

---

119   Wesley, "On Sin in Believers," in *Works* 1, IV.4.
120   Cf. fn. 44.
121   Cf. fn. 59.
122   Cf. fn. 55.
123   Wesley, "On Sin in Believers," in *Works* 1, IV.7.

resides in our human nature. According to Wesley, this carnal principle is "put under our feet" by "God through the blood of the cross." It has "no more dominion over us." But "it still *exists*," and it is contrary to another principle that resides in our human nature.[124] Wesley saw this latter principle as coming through divine grace, and referring to the Pauline term in Galatians 5:17, he named it the "Spirit," and the former principle the "flesh."[125] He then insisted:

> Resentment of an affront [i.e., the flesh] is sin; it is ἀνομία, *disconformity to the law of love*. This has existed in me a thousand times. Yet it did not, and does not reign ... if the resentment I feel is *not yielded to*, even a moment, there is no *guilt* at all, no condemnation from God upon that account. And in this case, it has no *power*. Though it "lusteth against the Spirit," it cannot prevail. Here, therefore, as in ten thousand instances, there is *sin* [i.e., *being*] without either *guilt* or *power*.[126]

It appears from this passage that Wesley describes the paradoxical aspect of our human nature. Specifically, there are two contrary principles in our human nature. One is the flesh (being) resulting from original sin. The other is the Spirit resulting from God's grace. Here the paradox comes into play: Both principles are in one way or another present in our human nature, but *paradoxically* our human nature plays at variance with these *logikoi*.[127] In other words, although a person tends toward each of these habitual principles, it is not by the independent operation of the flesh or the Spirit that the person *either* commits an outward or inward sin *or* grows in grace unto perfection (holy love). Human, after all, is not a puppet. There is always another factor at play. Wesley had already called this factor "freedom,"[128] and now in "On Sin in Believers" he linked it

---

124   Ibid., IV.6–7. Wesley writes: "And they [Christians] are likewise holy and undefiled, while they 'walk after the Spirit'; although sensible there is *another principle* in them, and that 'these are contrary to each other.'"

125   Ibid., III.3; V.1.

126   Ibid., IV.10.

127   Ibid., IV.13.

128   While preserving a God-given and polyvalent freedom (image) which results in either one's deviation from God's will or one's *félix* resignation to it (likeness), Wesley writes: "O that we may not be hearers of it [Matthew 5:48: Be perfect, therefore, as your heavenly Father is perfect.] only! – 'like a man beholding his

with the life of virtue (goodness and justice), which was the original destiny God gave to Adam, and then preached:

> Understand the proposition right[!] ... Though the flesh in you "lust against the Spirit," you may still be a child of God; but if you "walk after the flesh," you are a child of the devil. Now this doctrine does not encourage to obey sin, but to resist it with all our might ... [and] earnestly ... "watch and pray" against the enemy within.[129]

In "On Sin in Believers," Wesley retained a softened version of human depravity. Although the being of sin (original sin) still remains, Wesley saw that it does not reign to the extent that it does not cut man off from God altogether[130]; neither does it destroy freedom, one of the essential parts of God's image in man, nor does it border on the Manichean position in which evil has positive ontological status.[131]

All of Wesley's vocabulary about sin is now set in place. Hence, his doctrine of sin and nature would not substantially change from this time onwards. At the same time, his continued affirmation of total depravity – albeit in a qualified form – puzzles many Wesleyan scholars, as does his ambivalent attitude toward perfection. For instance, Wesley wrote in his 1759 sermon "Original Sin":

> Many of the ancient Heathens have largely described the vices of particular men. They have spoken much against their covetousness, or cruelty; their luxury, or prodigality. Some have dared to say that "no man is born without vices of one kind or another." But still as none of them were apprized of the fall of man, so none of them knew of

---

own face in a glass, who goeth his way, and straightway forgetteth what manner of man he was.' Nay, but let us steadily 'look into this perfect law of liberty, and continue therein.' Let us not rest, until every line thereof is transcribed into our own hearts." Wesley, "Upon Our Lord's Sermon on the Mount III," in *Works* 1, IV.

129 Wesley, "On Sin in Believers," in *Works* 1, IV.13; V.2.
130 Cf. fn. 44.
131 Wesley explicitly affirmed this Augustinian view that evil has no essence in his early Oxford sermon "On Mourning for the Dead (1727)": "It was, indeed, of man's own, not of God's creation; who may permit, but never was the author of, evil. The same hour gave birth to ... sin ... For neither did [it] exist before human nature was corrupted, nor will it continue when that is restored to its ancient perfection." Wesley, "On Mourning for the Dead," in *Works* 4, §5.

his *total corruption*. They knew not that all men were empty of all good, and filled with all manner of evil. They were wholly ignorant of the *entire depravation* of the whole human nature, of every man born into the world, in every faculty of his soul, not so much by those particular vices which reign in particular persons, as by the general flood of Atheism and idolatry, of pride, self-will, and love of the world.[132]

Even in his post-1763 sermons, "On Patience (1784)" and "Cause of the Inefficacy of Christianity (1789)," Wesley gave a clear exposition of total depravity:

> In the same proportion as he grows in faith, he grows in holiness; he increases in love, lowliness, meekness, in every part of the image of God; till it pleases God, after he is thoroughly convinced of inbred sin, of the *total corruption* of his nature, to take it all away; to purify his heart and cleanse him from all unrighteousness; to fulfill that promise which he makes first to his ancient people, and in them to the Israel of God in all ages: "I will circumcise thy heart, and the heart of thy seed, to love the Lord thy God with all thy heart, and with all thy soul."[133]

> Why has Christianity done so little good in the world? Is it not the balm, the outward means, which the great Physician has given to men, to restore their spiritual health? Why then is it not restored? You say, Because of *the deep and universal corruption of human nature*. Most true.[134]

In each case, to avoid any confusion, one must carefully attend to Wesley's full-fledged categorical/grammatical constructions of sin and nature – wherein the vocabulary of total depravity refers to what Wesley calls "the natural man," that is, to an ungraced person who does not exist in this world.[135] This cannot help but affirm the mature Wesley's theological-anthropological implication that human freedom is not entirely extinguished, but still comes out of the paradoxical nature of *imago Dei*, which

---

132   Wesley, "Original Sin," in *Works* 2, II.1. A year later, Wesley again shows in his 1760 sermon "Heaviness through Manifold Temptation" that he is convinced of human helplessness and its state of total corruption: "It is allowed, there will be a far deeper, a far clearer and fuller knowledge of our inbred sin, of our *total corruption* by nature, after justification, than ever there was before it." Wesley, "Heaviness through Manifold Temptations," in *Works* 2, III.9.

133   Wesley, "On Patience," in *Works* 3, §10.

134   Wesley, "Causes of the Inefficacy of Christianity," in *Works* 4, §1.

135   Collins, *The Theology of John Wesley*, 73–4.

both God and human cannot compromise.[136] The following table shows the sermon manuscripts that fully unfold Wesley's mature vocabulary of sin and nature:

Sermon Title	Bible Verse	Date of Sermon
Original Sin	Genesis 6:5	1759
The Wilderness State	John 3:7	1760
Wandering Thoughts	2 Corinthians 10:5	1762
On Sin in Believers	2 Corinthians 5:17	1763-03-28
The Lord Our Righteousness	Jeremiah 23:6	1765-11-24
The Repentance of Believers	Mark 1:15	1767-04-24
The Good Steward	Luke 16:2	1768-05-14
On Predestination	Romans 8:29–30	1773-06-05
The End of Christ's Coming	1 John 3:8	1781-01-20
On the Fall of Man	Genesis 3:19	1782-03-13
God's Love to Fallen Man	Romans 5:15	1782-03-13
The General Spread of the Gospel	Isaiah 11:9	1783-04-22
On the Education of Children	Proverbs 22:6	1783-07-12
What is Man?	Psalms 8:4	1787-07-23
On Conscience	2 Corinthians 1:12	1788-04-08
On the Discoveries of Faith	Hebrews 11:1	1788-06-11
On the Omnipresence of God	Jeremiah 23:24	1788-08-12

136   Cf. fn. 118.

Conclusion

Formed under the Augustinian tradition within the Church of England, Wesley saw Adam's fall as a historical event, just as did Augustine. He also shared the traditional belief – confirmed in his commentary on Romans – that all subsequent humans were present in Adam's loins. However, his unique theological style (*via media*) developed his view of sin into an original and wayward theological anthropology. This development went through three period as we discussed above. First, the early Wesley summed up sin primarily as a disease of nature. This clearly demonstrated Wesley's Anglican roots, while also why his anthropology and soteriology are couched in a therapeutic language.

Second, the middle Wesley established most of his vocabulary on sin at this time. His often-used vocabularies are guilt, power, outward, inward, habitual, commission (committing), infirmity, voluntary, involuntary, willful, and etc. Essential to this vocabulary was to surface a positive assessment of human will, which in turn helped the middle Wesley to understand man as a moral agent assisted by grace or as a graced partner of grace in the journey of salvation.

Finally, the mature Wesley completed his doctrine of sin by further integrating its vocabulary with his doctrine of perfection. In the process, he maintained an eschatological tension between "already" and "not yet." Also, he gave his consensual views of total depravity here and there. By doing this, he further complicated his nuanced theological anthropology, though this does not outweigh the positive evaluations of human nature that are evident in Wesley's early, middle, and later works: "He that made us without ourselves, will not save us without ourselves."[137] Rather, it makes us wonder where its position can be located within his doctrine of grace that we will now address in the next chapter.

---

137   Wesley quoted this phrase from Augustine to emphasize a dynamic and collaborative relationship of human nature to divine grace. Wesley, "On Working Out Our Own Salvation," in *Works* 3, III.7.

CHAPTER 3

John Wesley on Grace

The ability of human nature to cooperate with grace was a vexing issue of early Protestant scholastic theology. On the one hand was the formulation of semi-Pelagianism, with its emphasis upon human merit. On the other hand was the formulation of Augustinianism, with its emphasis upon divine sovereignty. If we look at Martin Luther's theology, we see how he was willing to countenance this kind of extreme Augustinian theology. But his solution to the issue appeared to create a new set of difficulties, positing a God who effectuates His saving grace by a simple, unilateral, absolute fiat:

> There is nothing else that leads to the grace of God, or eternal salvation, but the word and work of God – grace, or the Spirit, being that very life to which the word and work of God lead us.[1]

The same solution was proposed by another early Protestant theologian, John Calvin. Based on the Lutheran claim *sola gratia*,[2] Calvin denied the power of human nature to bring about justification and affirmed the absolute sovereignty of divine grace in salvation.[3] From Wesley's perspective, however, this solution of either Luther or Calvin robbed humans of moral responsibility, and since all were predestined to election or damnation, it made humanity into an automaton[4] and God into a God whose *actus purus* is not *one* but *double* in His act of love.[5]

---

1   Martin Luther, *On the Bondage of the Will Luther and Erasmus: Free Will and Salvation* (Louisville, KY: Westminster John Knox, 2006), 139.

2   John Calvin, *The Institution of the Christian Religion: The Four Books – Complete and Unabridged*, trans. Thomas Norton (San Bernardino, CA: Createspace Independent Publishing Platform, 2017), 341.

3   Ibid., 341–2.

4   Wesley, "Predestination Calmly Considered," in *Works* (Albany) 10, §52.

5   Ibid., §30; §42; §44.

Was there no third possibility, a doctrine that would maintain both the reality of our human helplessness and the necessity of our cooperative response to God's divine initiative? In fact, such a *via media* laid readily at hand in Wesley's theological tradition.[6] It is here that Wesley discovered the key, the doctrine of "prevenient"[7] and "convincing"[8] grace, a doctrine that became increasingly important as his relational-dynamic view of grace had developed in opposition to Calvinist/Augustinianism.[9]

In this chapter, our major consideration will be given to the doctrine of "prevenient" and "convincing" grace that Wesley came to depend upon as a viable alternative to both divine predestination and human self-determination. The goal is to offer a broader reading of Wesley that has often been overlooked; or more specifically, to capture Wesley's evolving concern in maintaining our God-imaged liberty alongside the efficacy of grace. In line with our methodology as in the previous chapter, this goal will be achieved by chronologically analyzing the primary sources starting during his days at Oxford and ending in his most mature statements on the matter, published in the 1780s. The synthesis of this chronologically ordered analysis will provide a proper understanding of how grace is described in Wesley's writings, and it will ultimately aid in furthering our own exploration in the comparative study of Chapter 6.

6   Randy L. Maddox, "John Wesley and Eastern Orthodoxy: Influences, Convergences and Differences," *The Asbury Theological Journal* 45, no. 2 (1990): 29–53, at 30; Kenneth J. Collins, *The Theology of John Wesley: Holy Love and the Shape of Grace* (Nashville, TN: Abingdon Press, 2007), 4; and Fred Sanders, *Wesley on the Christian Life: The Heart Renewed in Love* (Wheaton, IL: Crossway, 2013), 16–7.

7   Wesley, "On Working Out Our Own Salvation," in *Works* 3, II.1, fn. 24. As Albert C. Outler commented, the words "preventing" and "prevenient" are synonymous for Wesley, and they equally refer to "the Holy Spirit's activity in moving or drawing the will in advance of any conscious resolve." See Wesley, "On Working Out Our Own Salvation," *Works* 3, II.1, fn. 24.

8   Wesley, "On Working Out Our Own Salvation," *Works* 3, II.1.

9   For an insightful study of the main theological controversies in which Wesley was engaged, see Allan Coppedge, *Shaping the Wesleyan Message: John Wesley in Theological Debate* (Nappanee, IN: Francis Asbury Press of Evangel Publishing House, 2003).

A Preliminary Note: Early Protestant Approach to Grace from Weimar to England

Before turning this analysis, a historical overview of the early Protestant approach to grace may offer a proper context in which to better understand Wesley's teachings about grace – as well as the reason why Wesley struggled in the process of shaping his own doctrine of grace. In response to the monergistic view of Luther and Calvin, a Protestant theologian named Philip Melanchthon rose up in opposition. Melanchthon asserted a certain cooperation or synergism of a remnant of *imago Dei* (free will) in salvation at the Augsburg Confession in 1540. Historically, in his first 1521 edition of *Loci*, Melanchthon had once denied the capacity of human nature for cooperatively achieving salvation and insisted on the Lutheran *sola gratia*, emphasizing the absolute sovereignty of divine grace in salvation.[10] This unilateral view of Melanchthon began to change in his 1535 edition of *Loci*, and by the 1549 edition of his *Loci* it came to terms with the formula *facultas se applicandi ad gratiam* (that is, the power to dispose oneself naturally toward grace).[11] Although Luther with indulgent tolerance had accepted Melanchthon's theological shift, his generous response was bound to change as John Pfeffinger, superintendent at Leipzig, published in 1555 his *Propositiones de libero arbitrio* in defense of Melanchthon's synergism: "Man is not like a 'passive statue' during his conversion, but rather has the capacity to cooperate with the will of God."[12] Eventually, for the first time in Protestant history, a formal theological disputation about the precise extent of the role of grace in salvation took place in Weimar, Germany in 1560.

At the Weimar Disputation of 1560, some rigid Lutherans and radical Augustinian advocates (e.g., Nicholas v. Amsdorf, Matthias Flacius of

---

10 Johann Heinrich Kurtz, *Church History*, Vol. 2, trans. John MacPherson (New York: Funk and Wagnalls Company, 1889), 352.

11 Ibid.

12 Eric W. Gritsch and Robert W. Jenson, *Lutheranism: The Theological Movement and Its Confessional Writings* (Philadelphia, PA: Fortress Press, 1976), 56. See also Kurtz, *Church History*, 352–3.

Illyria, and John Wigand) argued that the fallen humanity is entirely dead to moral/spiritual impulses, and that the essence of human nature has been so corrupted by sin that evil is not simply an accidental attribute, but is rather part of the essential substance of human beings: "Original sin was not something accidental, in man, but something *substantial*."[13] Against this pessimistic view of humanity, Victorin Strigel, a protégé of Melanchthon's working at Jena, who was ironically appointed to assist Amsdorf, Flacius, and Wigand at Weimar, claimed the earlier consensual teaching that original sin has not totally destroyed human nature but simply limited it, and that no inward or saving transformation can be effected without the liberty and concurrence of the human will.[14]

According to Johann Heinrich Kurtz, the sympathy which Strigel evinced for synergism won in favor of the Duke John Frederick, who presided over the disputation at Weimar. But it was of short duration. Strigel was soon accused of a crypto-Catholic.[15] What is worse, however, was that Melanchthon died in 1560, and Jena University, the academic field of these two moderate Lutherans, was referred to the Inquisition.[16] Subsequently, this synergistic belief was gradually forgotten in Protestant Europe, while the controversy about the Calvinistic doctrine of supralapsarianism gradually gained prominence.

Does divine grace occur by simple, unilateral, absolute fiat? Or does God take into consideration the nature of *imago Dei* as endowed with free will? How do God and man relate to one another in the salvation encounter? This soteriological dilemma once again emerged as an important issue at an international Synod held in Dordrecht from 1618 to 1619 (now

---

13   Johann Heinrich Kurtz, *History of the Christian Church: From the Reformation to the Present Time* (London: T. & T. Clark, 1864), 116.

14   Luka Ilić, *Theologian of Sin and Grace: The Process of Radicalization in the Theology of Matthias Flacius Illyricus* (Göttingen: Vandenhoeck & Ruprecht, 2014), 150–5. See also Kurtz, *History of the Christian Church*, 116; and Thomas C. Oden, *The Transforming Power of Grace* (Nashville, TN: Abingdon Press, 1993), 99.

15   Hans J. Hillerbrand, ed., *The Oxford Encyclopedia of the Reformation*, 4 vols. (New York: Oxford University Press, 1996), 4:133.

16   Samuel Macauley Jackson, ed., *The New Schaff-Herzog Encyclopedia of Religious Knowledge*, 4 vols. (New York: Funk & Wagnalls Company, 1909), 4:322.

called the Synod of Dort). Delegates from most of the Reformed churches in Europe – for example, the Rhenish Palatinate, Geneva, Switzerland, Emden, Hesse, Bremen, and Nassau/Wetteravia – attended the Synod of Dort. There was also a British delegation from James I, who was still involved in a protracted war of liberation against Spain and Catholic domination.[17]

At the Synod of Dort, two opposing groups clashed. One was classical Calvinism led by Franciscus Gomarus,[18] and the other was moderate Arminianism led by Simon Episeopius.[19] The former was largely in the majority, and it soon appeared that the latter was there simply to be tried, not to consult or cooperate in equal debate. Episeopius and 13 other Arminians were condemned as heretics and excluded from the Synod, which then proceeded to formulate and confirm what true faith is in a series of doctrinal decrees.[20]

17 The British delegation was led by Bishop George Carleton of Llandaff and consisted mainly of Cambridge theologians who opposed the pro-Arminian views espoused by Bishop John Overall of Norwich and Professor Peter Baro of Cambridge in the 1590s. Mark Chapman, *Anglican Theology* (London: T&T Clark International, 2012), 140.

18 Franciscus Gomarus was a Dutch theologian who presided as the chair over James (or Jacob) Arminius' doctoral examination and granted Arminius the first doctorate from Leiden University. However, in later years Gomarus was so uncomfortable with Arminius' synergistic position that he tried to stop Arminius from becoming a professor at Leiden – though this attempt did not pay off as Arminius started his career at the university. For a more detailed description of the theological conflict between Gomarus and Arminius, see Peter Sammons, *Reprobation: From Augustine to the Synod of Dort: The Historical Development of the Reformed Doctrine of Reprobation* (Göttingen: Vandenhoeck & Ruprecht, 2020), 97–9.

19 Simon Episeopius is an ardent synergist with a high view of humanity as opposed to Theodore Beza's fairly extreme Calvinism, known as supralapsarianism. Daniel Coit Gilman, ⊠Harry Thurston Peck, and ⊠Frank Moore Colby, eds., *The New International Encyclopaedia*, vol. 2 (United States: Dodd, Mead and Company, 1902), 13. All future references to *The New International Encyclopaedia*, Vol. 2 will be listed as *TNIE* followed only by the page.

20 Episeopius was exiled from the country, and some 200 Arminians were expelled from their positions and then exiled. *TNIE*, 13.

Central to the doctrinal decrees of Dort – commonly known under the rubric of TULIP[21] – was the doctrine of unconditional election and reprobation. This doctrine was accepted by the Reformed churches in Holland and in France, along with those doctrinal decrees of Dort. But as the Stadtholder Maurice – who gave full credit to high Calvinism at the Synod of Dort – died in 1625, the Calvinist group soon lost its iron grip, and the exiled Arminians found their way back to their churches and seminaries.[22]

The situation hostile to Calvinism continued in other parts of Europe. For example, England received the Synod of Dort and its canons differently from Holland or France, where Calvinism prevails within its religious circle. Some British divines, whether within the Church of England or separated from it, supported the canons and expressed a strong affirmation of their pro-Calvinist flair for monergism.[23] However, other British divines, such as Bishop Lancelot Andrewes of Chichester and Bishop Richard Neile of Durham, stood on the other side and pursued an anti-Calvinist path for synergism, which gradually evolved in the later years of James I and in the reign of his son and heir.[24] In England, Calvinism was not so predominant, therefore the decisions of the synod of Dort were not able to have a strong impact on English Protestantism and reduce its pluralistic approach to grace and nature according to a Calvinistic paradigm.

Such diversity in theology in England opened up a new form of religious tolerance that was not biased to either Calvinism or Arminianism:

> Let us not magisterially imposed upon one another, and be so charitable as to believe well of Dissenters from us that live good lives, are of modest and peaceable deportment, and hold no Opinions, that directly oppose the design of the Christian religion, and of making men like to God; and then we shall see, that there will

---

21   Though it does not comprise Calvinism in totality, the acronym TULIP represents some of its main points: Total depravity, Unconditional election, Limited atonement, Irresistible grace, and Perseverance of the saints.

22   *TNIE*, 13.

23   Chapman, *Anglican Theology*, 140.

24   Ibid., 140–1.

be little reason to desire an Infallible Judge of Controversie, to make us all of one Opinion.[25]

The same motto was used by Bishop Edward Stillingfleet of Worcester and other prominent British divines, including Bishop Gilbert Burnet of Salisbury, and two Archbishops of Canterbury, John Tillotson and Thomas Tenison.[26] Without granting magisterial power to either Calvinist or Arminian theology, these England churchmen infused a pluralistic and ecumenical sentiment into the Church of England in the late seventeenth and early eighteenth centuries.[27] Although the sentiment was far from universally held in England,[28] one thing is certain: It evolved into the Declaration of Breda in 1660[29] and into the Act of Toleration in 1689, providing priests and theologians belonging to the Church of England with a measure of freedom and partial relief to adopt various theological views on grace and nature.[30]

John Wesley was born in 1703 into this pluralistic religious milieu. Here, doctrinal variation was permitted, and concern for toleration outweighed the desire to enforce theological uniformity. Thus, in his lifetime,

---

25 Edward Fowler, *The Principles and Practices of Certain Moderate Divines of the Church of England (Greatly Mis-understood), Truly Represented and Defended* (London: Lodowick Lloyd, 1670), 308–9.

26 Chapman, *Anglican Theology*, 165.

27 Ibid. See also John Marshall, "The Ecclesiology of the Latitude-men, 1660–1689: Stillingfleet, Tillotson and 'Hobbism,'" *Journal of Ecclesiastical History* 36 (1985): 407–27.

28 Chapman, *Anglican Theology*, 166.

29 In his famous Declaration of Breda on April 4, 1660, Charles II revealed his desire to allow a degree of *tolérance* in the future Church: "Because the passion and uncharitableness of the times have produced several opinions in religion, by which men are engaged in parties and animosities against each other (which, when they shall hereafter unite in a freedom of conversation, will be composed or better understood), we do declare a liberty to tender consciences, and that no man shall be disquieted or called in question for differences of opinion in matter of religion, which do not disturb the peace of the kingdom." Full text in Gerald Bray, *Documents of the English Reformation, 1526–1701* (Cambridge: James Clarke, 2004), 544–5; here, 545.

30 Kenneth A. Locke, *The Church in Anglican Theology: An Historical, Theological and Ecumenical Exploration* (Aldershot: Ashgate, 2009), 107.

Wesley moved around intellectually: first he received a Puritan background, next he engaged in a Greek Patristic reading program (Holy Club), then was spiritually shaken from his exposure to a Luther at Aldersgate, and finally he delved into Roman Catholic mysticism and Pietist spiritual writers.[31] Seeking to journey on a middle way between diverse emphases of various systems of theology,[32] Wesley was not afraid to cross lines. Nor was he reluctant to hold a diversity of truths in tension. To be sure, Wesley's unique account of prevenient grace and many other types of grace was one of the important outcomes that he had made by risking this *via media* pilgrimage, and it is to this outcome that this chapter now turns and discusses.

The Oxford Era (1725–1737)

God first operates before man can cooperate, as Gregory the Great wrote: "The divine goodness first effects something in us without our co-operation."[33] Preventing (or prevenient) grace is, therefore, the grace of God that works without us because it works before us (*gratia operans*). A broad understanding of this theological position was affirmed by the Second Council of Orange (AD 529). Then it was passed on to other subsequent ecumenical councils. In response to semi-Pelagianism, the concept asserted the necessity of grace for each and every step on the way to salvation, as Leo G. Cox well expressed: "Prevenient grace leads on to saving grace, prepares for it, enables a person to enter into it."[34]

Not all Protestant theologians have welcomed prevenient grace. Calvin, for example, took this concept very restrictively.[35] And those from

---

31   Collins, *The Theology of John Wesley*, 4.
32   Maddox, "John Wesley and Eastern Orthodoxy," 30. For more information about this philosophical pilgrim, see P. H. Hughes, *The Theology of the English Reformers* (London: Hodder and Stoughton, 1965).
33   Gregory the Great, *Moralia in Job* 16.10.
34   Leo G. Cox, "Prevenient Grace – A Wesleyan View," *Journal of the Evangelical Theological Society* 12/3 (Summer 1969): 143–9, at 144.
35   Calvin, *The Institutes of Christian Religion*, 183–92.

his theological system viewed it as a deviation from Calvin,[36] and they went on to treat prevenient grace as common grace, a universal form of conscience that has no soteriological significance, but only moral content that undergirds civil justice in human society.[37] For Calvin and Calvinists, prevenient grace can, at best, function for the convictions of sins, but even at this point, its operation is strongly limited to convicting the sins of the elect,[38] since they can hardly admit that "Christ by His atoning blood merited these blessings [i.e., prevenient grace] for the impenitent and reprobate."[39]

However, unlike Calvin or Calvinists, the concept of prevenient grace was important to Wesley, and it has now become a vital theological category for contemporary Wesleyan theologians. H. Ray Dunning, for instance, argues that this theological category serves as a norm or method in eleven different theological themes that Wesley develops, including theological epistemology, moral ethics, faith and repentance, free will, and synergistic soteriology.[40] Other Wesleyan theologians, too, affirm the importance of this grace in their theological system and insist that the doctrine must be presupposed to fully express "the entire work of God" that extends "from the first dawning of grace in the soul till it is consummated in glory."[41]

---

36 Gregory Crofford, *Streams of Mercy: Prevenient Grace in the Theology of John and Charles Wesley* (Lexington, KY: Emeth, 2010), 193.

37 H. Ray Dunning, *Grace, Faith, and Holiness: A Wesleyan Systematic Theology* (Kansas City, MO: Beacon Hill Press, 1988), 296.

38 Crofford, *Streams of Mercy*, 194. See also Neil R. Livingston, "A Calvinistic Concept of Prevenient Grace" (M. Th. Thesis, Dallas Theological Seminary, 1961), 57–66, 68.

39 Louis Berkhof, *Systematic Theology* (Grand Rapids, MI: Eerdman's Publishing, 1996), 438.

40 Dunning, *Grace, Faith, and Holiness*, 655.

41 Theodore Runyon, *The New Creation: John Wesley's Theology Today* (Nashville, TN: Abingdon Press, 1998), 36. Considering original sin and prevenient grace as the twin *foci* of Wesley's soteriology, Herbert Boyd McGonigle argued that prevenient grace serves as a theological axis for Wesleyans. Herbert Boyd McGonigle, *Sufficient Saving Grace: John Wesley's Evangelical Arminianism* (Carlisle, UK: Paternoster Press, 2001), 329. For another opinion that speaks of the importance of prevenient grace in the Wesleyan theological system, see Charles A. Rogers, "The Concept of Prevenient Grace in the Theology of John Wesley" (PhD dissertation, Duke

Yet, this was unfortunately not always the case for Wesley. In fact, the concept rarely appears in Wesley's early sermons. A review of other treatises and letters he wrote during this Oxford period leads to a similar conclusion. It was theologically formed and developed after the 1740s – and especially as Wesley entered into protracted debate with other Calvinists in the Methodist camp.[42] At the same time, this does not necessarily mean that one cannot find any theological work that characterizes this concept of prevenient grace in the earliest years of his theology. An example comes from his 1733 sermon, "The Circumcision of the Heart." Here, Wesley wrote:

> [W]e are convinced that we are not sufficient of ourselves to help ourselves; that without the Spirit of God we can do nothing but add sin to sin; that it is he alone "who worketh in us" by his almighty power, either "to will or do" that which is good – it being as impossible for us even to think a good thought without the supernatural assistance of his Spirit as to create ourselves, or to renew our whole souls in righteousness and true holiness.[43]

While the term "prevenient" grace was somewhat absent here, the concept was implicit in the logic chosen to explain the relationship between grace and nature. Firstly, Wesley affirmed that we are "not sufficient of ourselves to help ourselves." Only with the "supernatural assistance of [H]is Spirit," can the individual achieve such a blessed state that Wesley referred to in the sermon as the "circumcised" heart.[44] Secondly, one's incapability of spiritual progress included a *hypothetical* reality that would be totally negative were it not for Christ's atonement that works retroactively through the Spirit on his or her fallen nature and nullifies that hypothetical reality inherited from Adam. Finally, the pneumatological

University, 1967), 228; and Sondra Higgins Matthaei, *Making Disciples: Faith Formation in the Wesleyan Tradition* (Nashville, TN: Abingdon Press, 2000), 46.

42 For more support for this claim, see David C. Shipley, "Wesley and Some Calvinistic Controversies," *The Drew Gateway* XXV (1955): 195–210; Runyon, *The New Creation*, 36; William J. Abraham, *Wesley for Armchair Theologians* (Louisville: Westminster John Knox, 2005), 19; and Crofford, *Streams of Mercy*, 76.

43 Wesley, "The Circumcision of the Heart," in *Works* 1, I.3.

44 Referencing Romans 2:29, Wesley equated the circumcised heart with "holiness" or "habitual disposition of [the] soul ... [towards] those virtues in Christ Jesus." Ibid., I.1.

aspect of prevenient grace came into focus, for it is the Spirit who un-boundedly works as the agent – or in Wesley's words the "inspirer" or "perfecter" – of spiritual renewal.[45]

Later in the sermon, Wesley rearranged this logic more explicitly, as if he were describing prevenient grace, especially one of its characteristic attributes – that is, to come before our free decision, stirring up the will to do good:

> "If any man has not the Spirit of Christ, he is none of his." He alone can quicken those who are dead unto God, can breathe into them the breath of Christian life, and so *prevent, accompany*, and *follow* them with his grace as to bring their good desires to good effect. And "as many as are thus led by the Spirit of God, they are the sons of God."[46]

Perhaps this is the first explicit mention of prevenient grace in Wesley's entire writings. Also important were the words "dead," "quicken," "breathe," "prevent," "accompany," and "follow." As can be seen in connection with Wesley's mature doctrine of sin in Chapter 2, all humans were spiritually "dead," alienated from God, and thus insensible to the reality of spiritual good. God's work in Christ through the Spirit was to "quicken," to "breathe" spiritual/supernatural life into where none existed, and to "prevent," "accompany," and "follow" until one reaches out to desire the ultimate good. This series of words took their place in a pile of related terms that later Wesley increasingly used to describe a different set of circumstances for the grace that comes before (*praeveniens*) and the grace that accompanies (*comitans*) or follows (*sequens*). Therefore, although the doctrine was not of primary interest in Wesley's early writings, one must admit that the early Wesley had recognized that we humans need God's *prior* and *posterior* intervention to achieve spiritual life and progress to God. More complex theological implications of this fact evolved following Wesley's Aldersgate period, which we will discuss in the next sections.

45   Ibid., II.4.
46   Ibid.

The Aldersgate Era (1738–1758)

The second major period of Wesley's theological formation followed his Aldersgate experience on May 24, 1738. During this period, most of Wesley's theological energy was given to the doctrine of justification by faith; "justifying grace," which he regarded as a synonym for "faith," was frequently discussed at this time.[47] However, as the Calvinist doctrine of grace (represented by George Whitefield, Ann Allin, and Thomas Bissicks) emerged as part of the debate within his own Methodist camp, Wesley had to focus less on "justifying grace" *operatively* and *efficaciously* effecting justification, and focus more on his understanding of grace's co-operative role in perfecting human nature.[48]

Was God's grace available to all? Or was it reserved only for the elect? Unlike those Calvinists who favored the latter position, Wesley supported the former. This anti-Calvinist position of Wesley first appeared in his 1739 sermon "Free Grace." Taking Romans 8:32 as his text, Wesley organized "Free Grace" around two main points: (1) God's grace is free *in* all, and (2) God's grace is free *for* all. Throughout this sermon, Wesley expressed his theological frustration with Calvinism and criticizes supralapsarianism, a Calvinistic conception of *gratia perseverantiae* that would appear to make God the author of evil:

> You cannot deny that he says, "Come unto me, all ye that are weary and heavy laden." If then you say he calls those that cannot come, those whom he knows to be unable to come, those whom he can make able to come but will not, how is it possible to describe greater insincerity? You represent him as mocking his helpless creatures by offering what he never intends to give. You describe him as saying one thing and

47 William Ragsdale Cannon, *The Theology of John Wesley: With Special Reference to the Doctrine of Justification* (New York: Abingdon-Cokesbury Press, 1946), 115; cf. 248.

48 For a brief discussion of the so-called "free grace controversy" in the early Methodist movement, see Kenneth J. Collins, *John Wesley: A Theological Journey* (Nashville, TN: Abingdon Press, 2003), 114–7; and for a full explanation of its historical background, see Joel Houston, *Wesley, Whitefield and the "Free Grace" Controversy: The Crucible of Methodism* (London and New York: Routledge, 2019), 67–181.

meaning another; as pretending the love which he had not. Him "in whose mouth was no guile" you make full of deceit, void of common sincerity. Then especially, when, drawing nigh the city, "he wept over it," and said, "O Jerusalem, Jerusalem, thou that killest the prophets, and stonest them that are sent unto thee, how often would I have gathered thy children together ... and ye would not": (ἠθέλησα – καὶ οὐκ ἠθελήσατε). Now if you say, "They would," but "he would not," you represent him (which who could hear?) as weeping crocodile's tears, weeping over the prey which himself had doomed to destruction ... Such blasphemy this, as one would think might make the ears of a Christian tingle. But there is yet more behind ... It destroys all his attributes at once. It overturns both his justice, mercy, and truth. Yea, it represents the most Holy God as worse than the devil; as both more false, more cruel, and more unjust.[49]

While we were still sinners, Christ died for the ungodly. When we were dead in sin, God spared not his only begotten Son, but gave him up for us all. Christ died for all of us, so grace is "free *for* all" and its gracious enabling comes to everyone, not just to the elect.[50] What did Wesley actually mean when he said: "God's grace, whence cometh our salvation, is free *in* all"?[51] Wesley claimed that it

> does not depend on any power or merit in man; no, not in any degree, neither in whole, nor in part. It does not in any wise depend either on the good works or righteousness of the receiver; not on anything he has done, or anything he is.[52]

While it is true that he championed human responsibility elsewhere, Wesley made it clear in this passage that humans cannot merit grace. For him it is a gift, and this gift is called "free," since it is bestowed on a person beyond the capacity of nature. In other words, "Free Grace" was sensitive to the charge of semi-Pelagianism in which the *initium fidei* is considered the fruit of human action. So in this explanation of "free *in* all," it steered clear of the error and made it clear that divine grace precedes human action and the worth (*pretium*) of the latter depends on the dignity of the former (*dignitatem gratiae*).

49   Wesley, "Free Grace," in *Works* 3, §§24–5.
50   Ibid., §1.
51   Ibid., §2.
52   Ibid., §3.

However, Wesley did not call "evil" or "unmeritorious" what appeared to be "good" in our acts, words, or thoughts. This was because for Wesley, it could not necessarily be a way to avoid Pelagius' error. Moreover, it was only an exchange of one error for another (such as antinomianism).[53] What was good in Wesley's view could truly be and should be classified as such, so long as it was a reflection not of human merit, but of divine activity:

> [One's] good tempers, or good desires, or good purposes and intentions ... flow from the free grace of God. They are the streams only, not the fountain. They are the fruits of free grace, and not the root. They are not the cause, but the effects of it. Whatsoever good is in man, or is done by man, God is the author and doer of it. Thus is his grace free in all, that is, no way depending on any power or merit in man, but on God alone, who freely gave us his own Son, and "with him freely giveth us all things."[54]

In this process of creating a generous space for what is good in and of one's graced work, Wesley further argued that it merits the end of one's spiritual life (holiness)[55] and even the conversion of another person.[56] Although Wesley did not immediately follow up this argument with a consideration of whether the work done in grace is meritorious in proportion to the reward of eternal life, this semi-meritorious account of salutary acts (*actus salutares*) may appeal to the need for more research into his positive account of merit.[57]

---

53   Ibid., §§11–2; and §§18–9.
54   Ibid., §3.
55   Ibid., §11.
56   Ibid., §18.
57   One example that gives us a glimpse of his positive analysis of merit comes from the August 2, 1745 Conference *Minutes*, where Wesley refused to label the pious works of Cornelius (Acts 10) as "splendid sins," since they were not done antecedent but posterior to – and in tandem with – the "grace of Christ." Wesley, "Conversation 2" on August 2, 1745 in *Works* (Albany) 8, qq.1–25, especially on page 305. One can, however, find any number of similar examples from his "Preface to A Treatise on Justification" or from his 1765 sermon "The Lord Our Righteousness," where Wesley taught by warning, "O warn them that if they remain unrighteous, the righteousness of Christ will profit them nothing," that the language of *imputation* should relate only to justification, to forgiveness and acceptance, and not to sanctification itself. Wesley, "The Lord Our Righteousness," in *Works* 1, II.20. For further related examples of how Wesley expresses the dynamic role of grace in creating one's

Charles Allen Rogers, one of the pioneers in the study of Wesley's conception of prevenient grace, found in the excerpt from "Free Grace" given above some of the Christological foundations of prevenient grace. For the sake of Christ and his atoning work *pro nobis*, God had freely given us all the gifts we shall need for our lives and for godliness, and as Rogers well pointed out, this gift included the favor of a universal and prevenient grace.[58] Likewise, another pioneer, Kenneth J. Collins, remarked that for Wesley, prevenient grace was "based upon the salvific work of Christ."[59] Even though this Christological underpinning was more systematically dictated in the Conference *Minutes* of 1744[60] – and more prevalent in his later writings on the subject[61] – it seems arguably true that early Wesley

good/meritorious acts, see his two treatises, *The Principles of a Methodist* (1742) and *A Farther Appeal to Men of Reason and Religion* (1745), and his 1765 sermon, "The Scripture Way of Salvation." One can also add to the list of those examples the Conference *Minutes* of 1770, where Wesley said: "We have received it as a maxim, that 'a man is to do nothing in order to justification.' Nothing can be more false. Whoever desire to find favor with God, should 'cease from evil, and learn to do well.' So God himself teaches by the Prophet Isaiah. Whoever repents, should 'do works meet for repentance.' And if this is not in order to find favor, what does he do them for." Wesley, "Minutes of Several Conversations," in *Works* (Albany) 8, q.77, a.3, especially on page 374. Then, for a brief historical account of the debate over merit within the Methodist circle, see Collins, *John Wesley*, 221–7.

58 Rogers, "The Concept of Prevenient Grace in the Theology of John Wesley," 26.
59 Collins, *The Theology of John Wesley*, 74.
60 In the Conference *Minutes* of 1744, Wesley brought up his commentary on Romans 5:19 that we were "cleared from the guilt of Adam's actual sin" by virtue of the "merits of Christ." Moreover, according to Wesley, divine merits in Christ's obedience and death provided five benefits: (1) our post-resurrection bodies; (2) a "capacity of spiritual life" restored in our souls; (3) a true "spark" or universal "seed" of this spiritual life in all humans – each of these terms is a metaphor for prevenient grace, which Wesley frequently refers to with another term "light"; (4) our reconciliation to God as "children of grace"; and (5) our spiritual growth as a partaker of the divine nature. Here was another clear implication that Wesley understood the atonement as the theological basis of prevenient grace (especially, its universal availability). Wesley, "Minutes of Several Conversations," in *Works* (Albany) 8, q.16, aa.1–5, especially on page 297–8.
61 In his "Farther Appeal to Men of Reason and Religion," Wesley said that Christ is the cause and source for prevenient grace: "There is no more of power than of merit in man; but as all merit is in the Son of God, in what he has done and suffered for

had already viewed prevenient grace as a provision of the atonement, or, to put it differently, as a supernatural gift given to one's fallen nature retrospectively from this divine initiative of God in Christ.

Three years after the publication of "Free Grace," Wesley penned his 1742 treatise, *The Principles of a Methodist*. Here his positive sentiment toward divine initiative was reaffirmed.[62] Yet, central to this treatise was an additional clarification of prevenient grace that Wesley made in opposition to the charge imposed on him by Rev. Josiah Tucker of Madison.[63] Approvingly quoting Rev. Tucker, Wesley wrote:

> For the preventing grace of God, which is *common to all*, is *sufficient* to bring us to Christ, though it is *not sufficient* to carry us any further till we are justified ... The moment a man comes to Christ (by faith) he is justified ... and he has power over the stirrings and motions of sin, but not a total freedom from them.[64]

In this passage, Wesley put a threefold conceptual clarification into prevenient grace. First, it was a benefit commonly (or universally) applied to all by God. Secondly, it was "sufficient" in the sense that a person was enabled to heed God's call (*vocatio*) prior to conversion – that is, without

us, so all power is in the Spirit of God. And therefore, every man, in order to believe unto salvation, must receive the Holy Ghost." Wesley, "A Farther Appeal to Men of Reason and Religion," in *Works* (Albany) 8, Pt.1, I.6, especially on page 52. Likewise, Wesley wrote in his letter to Mr. John Mason on November 26, 1776: "[N]o man living is without some preventing grace; and every degree of grace is a degree of life ... Therefore, no infant ever was, or ever will be, 'sent to hell for the guilt of Adam's sin;' seeing it is cancelled by the righteousness of Christ, as soon as they are sent into the world." Wesley, "Letter to Mr. John Mason," in *Works* 12, especially on page 453.

62   Wesley, "The Principles of a Methodist," in *Works* 9, especially on page 47–66.
63   In 1742, Rev. Tucker penned a pamphlet critical of Wesley. There he accused Wesley of denying the moral component of Christian life by preaching justification by faith alone. Then he also pointed out Wesley's "combination of Calvinist and Arminian ideas" and "charged him with serious inconsistency." But this was a charge that Wesley rejected in his *Principles of a Methodist*. Donald A. Bullen, *A Man of One Book? John Wesley's Interpretation and Use of the Bible* (Eugene, OR: Wipf & Stock, 2007), 117.
64   Wesley, "The Principle of a Methodist," in *Works* (Albany) 8, §29.1, especially on page 415.

being effectively converted to God. Lastly, it did not guarantee conversion or post-conversion life and work. In other words, prevenient grace is "not sufficient" in the sense that it is not necessarily efficacious for salvation. This last point was further refined in his letter to Thomas Whitehead on February 10, 1748. Here Wesley opined that prevenient grace could only be effective when seconded by the non-resistance or voluntary acceptance of the recipient.[65] From this point of view, one might also rephrase the term "not sufficient" in the following way: For Wesley prevenient grace is "not sufficient" in the sense that it cannot actually or irresistibly save a morally responsible person without his or her own exercise of faith.

But unfortunately, it seems that he struggled in further elucidating the concept, especially in grafting it into his way of salvation (*via salutis*):

> When I shall have received farther light, I may be convinced that [prevenient grace] "is a necessary qualification, antecedent to justification." This appears to me now to be directly opposite to the gospel of Christ [Scripture]. But I will endeavor impartially to consider what shall be advanced in defense of it. And may He who knows my simpleness, teach me his way, and give me a right judgment in all things![66]

His theological difficulty, as seen in this passage above, may have come from his early judgment that there is no clear and adequate basis in Scripture for this concept of prevenient grace. However, given the historical context of early Methodism at the time, it may actually and more likely have come from a protracted debate about divine sovereignty and human responsibility, which flared up between the Calvinist and Wesleyan camps of early Methodism in the late 1730s and early 1740s.[67]

---

65   Wesley, Letter to Thomas Whitehead, 2/10/48 in *Works* (Telford) 2, especially on page 118.
66   Wesley, "The Principle of a Methodist," in *Works* (Albany) 8, §31, especially on page 415–6.
67   The debate flared up again in 1756 between John Wesley and James Hervey. Hervey was a member of the Holy Club, but he came to adopt a thoroughly Calvinistic creed. Then in his *Theron and Aspasio*, he argued that God's "grand end" is to "demonstrate the sovereignty of His grace." In response, Wesley said in his letter to Hervey on October 5, 1756: "Not so: to impart happiness to His creatures is His grand end herein. Barely to demonstrate His sovereignty is a principle of action fit

This controversy surfaced at the first meeting of a yearly conference that Wesley founded in 1744 for substantive colloquy with Methodist leaders on doctrine and discipline.[68] At the first conference, Wesley offered a commentary on Romans 5:19, where he provided the five benefits of Christ's death and obedience and then managed to address the divine sovereignty-human responsibility problem in a way that affirms divine initiative in a gracious and cooperative sense, not in a meticulous and exhaustive sense.[69] However, Wesley's teachings had no appeal to another leader of early Methodism: George Whitefield. Unlike Wesley, Whitefield upheld the matter in a Calvinist sense, which in turn sparked a theological break between Wesley and Whitefield, and then between Wesleyan and Whitefieldian Methodists.[70]

At this critical juncture in the movement of early Methodism, Wesley could not sit silently and watch this theological break passively as it slowly faltered toward a fully open split. Therefore, he came to reconciling with Whitefield: "I love Calvin, Luther more; the Moravians, Mr. Law, and Mr. Whitefield far more than either."[71] Then he helped to keep his camp collegial with Whitefield's and even those Calvinists that he felt were quarrelsome on the topics related to *gratia perseverantiae*. According to William J. Abraham, this theological compromise, with nominal reconciliation, further led Wesley to bend over backwards to try and satisfy his Calvinist opponents, even to the point where he somewhat allowed that "God might irresistibly bring some select, chosen souls to salvation."[72] "So long as Whitfield was

for the great Turk, not the Most High God." Wesley, Letter to James Hervey, 10/5/56 in *Works* (Telford) 3, especially on page 387–8.

68   Thomas C. Oden, *John Wesley's Scriptural Christianity: A Plain Exposition of His Teaching on Christian Doctrine* (Grand Rapids, MI: Zondervan, 1994), 201.

69   Wesley, "Minutes of Some Late Conversations," in *Works* (Albany) 8, qq.11–26, especially on page 296–9.

70   David C. Shipley, "Wesley and Some Calvinistic Controversies," *The Drew Gateway* XXV (1955): 195–210.

71   Wesley, Letter to Elizabeth Hutton, in *Works* (Telford) 2, especially on page 25.

72   Abraham, *Wesley for Armchair Theologians*, 19. Indeed, Wesley wrote: "God may possibly, at some times, work irresistibly in some souls. I believe he does." Wesley, *Predestination Calmly Considered*, in *Works* (Albany) 10, §81. He admitted as much elsewhere, too: Wesley, "The Question 'What Is an Arminian?' Answered," in *Works* (Albany) 10, §§ 7–10, especially on page 428; Sermon 63, "The General

alive," Abraham continues, "there was hope that they [the two opposing camps of early Methodism] could avoid theological warfare."[73]

However, such hopes began to falter much earlier than Abraham expected. Even when Wesley expressed some openness to the Calvinistic conception of irresistible grace, Wesley did not completely overturn his anti-Calvinistic position on grace. He rather continued to develop it with care – especially with the following characteristics:

(1) "Grace," which in some cases is called "free love" and in other cases "unmerited mercy," operates in us with God's "pardoning love (Christ *for us*)" and "[enabling] power (Spirit *in us*)," and in this Trinitarian operation, it *sufficiently* empowers man to seek God so that none are finally saved or condemned by necessity[74];

(2) The Holy Spirit is the agent of grace, and His light purifies our minds,[75] breathes new vitality and virtue into our lives,[76] and shines as a divine source of our power to walk (*actus*) in God's ways[77]; and

Spread of the Gospel," in *Works* 2, §12; and Wesley, *Journal* (8/24/43), in *Works* 19, especially on page 332–3. But in each case, one should attend to Wesley's overly hedged grammatical constructions, including his profuse conditionals, rhetorical questions, and subjunctives. For these did not eventually overshadow the gist of Wesley's *Journal*, written on August 24, 1743: "that the grace of God both before and after those [irresistible] moments, may be, and hath been, resisted; and that, in general, it does not act irresistibly, but we may comply therewith or may not." Wesley, *Journal* (8/24/43), in *Works* 19.

73   Abraham, *Wesley for Armchair Theologians*, 19.

74   Wesley, "The Witness of Our Own Spirit," in *Works* 1, §15.

75   John Wesley, *The Sunday Service of the Methodists in North America* (London: Stranhan, 1784; reprint ed., Nashville, TN: United Methodist Publishing House, 1992), 125.

76   Wesley, "A Farther Appeal to Men of Reason and Religion," in *Works* (Albany) 8, Pt.1, V.28, especially on page 171.

77   Wesley, "The Witness of Our Own Spirit," in *Works* 1, §16. This echoed his earlier sentiment from the treatise, *A Farther Appeal to Men of Reason and Religion*: "There is no more of power than of merit in man; but as all merit is in the son of God, in what he has done and suffered for us, so all power is in the Spirit of God. And therefore, every man, in order to believe unto salvation, must receive the Holy Ghost. ... Sometimes He acts more particularly on the understanding, opening or enlightening it [the soul]."

(3) God the Spirit applies God's grace from Christ's merciful work to all humans through "outward signs [scripture], words [prayer], or actions [sacrament]," which Wesley understood as the "means of grace [*gratia externa*]"[78] "whereby [God] might convey to men preventing, justifying, or sanctifying grace."[79]

These (1), (2), and (3) show that Wesley was forming grace's various expressions or types in an anti-Calvinist sense. Although portrayed here only descriptively, these expressions or types were gradually conceptualized, and as Wesley proceeded to the task of distilling his own taxonomy of grace in "The Witness of the Spirit, Discourse I," "Self-denial," "The Scripture Way of Salvation," and "On Working Out Our Own Salvation," they were typologically categorized into (1) grace as "preventing [prevenient]," (2) grace as "accompanying," and (3) grace as "following."[80] With this threefold division of grace, the later Wesley made it clearer what he believed about grace. Then he enunciated his theological argument regarding the dynamics of grace at work in the totality of our salvation: (1) God's "preventing [prevenient]" grace has initiated our spiritual life by graciously preceding any action on our behalf; (2) God's

---

78   Wesley, "The Means of Grace," in *Works* 1, V.1.

79   Ibid., II.1, III.1, 7, and 11.

80   Wesley, "The Witness of the Spirit, Discourse I," in *Works* 1, II.2–4: "[The Scriptures] describe in the plainest manner the circumstances which go *before*, which *accompany*, and which *follow*, the true, genuine testimony of the Spirit of God with the spirit of a believer …, [thereby laying] down those clear, obvious marks as preceding, accompanying, and following that gift"; "Self-denial," in *Works* 2, I.1: "[Having established that self-denial is utterly foreign to worldly logic, Wesley implores his reader to let God's grace] then go *before, accompany,* and *follow* what you are now about to read, that it may be written in your heart by the finger of God, so as never to be erased"; "The Scripture Way of Salvation," in *Works* 2, III.8: [In repentance, we are convinced] "of our utter inability to think one good thought, or to form one good desire; and much more to speak one word aright, or to perform one good action but through his free, almighty grace, first preventing us, and then accompanying us every moment"; and "On Working Out Our Own Salvation," in *Works* 3, III.8: "Go on in virtue of the grace of God, *preventing, accompanying,* and *following* you, in 'the work of faith, in the patience of hope, and in the labour of love.' … [And may God] 'make you perfect in every good work to do his will, working in you what is well-pleasing in his sight, through Jesus Christ, to whom be glory for ever and ever!'"

"accompanying" grace acts in order that we may come to co-act with God's "justifying" grace; and (3) God's "following" grace cooperates with us in doing God's will. At this point, we see how one must be careful in interpreting Wesley: He never describes grace in such a way that it tacitly places any and all goodness beyond the pale of human nature.[81]

Wesley also made some serious efforts to pave the way for prevenient grace. An example can be found in his 1752 treatise *Predestination Calmly Considered*:

> His first step is to enlighten the understanding by that general knowledge of good and evil. To this he adds many secret reproofs, if they act contrary to this light; many inward convictions, which there is not a man on earth who hath not often felt. At other times he gently moves their wills, he draws and woos them, as it were, to walk in the light. He instills into their hearts good desires, though perhaps they know not from whence they come. Thus far he proceeds with all the children of men, yea, even with those who have not the knowledge of his written word. But in this, what a field of wisdom is displayed, suppose man to be in some degree a free agent. How is every part of it suited to this end, to save man, as man; to set life and death before him, and then persuade (not force) him to choose life.[82]

And,

> I only assert, that there is a measure of free-will supernaturally restored to every man, together with that supernatural light which "enlightens every man that cometh into the world." ... God does not do the whole work, without man's "working together

81   For this reason, one must be careful about any and all attempts to systematize Wesley's relational-dynamic ideas of grace in a certain and overly flattening way. Unfortunately, such attempts have been made among a large number of Wesleyan theologians and commentators over the past 50 years or so. These theologians and commentators have developed a fairly coherent threefold model of grace, which has still been considered as an essential norm or criterion in discussing Wesley's teachings about grace: grace as *prevenient*, *justifying*, and *sanctifying*. The model, of course, is useful for capturing Wesley's emphasis on *sola gratia*. But since it is somewhat hardened by Calvinism, the model runs the risk of compromising his earnest attempts to maintain the efficacy of grace alongside the God-imaged liberty of human nature.

82   Wesley, *Predestination Calmly Considered*, in *Works* (Albany) 10, §51, especially on page 232–3.

with Him." ... [B]oth experience and Scripture ... make it clear to every impartial inquirer, that though man has freedom to work or not "work together with God," yet may God have the whole glory of his salvation.[83]

As seen in these two excerpts from *Predestination Calmly Considered*, Wesley attempted to construct an anti-Calvinist concept of divine prevenience that respected Scripture, saving a place for both divine sovereignty and human responsibility. Parallel to this attempt is seen elsewhere, too: Wesley's *NT Notes* on Matthew 25:14–30, John 1:9 & 6:44, and Romans 2:14–5; and Wesley's 1757 treatise *The Doctrine of Original Sin*. In each of these writings, Wesley first acknowledged the gratuity and necessity of divine prevenience in order for fallen humanity to have spiritual life. Then he tried hard to protect the universal and prevenient givenness of a *gratia Dei* that functions apart from any kind of either divine predestination or human self-determination:

> No man can believe in Christ, unless God give him power, He draws us first by good desires, not by compulsion, not by laying the will under any necessity; but by the strong and sweet, yet still resistible motions of his heavenly grace.[84]

Lastly, Wesley affirmed that by this *gratia Dei*, our corrupted nature can either "will" or "do" "what is pleasing to God," but one's capability of this divine duty is not a dismissal of "a measure ... given to all men" by that *gratia Dei*,[85] but a reflex of that which is graciously given to all of us. To sum up: The Aldersgate Wesley champions universally prevenient grace – free grace for all – in the face of predestination and its twofold corollary, total depravity and reprobation. As a soteriological antidote to total depravity and reprobation, this particular type of grace implies a gratuitous and supernatural gift of God the Spirit, derived from the merits of Jesus

83   Ibid., §§45–6, especially on page 271.
84   Wesley, *NT Notes* on John 6:44. Likewise, Wesley noted in his *NT Notes* on John 12:32 that not all follow God's "heavenly grace." Then he affirmed that God's grace, though sufficiently powerful in the *ordo salutis*, does not dictate outcomes at the expense of human response-ability.
85   Wesley, *The Doctrine of Original Sin*, in *Works* (Albany) 9, Pt.2, I, especially on page 274.

Christ, by which a person is enabled to make good ethical choices and respond *favorably* (but *not necessarily*) to God's universal offer of salvation.

But again, it seems clear that Wesley was not completely indifferent to Whitefield and other early Calvinist Methodists. Indeed, during the latter half of this middle period, Wesley avoided any direct or unhedged exposure of the term prevenient grace. He rather preferred to use some descriptive language or some indirect metaphors from the Bible, such as "conscience,"[86] "motion,"[87] or "talent,"[88] and acknowledged here and there that God's grace may indeed work irresistibly at various times. To be sure, this highly nuanced approach remained until the end of his Aldersgate ministry. But, as one can see in his 1759 sermon "Original Sin" or his 1765 sermon "The Scripture Way of Salvation," it also continued some time thereafter.[89] Therefore, to appreciate a more Wesleyan account of grace, including that of prevenient and convincing grace, one must move on to the latter part of his post-Aldersgate ministry, which this chapter will now discuss.

---

86 Wesley, *NT Notes* on John 1:9 and Romans 2:14–5.

87 Wesley, *NT Notes* on John 6:44.

88 Wesley, *NT Notes* on Matthew 25:14–30.

89 In 1759, Wesley published a sermon called "Original Sin." In defending the human incompetence described by Augustine, Wesley concluded in the sermon as follows: "By nature ye are wholly corrupted ... By grace ye shall be wholly renewed (III.5)." In addressing the gist of that conclusion, Wesley mentioned three possible means that would somehow counteract that human incompetence: (1) constitution, (2) education, and (3) prevenient grace. The first two of these means create some moral or epistemological differences between persons. But interestingly, Wesley did not provide any further explanation for the third means – for example, whether it makes any ontological or spiritual difference between persons. A similar sentiment appears in the sermon "The Scripture Way of Salvation," published by Wesley in 1765. In this sermon, Wesley said that if the *ordo salutis* were viewed in the broadest sense possible, it could include prevenient grace (I.2). He then argued that this prevenient form of grace was universally given to everyone. Suddenly, however, the flow of his argument for prevenient grace ceased and an unexpected twist emerged. Wesley limited the main argument of this sermon to defending justifying and sanctifying grace and no longer provided any further elaboration on it. In other words, this sermon, just as in the sermon "Original Sin," somewhat underplays prevenient grace in passing and as a parenthetical remark.

The Methodist Revival and Ensuing Schism Era (1759–1791)

When Whitefield died in 1770, the controversy between Wesleyans and Calvinist Methodists in early Methodism grew further, which eventually led to Wesley's establishment of a monthly magazine called the *Arminian Magazine*. The *Arminian Magazine* came off the press in January 1778, and it continued after Wesley's death in 1791 with material prepared by him. As a suitable alternative to the *Gospel Magazine* and the *Spiritual Magazine* – both of which were being published in England to advocate Calvinism while criticizing Wesley and his Methodist movement[90] – his new publication provided a venue for printing Wesley's later sermons, as well as publishing a catalog of books, pamphlets, and tracts sold by his publisher Methodist Book Concern. It was originally designed to be 50 to 60 pages and included four distinct parts: an introduction to Christian doctrines, a story about the lives of some saints, a psalm or letter from pious persons, and a series of comments on contemporary theological claims under consideration.[91] All of these parts, however, converged on the purpose of promoting Wesley's theology and spirituality both inside and outside of early Methodism.

Wesley's later sermons, published through the *Arminian Magazine*, largely kept their theological tone to be anti-Calvinistic, and all that it effected was a more pronounced defense of what Wesley had unfolded in his early sermon "Free Grace" – that "God willeth all men to be saved, and to come to the knowledge of the truth."[92] Since that defense is implicitly or explicitly present in all of these later sermons, it may be worth mentioning all of them here. Of particular note, however, are "The General Spread of the Gospel" and "On Working Out Our Own Salvation." For it is these two sermons by which one may come to appreciate a deeper, implicit nuance to Wesley's mature understanding of grace as "prevenient" and "convincing."

---

90 H. Newton Malony, Jr., *The Amazing John Wesley: An Unusual Look at an Uncommon Life* (Downers Grove, IL: InterVarsity Press, 2012), 149–50.

91 Thomas W. Herbert, *John Wesley as Editor and Author* (Princeton, NJ: Princeton University Press, 1940), 34.

92 Ibid.

First in a sermon of 1783, "The General Spread of the Gospel,"
Wesley wrote:

> Take one instance of this, and such an instance as you cannot easily be deceived in.
> You know how God wrought in your own soul, when he first enabled you to say, "The
> life I now live, I live by faith in the Son of God, who loved me, and save himself for
> me." He did not take away your understanding; but enlightened and strengthened
> it. He did not destroy any of your affections; rather they were more vigorous than
> before. Least of all did he take away your liberty; your power of choosing good or evil.[93]

Wesley made it clear in this passage that prevenient grace exercises a
causal influence on human nature. Then he explained that the causality
of prevenient grace is moral. Notice here that as a moral cause, this *gratia
Dei* has a *positive* effect: It elevates human nature to a higher and essentially different plane of being (existence), allowing our threefold faculties – understanding, affective volition*, and liberty* – to perform what is
metaphysically and theologically impossible for unaided human nature.[94]

But this mode of operation also presupposes a certain weakness of
human nature – *that is, concupiscence*, which is an effect of original sin – as
Wesley said from a few lines earlier in the same sermon:

> Are they as "holy as He that hath called them is holy?" Are they filled with "right-
> eousness, and peace, and joy in the Holy Ghost?" Is there "that mind in them which
> was also in Christ Jesus?" And do they "walk as Christ also walked?" Nay, they are
> as far from it as hell is from heaven! Such is the present state of mankind in all parts
> of the world! But ... God will be jealous of his honor: He will arise and maintain
> his own cause ... "The earth shall be filled with the knowledge of the Lord, as the

93 Wesley, "The General Spread of the Gospel," in *Works* 2, §11.
94 In his 1783 sermon, "Of Good Angels," Wesley reaffirmed that his concept of vol-
    ition – marked as affective volition with asterisks [*] above – is a natural function
    exerting itself in affection and many other forms, including intellect. Wesley, "Of
    Good Angels," I.1. Another concept marked with asterisks [*] above is liberty.
    Since Wesley's notion of liberty is about moral free agency without necessity, it
    concerns choice. Wesley insists that the proper act of liberty is choice, "a capacity
    of choosing the one and refusing the other." But he also ties it to reason, a cap-
    acity of "discern[ing] truth from falsehood, good from evil." Wesley, "The Original,
    Nature, Properties, and Use of the Law," in *Works* 2, I.1. See also Wesley, "The
    General Spread of the Gospel," in *Works* 2, §9.

waters cover the sea." The loving knowledge of God, producing uniform, uninter-
rupted holiness and happiness, shall cover the earth; shall fill every soul of man.[95]

In other words, the moral causality of prevenient grace has a *negative* effect
in addition to that positive above: It removes our natural infirmity resulting
from sin. In discussing the operation of prevenient grace in light of this twofold moral effect, Wesley signaled to us that an initial encounter with God's
grace harms *neither* the liberty *nor* the moral capacity of the soul in contact. It rather lays the foundation for the human dignity of our soul as a free
moral agent.

In addition to this moral conception of prevenient grace, Wesley also
presented two more theological inputs that are logically related to the development of an extended version of prevenient grace. One relates to Wesley's
mention of Mary, and the other to Wesley's recognition of the traditional
division of grace as operative and cooperative. With regard to the former,
Wesley wrote that Mary is an exemplary case of the twofold – positive and
negative – effect of prevenient grace:

> He did not force you; but, being assisted by his grace, you, like Mary, chose the better
> part. Just so has he assisted five in one house to make that happy choice; fifty or live
> hundred in one city; and many thousands in a nation; – without depriving ally of them
> of that liberty which is essential to a moral agent.[96]

As implied in this passage above, God's prevenient grace for Wesley is
not simply a moment or state in which God operates without our cooperation. It is a process or dynamic that always aims at subsequent ("justifying" and "assisting") grace, human responsibility, divine-human cooperation. Following Maddox's classification of prevenient grace, one
could therefore say that Wesley had both a "broad" and a "narrow" understanding of prevenient grace; but in this case, he was describing it in the
"broad" sense of the term – where prevenient grace is understood not as
a single occurrence of pre-conversion, but as a continuous ministration of

---

95   Wesley, "The General Spread of the Gospel," in *Works* 2, §§7–8.
96   Ibid., §11.

the Spirit that sufficiently enables God's people to convert (justification) and grow in holiness and happiness (sanctification).[97]

With regard to the latter, Wesley expended four paragraphs to discuss the paradoxical nature of God's grace at work in the soul. Here Wesley began his discussion by affirming that God's grace may operate irresistibly. But then he approvingly quoted St. Augustine's saying, "He that made us without ourselves, will not save us without ourselves."[98] How should one interpret these two disparate statements? Is it that Wesley – though not systematically – is trying to enunciate God's grace as operative and cooperative? Or is it that Wesley, as Collins interpreted, is simply saying that God's grace must act irresistibly at some point in the order of salvation because man is totally depraved?[99] Any judgment on this matter seems premature at this point in my thesis. But the latter position (Collins' interpretation) seems to have already lost its credibility for at least two reasons: It fits into *neither* Wesley's mature understanding of sin and nature[100] *nor* Wesley's own account of grace in his *Journal* entry for August 24, 1743:

> Yet I believe that the grace of God both before and after those moments [of prevenient grace], may be, and hath been, resisted; and that, in general, it does not act irresistibly, but we may comply therewith or may not.[101]

In addition to these two reasons, Wesley also made the following statement in this sermon that further discredited Collins' interpretation: "God *has* converted so many to himself without destroying their liberty."[102] He then supported this statement with his "inward and outward" motif that

---

97   Randy L. Maddox, *Responsible Grace: John Wesley's Practical Theology* (Nashville, TN: Kingswood, 1994), 30, 84, 159.

98   Wesley, "The General Spread of the Gospel," in *Works* 2, §12.

99   Collins, *The Theology of John Wesley*, 80.

100   As we have already discussed in the previous chapter, Wesley made a positive assessment of human nature and rejected the concept of pure nature because it is a hypothetical abstraction for him. From this point of view, Collins' interpretation seems to belittle human nature as created in God's image. Not only that, but it also seems to indicate at least at some point "that-before-which-we-simply-are-not."

101   Wesley, "Journal & Diaries" 8/23/43, in *Works* 19, especially on 332.

102   Wesley, "The General Spread of the Gospel," in *Works* 2, §12.

God's operative pardon generates our cooperative power both inwardly (*esse*) and outwardly (*operatio*).[103] Since this very motif broadly resonates with the scholastic maxim *agere sequitur esse*,[104] and since it is this maxim that results in the two aspects of God's grace, *operans et cooperans*,[105] one cannot help but admit that Wesley's prevenient grace can be or should be categorized as either operative or cooperative according to its effects. In other words, it is operative where prevenient grace essentially heals or restores some of the proper functionality of our faculties. It is cooperative where prevenient grace effects, at some point in the order of salvation, some inward or outward dispositional actions that also proceed from our genuine human cooperation. In view of this analysis, one can also say that operative prevenient grace is the formal principle of our God-rooted *esse*, that is, the state of *being graced*; cooperative prevenient grace, instead, is the formal principle of our God-reflective *operatio*, that is, the subsequent manifestation of God's universal and prevenient infusion of our souls.

Perhaps the sermon where Wesley offers the clearest explanation of these two concepts – grace as *operans* and grace as *cooperans* – is "On Working Out Our Own Salvation." Having provided an abbreviated version of his *via salutis* (way of salvation), Wesley concluded in this sermon of 1783:

103   Ibid., §18. As Albert C. Outler comments on Wesley's extended treatment of the Sermon on the Mount, Wesley repeatedly calls exegetical attention to the way in which Jesus' teaching proceeds from an inward to an outward focus – from what is inwardly disposed to what is outwardly exposed. A corollary implication of this treatment is that we may act holy because we are restored holy. Albert C. Outler, "An Introductory Comment [to Sermons 21–33]," in *Works* 1, especially on page 466. See also Wesley, "Upon our Lord's Sermon on the Mount, Discourse VI," in *Works* 1, §1.

104   This inward-outward motif is central to Wesley's interpretation of "the locus classicus of evangelical ethics, 'The Sermon on the Mount' (i.e., Matthew 5–7)." Throughout his 13 discourses thereon, Wesley repeatedly calls attention to the manners in which Jesus' teaching proceeds from an inward to an outward focus – from holy life/heart (i.e., our graced being) to holy act/temper (i.e., our graced action). Albert C. Outler, "An Introductory Comment [to Sermons 21–33]," in *Works* 1, especially on page 466.

105   Bernard Lonergan, *Grace and Freedom: Operative Grace in the Thought of St Thomas Aquinas*, ed. Frederick M. Crowe and Robert E. Doran (Toronto: University of Toronto Press, 2000), 47.

> For, first, God works; therefore you can work. Secondly ... God worketh in you; therefore you must work: you must be "workers together with him" (they are the very words of the Apostle); otherwise he will cease working.[106]

In a mere 37 words, Wesley summed up what he believed about grace – its operations, dynamics, and implications. God's initial grace is demonstrative of the divine initiative in salvation, and it stands as the cause of our response. Without it, our fallen nature can neither will nor do what is pleasing to God. With it, however, we are able to work out our own salvation. It is important to note here that Wesley was not saying that perseverance in grace (salvation) is automatically achieved by a singular infusion of God's prevenient grace. One's fall from grace is possible for Wesley; and our cooperative task is required if we are to sojourn along the way of salvation.

But at this point, one important question may arise: How is our cooperative task actualized or activated from potency to action? For Wesley, it seems clear that God's universally offered prevenient grace infused our souls with a potency whereby all people may cooperate with God's initial grace. Not only that, but it also seems clear that this possible reality must be in some sense fully actualized (action) because the necessity of our cooperation is openly assumed in Wesley's *via salutis*. From this, we can see that a careful appreciation of Wesley's treatment of potency and action is needed if we are to assess how Wesley understands God's grace. Although not explicitly depicted, one may probably find the key in the following excerpt from "On Working Out Our Own Salvation (1785)":

> Salvation begins with what is usually termed (and very properly) *preventing grace* [i.e., prevenient grace]; including the first wish to please God, the first dawn of light concerning, his will, and the first slight transient conviction of having sinned against him. All these imply some tendency toward life; some degree of salvation; the beginning of a deliverance from a blind, unfeeling heart, quite insensible of God and the things of God. Salvation is carried on by *convincing grace*, usually in Scripture termed *repentance*; which brings a larger measure of self-knowledge, and a farther deliverance from the heart of stone. Afterwards we experience the proper Christian salvation ... consisting of those two grand branches, justification and sanctification.[107]

106   Wesley, "On Working Out Our Own Salvation," in *Works* 3, III.2, 7.
107   Ibid., II.1.

In this passage, Wesley came up with a particular type of grace that does not fit into either prevenient grace or justifying grace – or "sanctifying grace" which Wesley had once mentioned in his 1778 sermon "A Call to Backsliders."[108] That particular type was termed "convincing grace" – or analogically "repentance" – in this sermon of 1785. As already assumed here, "convincing grace" seems to function as an extension or subspecies of prevenient grace that gives rise to the experience of "proper Christian salvation," that is, "justification and sanctification." However, by approaching "convincing grace" in light of two related sources – (1) Wesley's concept of repentance and (2) Outler's editorial notes on "prevenient" and "convincing" grace – one may come to discover that *graita auxilium* is assumed by Wesley, at least *criteriologically*. In other words, Wesley would probably solve the potency-action question with God's operative *auxilia*.

To see "convincing grace" in light of Wesley's concept of repentance, we must first explore Wesley's 1767 sermon, "The Repentance of Believers." Here Wesley argued that repentance was not just a pre-conversion, but a post-conversion human act:

> And this is undoubtedly true, that there is a repentance ... necessary at the beginning: A repentance, which is a conviction of our utter sinfulness, and guiltiness, and helplessness; and which precedes our receiving that kingdom of God, which, our Lord observes, is "within us" ... But, notwithstanding this, there is also a repentance ... which [is] requisite after we have "believed the gospel;" yea, and in every subsequent stage of our Christian course, or we cannot "run the race which is set before us." And this repentance ... [is] full as necessary, in order to our *continuance* and *growth* in grace, as the former [repentance was], in order to our *entering* into the kingdom of God.[109]

But in what sense are we to repent after we are graced to conversion? Wesley approached this question in two dimensions: (1) Why is it necessary? (2) How can it be done? First with regard to the former dimension,

---

108   Wesley, "A Call to Backsliders," in *Works* 3, I.3, II.10. Having approached sanctifying grace from a restorative/therapeutic perspective, Wesley wrote in this sermon that sanctifying grace works through love to restore the full image of God in us.

109   Wesley, "The Repentance of Believers," in *Works* 1, Preamble §§2–3.

Wesley argued that post-conversion repentance was necessary because of our postlapsarian reality in this world:

> There does still remain, even in them that are justified, a mind which is in some measure carnal; (so the Apostle tells even the believers at Corinth, "Ye are carnal;") an heart bent to backsliding, still ever ready to "depart from the living God;" a propensity to pride, self-will, anger, revenge, love of the world, yea, and all evil; a root of bitterness, which, if the restraint were taken off for a moment, would instantly spring up; yea, such a depth of corruption, as, without clear light from God, we cannot possibly conceive.[110]

After the Fall, all humans were spiritually corrupt. Although this reality was restored to some extent by the universal and nascent regenerative work of prevenient grace, it remains as a moral obstacle to salvation – or, more precisely, as an eschatological tension between the "already" of salvation's accomplishment and the "not-yet" of its final fulfillment and freedom – until we reach our final and highest end of beatitude in the bosom of God. In this regard, it would not be surprising that Wesley rephrased what Augustine stated in his *Confession* as follows: "Break off the yoke of inbred sin, And fully set my spirit free; I cannot rest till pure within, Till I am wholly lost in Thee."[111]

Having confirmed the need for a post-conversion act of repentance, Wesley now explained how it can be done in our Christian life. Central to his explanation of this latter dimension is that our post-conversion repentance cannot be thought of as a uniquely human act freed from divine moorings and instead independently anchored in purely natural traits. It should rather be understood as such an act that can only be achieved when it is properly (or fittingly) connected to a subsequent (or continuing) form of God's restoring grace:

> By all the grace which is given at justification we cannot extirpate them. Though we watch and pray ever so much, we cannot wholly cleanse either our hearts or hands. Most sure we cannot, till it shall please our Lord to speak to our hearts again, to

---

110   Ibid., I.10.
111   Ibid., III.2.

speak the second time, "Be clean!" And then only the leprosy is cleansed. Then only the evil root, the carnal mind, is destroyed.[112]

It is important to note here that Wesley did not say that our post-conversion repentance is achieved by a singular infusion of God's grace (whether operative or cooperative) or by our gracious cooperation (spiritual discernment or prayer) alone. He said it is accomplished by the subsequent fiat from God: "Be Clean!" Although he did not define this anomalous type of grace with precision, Wesley featured it descriptively with the following characteristic attributes: (1) "the mere gift of God" given to us "from moment to moment," not "all at once"[113]; (2) "the power of Christ every moment resting upon us … whereby we are enabled to continue in spiritual life"[114]; (3) God's "continual help" by which our gracious "actions are begun, continued, and ended in him"[115]; and (4) God's "ever interceding" Spirit from which "we receive help [*auxilia*] … to think, and speak, and act, what is acceptable in his sight."[116] Thus, if we look at "convincing grace" in light of Wesley's unique dialect, "repentance," it can be inferred that Wesley was not completely ignorant of a certain type of grace, traditionally called *gratia auxilium*.[117]

Further support for this analysis comes from Outler's editorial notes on "prevenient" and "convincing" grace. In the excerpt from "On Working Out Our Own Salvation" cited above, Outler provides editorial footnotes to two types of grace: "prevenient grace" and "convincing grace."[118] His notes point to a deeper understanding of what Wesley was trying to suggest with

---

112   Ibid., I.20.
113   Ibid., I.17.
114   Ibid., II.5.
115   Ibid.
116   Ibid.
117   For a similar view, see Outler's note in Wesley, "On Working Out Our Own Salvation," in *Works* 3, II.1, fn. 25: There Outler coined the term "the grace of repentance," which serves to encapsulate this anomalous type of grace in "The Repentance of Believers," and then proposed his analysis, that this term is considered within Wesley as equivalent to "convincing grace."
118   Outler's note in Wesley, "On Working Out Our Own Salvation," in *Works* 3, II.1, fn. 24 and fn. 25.

prevenient and convincing grace. The note to "prevenient grace" begins with a repeated explication of Wesley's existing position:

> "Preventing" and "prevenient" had long since become synonyms denoting the Holy Spirit's activity in moving or drawing the will in advance of any conscious resolve. In III.4 below, Wesley relates it to natural conscience even while denying that anything natural is good in and of itself alone.[119]

Following this note, however, Outler references the works of two Anglican priests Thomas Manton (1620–77) and William Tilly (1675–1740), which Wesley accepted as a theological legacy when he was finalizing his doctrine of grace. Manton offers a threefold division of grace in his *Works* (1681): "*gratia praeveniens, operans*, and *co-operans*."[120] By "*gratia praeveniens*," Manton means something similar to what Wesley came up with in "The General Spread of the Gospel": It is the grace of conversion (from *malum* to *bonum*) and the infusion of grace into the soul. "*Gratia operans*" then strengthens the infused grace (or, to borrow Manton's term, the "habit"), and "*gratia co-operans*" is divine assistance that our soul requires in order to act:

> There is *gratia praeveniens, operans*, and *co-operans*; there is preventing grace, working grace and co-working grace. Preventing grace that is when God convers us, when the Lord turns us to himself and doth plant grace in the soul at first. Working grace that is when God strengthens the habit. Co-working grace when God stirs up the act and helps us in the exercise of the grace we have.[121]

---

119   Ibid., fn. 24. As Outler well pointed out, Wesley saw grace as the active, dynamic presence of the Holy Spirit in nature, especially in conscience. More precisely, a very important link exists in Wesley's thought between prevenient grace, conscience, and the Holy Spirit. This link indicates that all of creation, even after the Fall, does not suffer from a total privation of grace, but rather enjoys a general divine presence for all creation, that is to say, the dynamic presence of the Holy Spirit at work in nature. A similar nuance appears as important in Thomas as in Wesley. Indeed, Thomas connects grace with the Holy Spirit and emphasizes the pneumatological implications of this connection, namely, the dynamic presence of the Holy Spirit working graciously in nature. A more detailed discussion of this teaching by Thomas can be found in Part 2. Catholic Tradition: Thomas Aquinas and His View of Grace and Nature.

120   Ibid.

121   Ibid.

Thus, one might say that Manton's "*gratia praeveniens*" is near to what is traditionally called *gratia habitualis*, whereas Manton's "*gratia operans*" and "*gratia co-operans*" are near to the operative and cooperative forms of what is traditionally called *gratia auxilium*.

Outler continues his editorial notes on Wesley's "prevenient" and "convincing" grace by referencing William Tilly's first sermon on Phil. 2:12–3 (Sermon VIII, in *Sermons*, pp. 245 ff).[122] In that first sermon, Tilly marks out two species of grace: "prevenient" and "assisting" grace. Then he describes:

> Prevenient grace removes man from bondage to the corruptions of his nature and breaks the power of temptation, placing him in a condition where, if he will, he can come to desire obedience and salvation ... Because God has given to man His assisting grace, man can and should use his "most diligent endeavours" to work out his salvation. God's grace supplies the "defects" in man's nature, and He intends that man should use his own strength as far as it will go. "Where we fail, and He sees the labour too much for us, there He is ready to come in to our relief." Furthermore, the continuance of God's assistance is dependent upon man's working with Him. Unless man is diligent in his endeavours to be obedient to God's will, the Spirit will withdraw Himself from us. Man should, therefore, pursue his true end and happiness with the "liveliest and strongest affections," and with all seriousness of mind engage in "constant preparation to fulfill all righteousness."[123]

By "prevenient grace," Tilly means something similar to what Wesley had unfolded in a moral sense in his "General Spread of the Gospel": It is a moral concept, a volitionally working effect that offsets certain losses caused by the Fall and non-coercively ushers in our genuine human response to the point where it is positioned somewhere between potency and action. "Assisting grace" then actualizes or activates what prevenient grace has morally enabled in the soul.

It is worth mentioning here that Outler's editorial note to "convincing grace" shows an interesting link between Tilly's "assisting grace" and

---

122   Ibid., fn. 24 and fn. 25.

123   The original text is not available, so the above quote is taken from an abbreviated version edited by Charles A. Rogers. Charles A. Rogers, "John Wesley and William Tilly," *Proceedings of the Wesleyan Historical Society* 35 (June 1966): 137–41, at 140.

Wesley's "convincing grace."[124] In his early days at Oxford, Wesley had abridged and preached five of Tilly's sermons.[125] Among them was Tilly's first sermon on Phil. 2:12–3. According to Charles A. Rogers, Wesley preached the sermon twice: on August 14, 1732, and October 1, 1732, at the Castle prison in Oxford.[126] But for some reason, he stopped preaching it. Perhaps it was because the sermon might put Wesley in trouble – in fact, the young Wesley was accused of supporting a doctrine of simple "work-righteousness" at this particular period of time.[127] After about 50 years, Wesley returned to Tilly and picked up his sermon on Philippians again. But this time, it wasn't just about making another abridged version of Tilly's. Wesley remastered it with his own vocabulary – and then published under the title "On Working Out Our Own Salvation." This very change was captured by Outler's editorial note to "convincing grace." Of particular note there is that the note has referenced one of the important translations that stands out in this remastered version of Tilly's Sermon VIII: where Tilly goes on to say "assisting grace" as a kind of operative *gratia auxilium*, Wesley employs the language of "convincing grace."[128]

What are we to make of Wesley's concept of repentance and of Outler's editorial notes on "prevenient" and "convincing" grace? It is impossible to assert that Wesley had in mind a Thomistic doctrine of grace when describing prevenient and convincing grace in "On Working Out Our Own Salvation." At the same time, seeing Wesley's use of "prevenient" and "convincing" grace through suggests that these two concepts reflect the scholastic notions of *gratia habitualis* and *gratia auxilium*. For Wesley, prevenient grace gives us the potential for gracious action – in the form of repentance. But prevenient grace does not reduce itself to action. For that, the other grace, of convincing grace, is needed. By convincing grace,

124 Outler's note in Wesley, "On Working Out Our Own Salvation," in *Works* 3, II.1, fn. 25.

125 Richard P. Heitzenrater, "Appendix C: Sermons Abridge from Other Authors," in *Works* 4: 531.

126 Rogers, "John Wesley and William Tilly," 139.

127 Ibid., 141.

128 Outler's note in Wesley, "On Working Out Our Own Salvation," in *Works* 3, II.1, fn. 25.

God reduce us to gracious action. Both graces are necessary if we are open to sojourn along the way of salvation – or, more precisely, to generate actions befitting divinity, which is beyond our natural capacities. Thus, Wesley seems to be saying here that God's prevenient grace instills a gracious semi-*habitus* that restores our moral capacity – but it stands in need of the actualization or activation of "convincing grace." So, arguably, the effect of Wesley's "prevenient grace" presupposes that of "justifying grace" and is parallel to operative habitual grace. Similarly, Wesley's "convincing grace" is analogous to operative *auxilium*, that is, to a specific form of grace that elevates one's cooperant experience of God's grace from "preventing [prevenient]" to "accompanying" and "following."[129]

Conclusion

Throughout the course of his life, Wesley was reluctant to fully reveal his views on grace because of various theological or church-political conflicts with Calvinists in the early Methodist movement. However, a review of Wesley's early, middle, and later references to grace in this chapter showed that Wesley continued to develop the following types of grace: (1) prevenient grace, (2) convincing grace, and (3) preventing-accompanying-following grace. First, with regard to prevenient grace, Wesley grounded it both Christologically and pneumatologically, teaching its sufficient (but not efficacious) universality as a consequence of Christ's atonement and the unbounded work of the Spirit. Wesley then described its twofold characteristic effect: One is to heal our fallen nature, and the other is to restore our moral capacities: understanding, affective volition, and liberty. According to Wesley, this healing and restoring of prevenient grace was graciously infused into the soul as a quality, a sort of habit capable of supernatural *esse* and *operatio*.

But ever since the quality was given exactly as quality, not equality, it was positioned somewhere between potency and action. In other words, the

129   Wesley, "The Witness of the Spirit, Discourse I," in *Works* 1, II.2–4.

life of grace is still a possibility in progress, and it always awaits activation. Wesley devoted his two later sermons – "The Repentance of Believers" and "On Working Out Our Own Salvation" – to discuss this potency-action problem. And in light of his Church of England theological heritage, he talked about the grace – a Wesleyan form of *gratia auxilium* – that works perseverance in grace (salvation), by enabling the graced person to overcome temptation (in the form of repentance) and continue on the path to God, to the experience of "proper Christian salvation," that is, "justification and sanctification."[130]

Besides "convincing grace," there were still other types or expressions of grace in Wesley. This type or expression of grace appeared almost descriptively in the early and middle periods of his writings, but in his post-Aldersgate sermons, it was unpacked according to his threefold division of grace: "preventing [prevenient]," "accompanying," and "following" grace. As discussed above, this threefold division of grace was a taxonomy upon which Wesley continued to rely in order to tell how grace works *operatively* or *cooperatively* with the soul for *justification* and *sanctification*. So all of these types or expressions of grace in Wesley can be synthesized into the following diagram:

Prevenient Grace with the efficacy of Justifying Grace	Parallel to	Operative Gratia Habitualis
Accompanying Grace		Cooperative Gratia Habitualis
Following Grace		Cooperative Gratia Auxilium
Convincing Grace		Operative Gratia Auxilium

---

130 Wesley, "On Working Out Our Own Salvation," in *Works* 3, II.1.

PART II

Catholic Tradition: Thomas Aquinas and His View of Grace and Nature

CHAPTER 4

Thomas Aquinas on Sin and Nature

This chapter will explore Thomas' understanding of sin and nature. His view of sin and nature, like Wesley's, retrieves many themes of Augustinian theology: (1) the literal-historical interpretation of Genesis 3 and Romans 5:12 that claims that all sinned in Adam,[1] (2) the cleansing power of Christ through baptism,[2] (3) the communication of original sin through carnal concupiscence (semen),[3] and etc. As he carefully glosses over Augustine, particularly his doctrine of communal guilt, in order to emphasize human dignity, authentic human autonomy, and moral responsibility, Thomas offers a new anthropological and metaphysical view of sin and nature. Thomas' view is articulated in his major works, *De Veritate* (1256–9), *Summa Contra Gentiles* (1259–65), and *Summa Theologiae* (1265–73). Chapter 4 will focus on engaging these three texts, each of which will help us get a clear glimpse of Thomas' original thinking on the subject.

Thomas's Views of Sin and Nature

To properly discuss the vast topic of sin and nature in Thomas' theology, one must first set some of the basic parameters of that discussion. In Thomas' extensive theological output, there are two representative works on sin and nature: One is Thomas' *Summa Contra Gentiles IV* and another is Thomas' *Summa Theologiae I-II*. In each case, the pedagogical context and intent of the discussion are somewhat different. In *Summa*

---

1   *SCG* 4, c.50.11. See also *ST* I–II, q.81, a.1, *sed contra.*
2   Ibid., c.52.16; c.55.30; and c.73.5.
3   *ST* I–II, q.81, a.1 ad 2.

Contra Gentiles IV, the context of Thomas' account of sin and nature is the discussion of original sin and the suitability of the Incarnation.[4] In *Summa Theologiae I-II*, Thomas considers original sin in a metaphysical context that brings original justice and concupiscence together through the use of Aristotelian categories.[5] For all the diversity of pedagogical contexts,[6] in each case Thomas comes to a similar conclusion regarding original sin, and importantly for the purposes of this chapter, provides essentially the same account for the state of pre- and postlapsarian human nature. In what immediately follows, the chapter will provide an overview of Thomas' account of sin and nature in *Summa Contra Gentiles IV* and *Summa Theologiae I-II*. Then it will look at Thomas' *De Veritate* and *Summa Theologiae I*, which assign a more specific content to the theological-anthropological insights gained through the overview of *SCG* IV and *ST* I–II. Here one will come to see Thomas' account of what is left to human nature after sin: *synderesis* and *liberum arbitrium*. As we shall see, these accounts will ultimately serve as the basis for comparative studies in the final chapter of this book.

Summa Contra Gentiles IV

Within his *Summa Contra Gentiles* (*SCG*), Thomas' discussion of sin and nature arises in the context of his examination of the *convenientia* (suitability) of the incarnation in Book IV. As we will see, the discussion unfolds through his particular observations of original sin and

---

4   *SCG* 4, cc.50–5.

5   *ST* I–II, qq.81–3 and q.85.

6   Thomas unfolds his discussion of morals in the *Prima Secundae* of *Summa Theologiae* in seven pedagogical contexts: (1) man's last end, (2) human acts, (3) passions, (4) habits, (5) vice. and sin, (6) law, and (7) grace. Each of these contexts is also considered from two points of view: from the point of view of the moral matter itself and of the pre- and/or postlapsarian state of humankind. See also Thomas' own introduction to *Prima Secundae* at the outset of the *Secunda Secundae* of *Summa Theologiae* (*ST* II–II, prologus).

original justice: Original sin is the counterpoint to original justice, and this opposing order is the bedrock of the incarnation's suitability. To figure this out more clearly, let us turn first to the conception of original justice – and then of original sin and the Incarnation.

In the *SCG 4*, Thomas calls our attention to the doctrine of *iustitia originalis* (original justice or righteousness). Original justice is a term used to express the prelapsarian state of human nature. It was Anselm of Canterbury who first set forth the term in relation to the doctrine of original sin.[7] In this state of original justice, human nature was established with an internal harmony that holds "all the soul's parts together in one."[8] The harmony in nature was a threefold subjection: "The inferior powers were perfectly subject to reason, the reason to God, the body to the soul."[9] This was not a purely natural state, but a state of grace: Original justice was a gift from God to the first man God created.[10] According to Thomas, Adam received from God this gift of *justitia originalis*, and the gift enabled his parts (soul and body) and powers (intellective, sensory, and appetitive) to function properly and optimally, in harmony with God, but removed neither his freedom nor his essential fallibility. Thus, Adam was able to follow God freely, and to attain a distinctively supernatural end – that is, unending communion with God – beyond what he could attain by nature alone, but he was also able to fall away from such a state and turn away from God.[11]

As Thomas further understands it, the gift of original justice was meant to be handed down to all the descendants of the first man Adam.[12] But this divine purpose was thwarted by original sin:

---

7   Whereas Augustine had understood original sin positively, that is, as a culpable active inclination of one's will against God, Anselm defined original sin negatively as the privation or absence of original justice. *Liber de Conceptu Virginali et Originali Peccato*, ch. XXVII (*PL, CLVIII*, 461); ch. III (*PL, CLVIII*, 435–6). For a more detailed summary of Anselm's notion of original justice, see G. Vandervelde, *Original Sin: Two Major Trends in Contemporary Roman Catholic Reinterpretation* (Amsterdam: Rodopi N.V., 1975), 26–8.

8   *ST* I–II, q.82, a.2, ad.3.

9   *SCG* 4, c.52.6.

10   *ST* I, q.95, a.1.

11   *SCG* 4, c.52. For comparable accounts, see *ST* I, q.95, a.1 and *QDM*, q.4, a.1.

12   Ibid., c.52.6. See also *ST* I, q.100, a.1.

"[O]riginal justice" was conferred on the first man in such wise that he was propagate it to his descendants along with human nature. But in the sin of the first man reason withdrew itself from the divine subjection. And it has followed thereon that the lower powers are not perfectly subject to the reason nor is the body to the soul; and this is not only the case for the first sinner, but the same consequent defect follows into his posterity and to the posterity in whom the original justice mentioned was going to follow. Thus, then, the sin of the first man from whom all other men are derived according to the teaching of faith was not only personal in that it deprived him and consequently his descendants of the benefit bestowed on the entire human nature.[13]

In this passage, Thomas shows that original justice has a social character, as in the case of original sin. In other words, it should have been passed on together with human nature through generation to all of Adam's posterity. The primal sin, however, deprived Adam and his descendants of original justice. Here the relationship between original justice and original sin becomes explicit: Original justice and original sin are exact opposites. As such, they are part of the same class or genus: To borrow one expression from Thomas' *ST* I, q.100, a.1, co., both original justice and original sin are related to "human nature as a whole" and so they both are (or would have been) effective in all human beings and thus are (or would have been) transmitted in the same way from one generation to the next.[14]

This was, for Thomas, the pre- and/or postlapsarian state of humankind. By virtue of original justice, humans were able to order their entire being or operation toward its proper and spiritual end, God. In this prelapsarian state, they were not constrained by "death and the necessity of dying."[15] *Iustitia originalis* was to be passed on to them, along with human nature. They were free, however, to rebel against this gift from God, and did so in the Fall. This first rebellion against the state of original justice then resulted in a state of original sin in Adam (and thus in his descendants).[16]

---

13   Ibid.

14   *ST* I, q.100, a.1, co.

15   *SCG* 4, c.50.3.

16   Adam's failure to transmit original justice makes the lack of original justice sinful in his posterity. Thomas uses Augustine's language concerning this corruption of nature by sin. An example comes from *SCG* 4, where he cites Augustine's *De haeresibus*, 88 (*PL*, 42, col. 48) to confirm: "since the Pelagian heretics denied original sin, we must show that men are born with original sin" (*SCG* 4, c.50.2).

So, for Thomas, it can be said that original sin is primarily under-stood in relation to the state of original justice. In his *ST* I–II, he also claims: "Original sin denotes the privation of original justice."[17] But as we shall see, there is a methodological difference between these two works: In *ST* I–II Thomas uses an Aristotelian framework (form and matter) to relate original sin to original justice and concupiscence, whereas in *SCG* IV, Thomas takes a strictly theological approach that discusses original sin in relation to the question "Was the Incarnation suitable?"

Following the Apostle Paul, who teaches that Christ reconciled sin-ners to God, Thomas argues that the Incarnation was *conveniens* because of original sin.[18] To further support this argument, Thomas develops in *SCG* 4, cc.50–2 the teaching of original sin in the form of a *Quaestiones Disputatae*. Next in *SCG* 4, c.53, he summarizes a number of arguments to the effect that the Incarnation was not *conveniens*. Then in *SCG* 4, c.54, he explains why he takes the Incarnation to be *conveniens*, while going on in *SCG* 4, c.55 to reply to the arguments listed in *SCG* 4, c.53.

Here the main objection to which Thomas must respond is the claim that the first sin committed by the first man as an act of the will cannot be passed on to the entire human race and therefore it is irrational to con-clude that original sin is true.[19] In providing his response to this objection, Thomas begins by pointing out that "the human race commonly suffers various penalties, both bodily and spiritually."[20] Humans are beset by obs-tacles. Humans are often frustrated and are all subject to death. Thomas notes that one might put all of this down to natural factors:

However, when he explains this usage, he indicates that it is improper (e.g., *QDM*, q.5, a.2): Thomas relies on Denys the Areopagite to argue that "strictly speaking, human nature survives the Fall." Daniel W. Houck, *Aquinas, Original Sin, and the Challenge of Evolution* (Cambridge: Cambridge University Press, 2020), 11–2.

17 *ST* I–II, q.82, a.1, ad.1.

18 *SCG* 4, c.50.2: "Now, the reason for this suitability the Apostle seems to situate in original sin, which is passed on to all men; he says: 'As by the disobedience of one man many were made sinners: so also by the obedience of one many shall be made just' (Rom. 5:19)."

19 Ibid., c.51.2.

20 Ibid., c.52.1.

For all that, one could say that defects of this kind, both bodily and spiritual, are not penalties, but natural defects necessarily consequent upon matter. For, necessarily, the human body, composed of contraries, must be corruptible; and the sensible appetite must be moved to sense pleasures, and these are occasionally contrary to reason.[21]

But he goes on to say, "one [must] weigh matters rightly," meaning that God could have arranged for us not to suffer the woes (or evils) that beset us. He then suggests that this fact gives us reason to think they are not just natural defects, but penalties of some kind: penalties for *peccatum*. So Thomas writes:

> Of course, although defects of these kinds may seem natural to human beings in an absolute consideration of human nature on its inferior side, nonetheless, taking into consideration divine providence and the dignity of human nature on its superior side, it can be proved with enough probability that defects of this kind are penalties. And one can gather thus that the human race was originally infected with sin.[22]

With that thought in place, Thomas responds to the main objection he noted in *SCG* 4, cc.50–2. In doing so, he makes the following points: *Originale peccatum* is propagated to all in their origin, "even though each individual is praised or blamed according to his [or her] own act."[23] The remission of original sin is necessary, and this necessity provides an appropriate context for explaining, to some extent (*aliquatenus*), that the incarnation was *conveniens*:

> God should not remit sin without satisfaction. But to satisfy for the sin of the whole human race was beyond the power of any pure man, because any pure man is something less than the whole human race in its entirety. Therefore, in order to free the human race from its common sin, someone had to satisfy who was both man and so proportioned to the satisfaction, and something above man that the merit might be enough to satisfy for the sin of the whole human race. But there is no greater than man in the order of beatitude, except God ... Therefore, it was necessary for man's achievement of beatitude that God should become man to take away the sin of the human race.[24]

21   Ibid., c.52.2.
22   Ibid., c.52.4.
23   Ibid., c.52.6.
24   Ibid., c.54.9.

It is important to note here Thomas' reference to the term "satisfaction" and the distinction he made between original and actual sin.[25] Thomas stands in a long Christian tradition, one most famously, perhaps, expressed by St. Anselm of Canterbury in *Cur Deus homo?*: Original sin requires a release or satisfaction of some sort because it is a guilt (*culpam*) of some kind.[26] Given that each individual can be praised or blamed for what he or she performs (actual sin), not for what he or she is born with (original sin), Thomas modifies two important notions of the Christian tradition coming from *Cur Deus homo?*: (1) satisfaction and (2) guilt.

The first notion relates to the understanding of Christ as satisfying for sin. Unlike Anselm, who emphasizes *why* we need a God-man in order to be saved, Thomas stresses the primacy of the *divine initiative* in the economy of salvation.[27] This shift of emphasis also appears in relation to the second notion of guilt. In *Cur Deus homo?* I, 24, Anselm sees the loss of original justice as a kind of debt and does link it with guilt (*culpa*); but in *SCG* 4, c.52.6–7, Thomas distinguishes the loss of original sin from guilt and suggests a fresh and original interpretation: The fault imputed to Adam has been transmitted to all of his heirs, not as personal *culpa*, but as "inherent in human beings fathered by Adam."[28] Thus, Thomas argues, while actual sin is "in act," original sin is "in principle" toward acting.[29] In other words, original sin is sin *secundum analogiam*, inherited rather than committed; as such, it involves no (actual) turn to what is not the ultimate good and

25 Ibid., c.52.7: "[Human beings] were present in Adam ... not in act, but only in ... principle [toward acting]." For a similar account of the difference between original sin and actual sin, see *ST* I–II, q.81, a.1, c.

26 "*Quod cum non sit actuale, non est actus sive motus animae vel corporis.*" Peter Lombard, *Sententiae* II, d. 30, c.8, in *Sententiae in IV libris distinctae*, ed. Ignatius Brady, vol. 1 (Grottaferrata: Editiones Collegii S. Bonaventurae Ad Claras Aquas, 1971–81), 500, 4–6.

27 For Thomas, divine mysteries such as the Incarnation do not take place by any form of necessity, but rely entirely on the divine will. So he argues, "All things that are done by God are foreseen and ordered from eternity by divine wisdom," and as such "there can be no cause of the divine will and providence." *SCG* 3/2, c.163.1, 3.

28 Brian Davies, *Thomas Aquinas's Summa Contra Gentiles: A Guide and Commentary* (Oxford: Oxford University Press, 2016), 355.

29 *SCG* 4, c.52.7.

the person with it still loves God – it is in this particular context that Thomas insists that unbaptized infants who die with only original sin will be "joined to God through participation in natural goods; they will even be able to enjoy him by natural knowledge and love."[30]

If one accepts this argument, then the question will come to mind: Where does original sin fit in? What exactly is it? A proper answer to this question is probably coming from *De Malo*, which this chapter will not cover since in *ST I–II* Thomas takes pretty much the same line as he does in the *De Malo*. Suffice it to say that Thomas writes in *De Malo*:

> The formal element in original sin is the lack of original justice, the material element is concupiscence. We may draw an analogy with actual and personal sin: there the turning away from God is formal, and the turning to creatures is material. Likewise original sin; it estranges us from God, and commits us to this world.[31]

For Thomas, original sin is not a total corruption of the *imago Dei* in human nature. The higher part of our human nature, represented by the soul and rational faculty, is still capable of perceiving that one has turned away from God, and that it still expresses something of *justitia originalis* in its affirmation of what Thomas later calls "human virtue."[32] So Thomas says in his book on evil that original sin is not "a fault of the person" but "a fault of human nature."[33] This implies the metaphysical character of original sin that *originale peccatum* is not biological or genetically natural; it is, as we have already seen, a disordering and weakening of human nature, particularly the will:

> [O]ur first parent lost the gift of original justice because he turned away from the immutable good. And his lower powers, which should have been elevated to reason, have been dragged down to lower things because he inordinately turned toward a transient good. Therefore, even regarding those who come from his stock, both the

---

30 *Scriptum* II, d.33, q.2, a.2, ad. 5.

31 *QDM*, q.4, a.2.

32 *ST* I–II, q.71, a.2.

33 *QDM*, q.5, a.2, co: "Therefore, it can be due to a fault of human nature or a personal fault that persons suffer harm regarding things superior to human nature, but it seems that it can be due only to a person's own fault that persons suffer harm regarding things that belong to human nature."

higher part of the soul lacks the requisite ordination to God, which it had through original justice, and the lower powers are not subject to the power of reason. Rather, the lower powers by their own impulse are turned toward lower things, and even the body itself tends toward dissolution by the inclinations of the contraries of which it is composed.[34]

A similar sentiment, however, is also being made in *SCG* 4, cc.50–5. One will probably find it as Thomas writes:

> "… when reason turned away from God, not only did the inferior powers rebel from reason, but the body also sustained passions contrary to that life which is from the soul."[35]

In addition,

> The nature's origin passes along the defects mentioned [suffering and death] because the nature has been stripped of that help of grace that had been bestowed on it in the first parent to pass on to his descendants along with the nature.[36]

Here Thomas makes it clear that the damage that original sin has done to human beings, and to human nature more specifically, is not merely biological but metaphysical. In other words, while Thomas does hold the teaching of Augustine that original sin, *qua* lack or privation of original justice, is transmitted to the first human's posterity by way of procreation, he does not regard it as constitutive of our biological nature (or genetic make-up) since it is not a fault or biological defect but a privation of that extra gift bestowed out of God's generosity (original justice).[37] Thus, in

---

34   Ibid., q.4, a.2, IV, co.

35   *SCG* 4, c.52.3.

36   Ibid., c.52.10.

37   In *SCG* 4, c.52.16, one can actually see that Thomas accepts Augustine's biological model of original sin, yet carefully overcomes it with his distinct view of original sin and actual sin: "Let one by the sacraments of grace be cleansed from original sin so that it is not imputed a fault in him (and for him personally this is to be freed from original sin); for all that, the nature is not entirely healed; therefore, in an act of the nature the original sin is transmitted to his descendants. Thus, in a man who generates there is no original sin insofar as he is a given person; and it also happens that in the act of generation there is no actual sin, which the eleventh argument was proposing. But so far as the man who generates is the natural principle of generation,

SCG 4, cc.50–5, one cannot point – at least in a metaphysical sense – to any part or power of the soul that has been totally corrupted or destroyed by sin. On Thomas' account, we are only damaged because of what we have lost, or more precisely, because of what we have not gained as a result of Adam's loss of that which is above human nature.[38] And as such, this damage (original sin) does not fundamentally alter or totally destroy our human nature – nor does it make us (including infants) lose anything that is ours by nature – though it leaves us in a certain state where we humans are ill-disposed to virtue and indirectly inclined to vice.[39]

Summa Theologiae I–II

Early in the *Summa Theologiae* I–II, Thomas reveals his plan for discussing original sin:

> the infection of the original sin which bears on nature *remains* in him and in his act of generation." From this excerpt, one should also note that Thomas appended the verb "remain" to the original sin. Of course, it relates to his conception of *fomes peccati*, a term from Peter Lombard's 2 *Sent.* 30.8(2): "*Originale peccatum dicitur fomes peccati, scilicet concupiscentia vel concupiscibilitas, quae dicitur lex membrorum, sive languor naturae, sive tyrannus qui est in membris nostris, sive lex carnis.*" More importantly, however, it seems to imply that Thomas' notion of *fomes peccati* is analogous to a Wesleyan concept of sin introduced in Chapter 2: "sin remaining," that which means sin as an inclination not as an action. A further comparison of these two concepts is made in Chapter 6.

38 In his commentary on Peter Lombard's *Sentences*, Thomas thinks that original justice was natural only in a sense that it was good for nature and sexually transmissible. But since original justice was not "due" to nature, Thomas argues that it was above nature and God could have withheld it without depriving the good of nature – that is, the principles of human nature (the animal body and rational soul) and what follows these principles (like the powers of the soul). In understanding Thomas' notion of original justice, one must therefore always keep in mind the two-fold and paradoxical character it possesses: original justice is natural and supernatural to humans. For more details, see *Scriptum* II, d.20, q.2, a.3.

39 *SCG* 4, c.54.8.

As will be explained later, through the sin of the first parent the supernatural gift divinely given to humanity was subtracted, and nature was left to itself. Thus we need to consider the natural reason why the motion of these members especially does not obey reason.[40]

Following this plan, Thomas explains his conception of original sin near the end of *Prima Secundae*, especially in the 13 articles of Questions 81–3. Here, says Thomas, there is a *formal* and a *material* element of original sin. He then links the former to the absence of original justice and the latter to "the disordered disposition rising from the dissolution of that harmony in which original justice consisted."[41] Basically, it is within this twofold metaphysical aspect of original sin that Thomas develops his mature view of sin and nature. But to appreciate it more plainly, one needs to see how Thomas understands nature, more specifically, which part of it is vulnerable to sin.

In Question 85 of the *ST* I–II, Thomas posits that there is a threefold good of nature (*bonum naturae*) – of which each aspect is variously affected by *peccatum* (sin): (1) the principles that constitute nature together with the capacities or properties that proceed from these principles; (2) the natural inclination or disposition to virtue that is rooted in the soul's rational nature; and (3) the divine gift of original justice.[42] According to Thomas, the third *bonum naturae* was additionally granted to the "entire human nature" as an accidental quality of that nature (not of the individual human being),[43] and it was a good of nature, nature's health, and order.[44] Thus, original justice was, in a sense, natural to Adam, and as such, all descendants from Adam could have been born in a state of original justice.[45]

40　*ST* I–II, q.17, a.9, ad 3.

41　Ibid., q.82, aa.1–3.

42　Ibid., q.85, aa.1–2.

43　*ST* I, q.100, a.1: "[Original justice was a] concomitant of the nature of the species [*accidens naturae speciei*] not as being caused by the basic elements of the species, but as a gift given by God to human nature as a whole."

44　*ST* I–II, q.82, a.3, co. See also *ST* I, q.95, a.1, co.

45　Paul A. McDonald, Jr., "*Original Justice, Original Sin and the Free-Will Defense*," *The Thomist* 74 (2010): 105–41, 138.

But when Adam rebelled against God, the divine gift of original justice was withdrawn[46]; and correspondingly something bad for nature had arisen: Adam lost the power to know God, to control his bodily appetites/desires, and to perform salutary acts.[47] He had to live the mortal life of "ignorance," "malice," "weakness," and "concupiscence."[48] His nature was "left to itself": "But because *human nature*, by the sin of the first parents, is *left to itself*, as will be said later on, for the supernatural gift which had be given to man by God was taken away from him."[49]

Adam's primal sin did not, however, destroy his nature itself. What was destroyed (or, as it turns out, taken away) was a gift from God – that is, the third *bonum naturae* that Adam had accidentally (but not substantially) received from God. In other words, original sin for Thomas is not like the concept of *peccatum* claimed by Augustine as concupiscence. It is the privation or absence of original justice rather than the incoming or entering of concupiscence. Therefore, concupiscence is not original sin per se for Thomas, but an effect of original sin – with which "all the powers of the soul are ... lacking an order proper to them."[50]

This is one of the important reasons why Thomas, unlike Augustine, assigns to concupiscence a material and not a formal role in original sin.[51] For Thomas, concupiscence could not have been part of original sin, insofar as original justice was present in human nature. In fact, Thomas had even claimed that sexual reproduction, although now distorted, was part of God's plan. In other words, concupiscence is a natural good, and it can never be the material cause of original sin unless it is against nature and then inherited from Adam.[52] For Thomas, the loss of original justice precedes concupiscence. What all humans inherit from the primal sin of Adam is, accordingly, not a broken reality, but a privation of order, or due harmony,

---

46   *ST* I–II, q.82, a.3, co.
47   Ibid. See also *ST* I, q.95, a.1, co.
48   Ibid., q.85, a.3, co.
49   Ibid., q.17, a.9, ad 3.
50   Ibid., q.85, a.3.
51   M.-D. Chenu, O.P., *Toward Understanding Saint Thomas* (Chicago: Henry Regnery Co., 1963), 175 citing *ST* I–II, q.82, a.3.
52   *ST* I–II, q.82, a.3, ad 1. See also *ST* I–II, q.85, a.3, ad.3.

in nature by which one can no longer achieve what he or she could have achieved in the state of original justice before the Fall.

Having established the twofold (*formal* and *material*) elements of original sin, Thomas now turns to the question of how original sin is transmitted from Adam to his posterity. With regard to this matter, Thomas holds the Augustinian principle that Adam imparted original sin to his offspring. We inherit the primal sin of Adam by way of procreation. We are sinners even prior to any willful act (or free choice) of evil. Thomas, however, does not maintain that the concupiscence of Adam and Eve causes sin in their posterity. The sexual act of the first man and woman, even if done in concupiscence, does not generate *peccatum* or *culpa* in their children, since it is itself a natural process:

> The semen is the principle of generation, which is an act proper to nature, by helping it to propagate itself. Hence the soul is more infected by the semen, than by the flesh which is already perfect, and already affixed to a certain person.[53]

Although it is grafted on evil concupiscence, concupiscence is itself not *malum*, but just a manifestation of *poena* which we humans pay for original sin.[54] In other words, Thomas drives a sharp wedge between original sin and actual sin in his speculation about the mode of transmission. He avoids some position – especially those following Augustine – that original sin is an act swept along by inordinate desire, or some kind of *active* concupiscence, and that it is this positive (not privative) disorder that Adam conveys in the act of generation.[55] As opposed to original sin, actual sin, reasons Thomas, is *in actu*: It stresses action over mere inclination.[56] More precisely, actual sin is the result of an act of willing *malum*, whereas original sin is a habit of inordinate disposition into which Adam was cast as a result of his actual sin. With regard to the original sin understood in this logic, Thomas says that it is voluntary only by the will of

---

53   Ibid., q.82, a.1, ad.4.

54   Ibid., q.85, a.3, ad.2.

55   J. A. Di Noia, O.P., "Not 'Born Bad': The Catholic Truth about Original Sin in a Thomistic Perspective," *The Thomist* 81 (2017): 345–59, 351.

56   *ST* I–II, q.71.5.

Adam, not by the will of the individual agent. And for the same reason, he contradicts the view that all humans ratify Adam's actual sin, or that they *acted in* – or were *represented by* – Adam:

> So too the disorder which is in an individual man, a descendant of Adam, is not voluntary by reason of personal will, but by reason of the will of the first parent, who through a generative impulse exerts influence upon all who descend from him by way of origin, even as the will of the soul moves bodily members to their various activities.[57]

This is a hugely important point. In Thomas' argument, Adam's causality is limited: We are given original sin "by way of origin," yet not given actual sin. We share in "the character of a habit" that originated in Adam's nature (with God's gift stripped off), not in "the character of guilt."[58] Thus, unlike Augustine, Thomas holds that *originale peccatum* is not identical to Adam's act of willing *malum* (actual sin), nor to any sinful or evil concupiscence.

Taking this position from his mature work *Prima Secundae*, Thomas goes further to add a new analogy to the traditional explanation of original sin's transmission. He insists that original sin cannot best be explained by comparison to a hereditary disease – that is, the Augustinian biological model devised to analogously describe the transmission of original sin. Thomas finds this comparison inapt: It does not do justice to the link between Adam's will and ours[59]; nor does it take into account the distinction between original sin (the inherited sin of nature) and actual sin (the committed sin of the person). According to Thomas, original sin is better compared to the analogy of a murderer moving his hand to kill.[60] The hand, in itself, is not guilty. It is guilty only insofar as it is moved to an act of the will. Likewise, the unbaptized infant, in himself – simply lacking *justitia originalis* – is not guilty. He is guilty only insofar as he is moved to the willful act of sin. Thomas does not think that the primal sin of Adam that has been passed on to us by way of origin is an act or a vice *in actu*: "It

57 Ibid., q.81, a.1.
58 Ibid., q.82, a.1.
59 Ibid., q.81, a.1, co.
60 Ibid.

does not *directly* incline one to act badly, only *indirectly*, insofar as original justice is removed."[61]

Accordingly, Thomas does not regard original sin as a broken state of the original human nature created by God; and its transmission as a biological mode in which Adam brings about the non-natural state of human *esse* into which Adam was cast. When the primal sin of man passes by way of origin to posterity, it does not destroy or entirely corrupt human nature. Such human wounds as "ignorance," "malice," "weakness," and "concupiscence" do not imply the tragically broken state of human nature.[62] They only indicate what Thomas calls the "sin of nature" – that is, a disorder that exists in nature due to the will of Adam who by motion of generation moves all who derives their origin from him.[63] Under these conditions, the postlapsarian state of human nature remains essentially intact, yet is deprived of God's gift of original justice.

As discussed above, original justice is a supernatural gift. It is also, in Thomas's view, a habit (*habitus*) of the soul itself, which God has given to man in order to perfect the human existence as a body-soul composite.[64] In other words, the perfection of human nature is a gift, and in this sense the state of being deprived of this gift cannot refer to human perfection or sinlessness. Ironically, it also cannot refer to any state of nature that is essentially destroyed from Thomas' point of view. Then what does this paradoxical state of nature imply? Or, to put it differently, how does Thomas describe the effects of original sin upon human nature? To get a suitable answer to this question, one must return to what was previously introduced as the threefold good of nature (*bonum naturae*).[65]

Affected in the post-original sin state was the second, not the first or third good of nature: the natural inclination or disposition to virtue that is rooted in the soul's rational nature. This seems to reflect Thomas' belief

---

61 Daniel W. Houck, "*Natura Humana Relicta est Christo*: Thomas Aquinas on the Effects of Original Sin," *Archa Verbi* 13 (2016): 68–102, 84. See also *ST* I–II, q.82, a.1, ad.3.
62 *ST* I–II, q.85, a.3, co.
63 Ibid., q.81, a.1, co.
64 McDonald, Jr., "*Original Justice, Original Sin and the Free-Will Defense*," 116.
65 *ST* I–II, q.82, a.3, co. See also *ST* I, q.95, a.1, co.

that "we are not born bad."[66] With this belief, Thomas explores the relation of original sin's effects to the second *bonum naturae* in Question 85 of the *ST* I–II. Here he points out that the natural inclination or disposition to virtue is "a kind of intermediate magnitude, for it lies between its *soil*, man's rational nature, and its *goal*, virtue."[67] With respect to its soil, the second *bonum naturae* is in no way destroyed or entirely corrupted by sin, for it is rooted in our rational nature.[68] But it can be diminished – teleologically – with respect to the attainment of its goal (virtue), for it is frustrated positively by actual sin and negatively by original sin.[69] To be more specific, actual sin, on the one hand, counteracts the second good of nature and thus puts an obstacle between the inclination to and the attainment of virtue.[70] Original sin, on the other hand, causes the loss of the third *bonum naturae* (original justice) by which the second *bonum naturae* is properly oriented; and as such, it deprives a proper orientation of our natural inclination or disposition to virtue and makes its goal elusive.[71] Here Thomas speaks of the teleological disorder of nature – instead of the ontological depravity of that which makes us who we are. This disorder of one's goal is later described as the four wounds of nature, each of which implies "the deprivation of a specific power of the soul of its proper orientation to a specific virtue"[72]:

> Again, there are four of the soul's powers that can be subject of virtue, as stated above (I–II:61:2), viz. the reason, where prudence resides, the will, where justice is, the irascible, the subject of fortitude, and the concupiscible, the subject of temperance. Therefore in so far as the reason is deprived of its order to the true, there is [1] *the wound of ignorance*; in so far as the will is deprived of its order of good, there is [2] *the wound of malice*; in so far as the irascible is deprived of its order to the arduous, there is [3] *the wound of weakness*; and in so far as the concupiscible is deprived of its order to the delectable, moderated by reason, there is [4] *the wound of concupiscence*.[73]

---

66   Noia, O.P., "Not 'Born Bad,'" 353.
67   Vandervelde, *Original Sin*, 31. See also *ST* I–II, q.85, a.2, co.
68   *ST* I–II, q.85, a.2, co.
69   Ibid., q.85, a.4, co.
70   Ibid., q.85, a.2, co.
71   Ibid., q.85, a.3, co.
72   Vandervelde, *Original Sin*, 32.
73   *ST* I–II, q.85, a.3, co.

Considering the cumulative effect of these four wounds – ignorance, malice, weakness, and concupiscence – it is not surprising to see that Thomas sees original sin itself as a *languor naturae* (sickness of nature).[74] But more important than that, one should not be surprised to see that however detrimental the sickness of nature is, Thomas does not claim that such wounds have nothing to do with a *status naturae lapsae* (state of lapsed nature) as Augustine did – that is, original sin with its consequences:

> [T]here is a good belonging to the very substance of nature, which good has its mode, species and order, and is neither destroyed nor diminished by sin. There is again the good of the natural inclination, which also has its mode, species and order; and this is diminished by sin, as stated above (Articles 1 and 2), but is not entirely destroyed.[75]

So for Thomas, the postlapsarian state of human nature remains essentially intact, and even with the Augustinian premise that original sin is sexually transmitted with what Thomas calls the "infection of nature,"[76] it does not work on to break and ruin the inviolable boundaries of *bonum naturae*, namely, the inalienable principles and properties of human nature. Hence the "*in naturalibus vulneratus*," that is, the disorderliness of our rational soul and bodily appetites/desires, is not un-natural or non-natural but completely natural. It is the way nature operates when left to itself.[77]

It is important to note here that Thomas distances himself significantly from the Augustinian concept of original sin. It is, as it were, the

---

74   Ibid., q.82. a.1, co.
75   Ibid., q.85, a.4, co. See Chapter 1 of this paper, especially the discussion of infant baptism referenced by Augustine to highlight the negative effects of original sin on human nature.
76   Ibid., q.81, a.1.
77   This is, indeed, how Thomas had once commented on *Glossa Ordinaria*'s famous statement about nature's vulnerability. There Thomas, as in this mature work on the natural state of fallen man, states that humans are in *naturalibus vulneratus* in the sense that they lost the *bonum naturae* for their nature that helped them reach the ultimate end. But ultimately, with Denys, Thomas affirms that the natural gifts (principles and properties) – endowed by God with the gift of original justice – have neither been lost nor diminished. Houck, "*Natura Humana Relicta est Christo*," 76.

naturalization of fallen man (Adam). To make it more specific, one needs to look more closely at the character of original justice in his theological anthropology. In Questions 82 and 95 of the *ST* I–II, Thomas claims that original justice is characterized by a hierarchical threefold subjection, the first of which relates to the relationship between God and man, and the second and third subjections to the relationship between the various constituents of man (such as our rational soul and bodily appetites/desires).[78] Prior to sin, human nature was characterized by the harmonious order of this threefold subjection: The will was subject to God, the lower powers in man to reason, and the body to the soul.[79] But after sin, original justice was no longer there in human nature. This meant to Thomas that as long as they were curbed by God's supernatural gift of original justice, humans were immortal and free from disorderliness – from any type of natural defect in the person. But when they disobeyed, and thereby God removed the gift of original justice, what remains of our nature is a *status naturae*, whose *languor naturae* had once been curbed by original justice yet was resuscitated after the loss of original justice.[80] As such, original sin for Thomas is essentially privative, not positive; and as such it is the opening up of the natural yet tragic state of human existence, not the destroying down of the natural state, the intrinsic goodness by which humans can do good.

De Veritate and Summa Theologiae I

At this point, we can ask what remains in human nature despite the Fall. Theologically speaking, one could say that it is the *imago Dei*. Indeed, Thomas also says: "The image of God remains continuously (*permanere semper*) in the mind, regardless of whether 'this image of God' is so thinned out [*sit obsoleta*]."[81] But if we are to take Thomas seriously regarding the image of God, we will see that he further links the *imago Dei* to the moral faculty of humanity like *synderesis* or *liberum arbitrium* and,

78   *ST* I–II, q.82, a.3, co. See also *ST* I, q.95, a.1, co.
79   Ibid.
80   Ibid., q.17, a.9, ad.3.
81   *ST* I, q.93, a.8, ad.3.

through this linking, he confirms that man is not exempt from his moral agency in sin.[82] In other words, the image of God was not destroyed after the Fall. It is preserved in the form of either *synderesis* or *liberum arbitrium* to inform the soul of good and order it to good. To appreciate this iconic dignity of human nature in more detail, we need to consider it through Question 16 of the *De Veritate* and Question 83 of the *Summa Theologiae* I.

So first, what is *synderesis*? According to Thomas, *synderesis* is a "habitual light" which proclaims that good is to be done and evil avoided.[83] "This light," says Thomas, "belongs to the nature of the soul, since by reason of this the soul is intellectual."[84] And it operates in a way that parallels what one may easily think of – or, to be precise, misunderstand – as *conscientia* (conscience).[85] Here one may be tempted to read Thomas as a humanist *par excellence* – the kind of intellectual opponent that John Wesley seeks to refute.[86] However, Thomas' next line points us to the præter-natural dimension of *synderesis*: "In Psalms (4:7) it is said of this: 'The light of thy countenance, O Lord, is signed upon us,' so that it shows good things to us."[87] As seen in this excerpt from *De Veritate*, Thomas does not simply correlate *synderesis* to innate knowledge or any independently actionable content. He rather underpins it theologically by appealing to the light of God engraved in us. In other words, Thomas does not stray to atheistic humanism.

---

82   Like Augustine, Thomas rejects the Manichaean idea of sin that we unwillingly sin, that is, humans are compelled by the principle of evil, the independent reality against God. See *ST* I–II, 1.5, aa.1–3.

83   *DV*, q.16, a.1, co.

84   Ibid., q.16, a.3, co.

85   *ST* I, q.79. a.12, co. In Questions 79 of the *ST* I, Thomas makes a distinction between *synderesis* and *conscientia*. The former is a natural habit, whereas the latter is an act that works with the knowledge of that natural habit. In this respect, the former belongs to a higher concept or category than the latter: while the former is infallible and universal, the latter can err or fade. See *ST* I, 1.79, aa.12–3.

86   See, for example, Wesley, "The Imperfection of Human Knowledge," in *Works* 2, I.1–3.

87   *DV*, q.16, a.3, co.

But with this theological rendering, neither does Thomas link *synderesis* to a command or norm that is arbitrary or external to human nature. Here comes a *via media*: With his own Aristotelian philosophical system, Thomas reconstructs that theological feature of *synderesis* into a self-evident part of human nature. Or to use the word of Tim Murphy, *synderesis* refers to "the moral experience of being human, or, to put it another way, to the responsibility intrinsic to being human."[88] Hence, for Thomas *synderesis* is an intrinsic moral sense or ability rooted in its theological foundation (*imago Dei*).

This idea of *synderesis* is further compared to "the universal principle of natural law"[89] or "the universal precept of [practical] reason."[90] The point here is that *synderesis* is a kind of enduring natural image of God: *Synderesis* is part of what it means to have an intellectual soul and so to be made and continuously existing in God's image.[91] If we make good use of this image, *bonum* will be done and *malum* can be avoided.[92] However, it is worth noting that *synderesis* is not identical to *actus purus* – meaning it cannot, on its own, actually (*in actu*) realize or put into action the wise knowledge or inclination that it has made in relation to the pursuit of good. Indeed, Thomas regards it not as an action itself, but as a habit of moral knowledge or inclination that unerringly prompts its realization. In the life of *synderesis*, there is always a tension between potency and action, orientation and attainment – similar to that seen in Aristotle's distinction between *episteme* and *techne*, or between practical knowledge and *phronesis* (oft-referred to as practical action or virtue).[93] This tension sets Thomas apart from the Pelagians, who appeal to the absolute power of human nature, and turns to the human need for divine grace, the main issue we will address in the next chapter. But at this point, suffice it to say that as long as the image of

---

88   Tim Murphy, "Natural Law and Natural Justice: A Thomistic Perspective," in Jonathan Crowe and Constance Youngwon Lee, eds., *Research Handbook on Natural Law Theory* (Cheltenham, UK: Edward Elgar Publishing, 2019), 320.

89   *DV*, q.16, a.1, co.

90   *ST* I–II, q.62, a.3.

91   *DV*, q.16, a.3, co.

92   *ST* I–II, q.94, aa.1–2.

93   Ibid., q.62, a.3 and q.94, aa.1–2.

God as *synderesis* holds the natural state of human existence, our moral life and dignity are still present (if not perfect) after the Fall and are not "taken even from the damned."[94]

Next, what is *liberum arbitrium*? In Question 83 of the *ST* I, *liberum arbitrium* does not easily map onto a colloquial understanding of free will or freedom. As Brian Davis notes well, Thomas never uses the term free will (i.e., *libera voluntas* or *libertas voluntatis*),[95] but he thinks of the *liberum arbitrium* as the *sine qua non* of rational creatures created in the image of God.[96] The belief that one lacks this *liberum arbitrium* is "not only contrary to faith but also subverts all the principles of moral philosophy," writes Thomas.[97] If nothing is left in our human nature and we are *necessarily* moved to will things, our "counsels, exhortations, commands, prohibitions, rewards, and punishments," of which moral life and virtue consists, will all be "in vain."[98] Hence one may not readily equate it with free will or freedom, but from this account of *liberum arbitrium*, it can be inferred that Thomas speaks of it as a kind of human liberty, something that safeguards our moral agency or dignity against the various forms of necessity in human life and behavior. Yet – we may still ask – what exactly is it?

To appreciate it more clearly, one should first look into under what category Thomas is treating *liberum arbitrium*. Thomas subsumes *liberum arbitrium* under the broader category of the will. He then treats it as an appetitive power of *electio* (choice) that proceeds from the judgment of reason.[99] *Liberum arbitrium* is, decidedly, not a separate faculty of the soul that can act upon the intellect and will alike. Indeed, it is of the same *potentia* as the will: "The will and the free-will [i.e., *liberum arbitrium*] are not two powers, but one."[100] As Eleonore Stump has rightly pointed out,

94   *DV*, q.16, a.3, ad.5.
95   See Brian Davis' editorial "Introduction" to *De Malo*, 35–6. Like many other con-
      temporary scholars of Thomas have noted, it seems best to leave *liberum arbitrium*
      untranslated so as to avoid linguistic confusion and anachronistic implications.
96   *ST* I, q.83, a.1, co.
97   *QDM*, q.6, a.1, co.
98   *ST* I, q.83, a.1, co.
99   Ibid., q.83, aa.3–4.
100   Ibid., q.83, a.4, co.

liberum arbitrium is not "a property of the will alone" but "a property of the will only insofar as the will itself understood to be the rational appetite and to have a close tie to the intellect."[101] The intellect turns things over discursively and has the capacity for comprehending goodness as good. On its own, though, the intellect is insufficient to enact motion toward what it knows to be good. Movement requires desire, and this "desire-working-with-reason" is the will.[102] In a way, *liberum arbitrium* is suspended between these two essential posts of human nature: without intellect or will, *liberum arbitrium* would sink, and without *liberum arbitrium*, intellect and will are two stanchions that are morally purposeless in human nature.[103] Only the dynamic interaction of intellect and will within our human nature produces *liberum arbitrium*, that is, our choices (or actions) that are true, free and unforced.

Are humans necessarily moved or determined – by fate or by fiat? This is another key question from Thomas exploring the *liberum arbitrium* in Question 83 of the *ST* I. Here Thomas writes: "Forasmuch as man is rational it is necessary that man have a free will [i.e., *liberum arbitrium*]."[104] The word "rational" here includes intellect and will in that it means the intellectual nature (or rational appetite) that defines humans. Hence the above statement implies that, as long as humans after the Fall remain essentially intact as rational beings with intellect and will, they must have *liberum arbitrium*. To ask this from this opposite perspective, any form that denies *liberum arbitrium* can be said to Thomas as a negation of what makes a human essentially human. He admits as much elsewhere, too: In Question 6 of the *De Malo*, for example, Thomas adds "*determinat non ex necessitate* [determined not by necessity]."[105] He then argues that one's intellect involuntarily converged to the will within the act of choice – or one's

101   Eleonore Stump, "Aquinas's Account of Freedom: Intellect and Will," *The Monist* 80, no. 4 (1997): 576–97, 587.

102   Rebecca Konyndyk DeYoung, Colleen McCluskey, and Christina Van Dyke, *Aquinas's Ethics: Metaphysical Foundations, Moral Theory, and Theological Context* (Notre Dame, IN: University of Notre Dame Press, 2009), 62.

103   *ST* I, q.83, a.4.

104   Ibid., q.83, a.1, co.

105   *QDM*, q.6.

will "necessarily moved to choose things" – is an affront to the Scripture, the Christian tradition, the wisdom of moral philosophy, and so forth.[106] Necessity renders human nature *non*-human, and human *non*-agent.[107] And if we are not agents, our actions can neither be genitive nor genuine. It is only because of *liberum arbitrium*, our actions are truly genitive of our nature (i.e., "ours") and really genuine to our nature (i.e., "really ours"). Thus, even though he does not treat it adamantly as a separate faculty of the soul that can act upon the intellectual nature or rational appetite of human beings, we can fully see it at a practical level that Thomas has a two-fold concern regarding humans, choice and necessity, and affirms a positive reading of fallen humans in the dissolution of that concern into *liberum arbitrium* – to reiterate, Thomas affirms that not only our dependence and rootedness in God, but also the true worth and possibility of freedom that emerge therefrom continue to hold the natural state of man after the Fall.

Conclusion

From his early commentary on Peter Lombard's *Sentences* to his own unfinished *Summa Theologiae*, Thomas discussed sin and nature in a consistent manner. This chapter looked at his *Summa Contra Gentiles* IV and *Summa Theologiae* I–II in particular and discussed how he dealt with that topic in them. First in his *SCG* IV, Thomas developed his discussion in the context of incarnation. Incarnation is necessary because of original sin. In this regard, Thomas agrees with Anselm. However, unlike his doctrine of satisfaction or guilt, Thomas linked the incarnation to the manifestation of God's goodness, and the privative notion of original sin to the disorder, not the guilt of nature. Through this linking, Thomas showed in his *SCG* IV that the moral dignity of human nature, created in the image of God, can still be preserved in the natural state of human existence after the Fall.

---

106 Ibid., q.6, co.
107 Ibid., q.6. See also *ST* I, q.83, aa.3–4.

This positive assessment of human nature was reaffirmed in his *Prima Secundae*, but the approach that Thomas had adopted in this text was different from that of *SCG* IV. It was philosophically styled, through which Thomas grafted the Aristotelian framework of form and matter into the two terms, original justice and concupiscence, that Christian theology had adopted from Anselm and Augustine to define original sin. This methodological shift helped Thomas reaffirm his privative notion of original sin, while providing a rationale for his naturalization of the fallen state of humanity. As a result, Thomas came to the same conclusion as in *SCG* IV, that the postlapsarian state of human nature, at least in an ontological sense, is identical to the *natural* state of the first man Adam.

Finally, this chapter reviewed Thomas' *De Veritate* and *Summa Theologiae* I. This review has shown that in Thomas' theological anthropology it is *synderesis* and *liberum arbitrium* that holds the natural state of human existence. Thomas did not, however, see the presence in human nature of these two moral powers as implying human perfection or sinlessness: It only indicates God's image, our natural roots in that image, and our moral constitution therefrom. The perfection of human nature is, for Thomas, a gift from God, from the relational and dynamic action of divine grace with human nature, which we will now address in the next chapter.

Thomas Aquinas on Grace

The second chapter of Part II, called "Thomas Aquinas on Grace," begins by exploring how Thomas came to understand the general nature of grace. Thomas addresses the idea of God's grace in all of his major works, approaching it in terms surprisingly similar to those of Wesley – God's free gift and healing/elevating favor. To map Thomas' teaching on grace, I chose to explore the *Summa* in conjunction with many of the commentators that have read it over the course of the centuries: Reginald Garrigou-Lagrange, Joseph P. Wawrykow, and Paul O'Callaghan, Jacobus M. Ramirez, and Bernard Lonergan. This approach will help us develop a Catholic understanding of grace, which will be used for the sake of critical comparison and comprehension in the final chapter of this book.

Grace under various forms (or terms) is not just discussed in its allocated segment, qq. 109–14 of the *Prima Secundae*. It is present in the entire *Summa Theologiae*. In fact, Thomas presents his nuanced view of grace, from *Prima Pars* to *Tertia Pars*, in conjunction with a variety of theological topics, including predestination (I.23), virtues (I–II.62), law and grace (I–II.90–108), gifts (II.171–8), incarnation (III.1–26), redemption (III.46–9, 53–6, 57), and sacraments (III.60, 62). However, this thesis is primarily concerned with the theological comparison of Thomas and Wesley, and their similar views on – and approaches to – the dynamic relationship between divine grace and human nature. Thus, this chapter will devote most of its attention to the treatise of grace (I–II. 109–14) where this point of Thomas is matured and discussed more explicitly than any other segment in *Summa Theologiae*.

However, it is worth noting that there has been a scholarly debate over the scope of his treatise on grace. Cornelius Ernst, for example, claims that Thomas has begun his discussion of grace with q.106 in questions dealing with the Law of the Gospel.[1] It is beyond the question that *ST* I–II. qq.106–8 are crucial: This particular segment shows that what comes preveniently – on law in its various expressions, including the Old Law – adds nothing to what comes subsequently – on grace in its various expressions, including the New Law; indeed, at every point, the substance of the latter is entirely in the former.[2] Not only that but it has also gained considerable support for its inclusion into the treatise on grace from Thomists like Ernst who argue that the impact of grace in Thomas should always be grasped as a process that unfolds in time:

> The theological locus [for grace in Thomas] is ... "the intersection of the timeless with time"; the dimension of metaphysical origination only acquires its full depth when it is allowed to exhibit the transcendent significance of a coherent historical process conceived of as the expression of an eternal divine purpose. The same pattern is exhibited at the end of the *Prima Secundae*, where three Questions (106–8) on the New Law lead directly into the formal treatment of grace in Questions 109–14.[3]

Nonetheless, the segment adds little to the presentation of grace itself; and its major insight – the interiority of the New Law, as the inward prompting of the "*gratia Spiritus Sancti quae datur per fidem Christi*"[4] – is adequately discussed, and advanced, by Thomas in the course of his detailed teaching on grace. Thus, one can safely start and end with *ST* I–II.

---

1   See Cornelius Ernst's Introduction to Thomas Aquinas, *Summa Theologiae, Vol. 30 (Ia2ae. 106-114): The Gospel of Grace* (Cambridge: Cambridge University Press, 1972), xv–xxvii. The same goes for Paul O'Callaghan. In his *Children of God in the World*, O'Callaghan also notes that Thomas' treatise on grace begins with q.106 and ends with q.114: "The study of grace, in fact, is situated at the end of his treatise on the foundations of moral life," that is, "*S.Th.* I–II, qq.106–14." Paul O'Callaghan, *Children of God in the World: An Introduction to Theological Anthropology* (Washington, DC: Catholic University of America Press, 2016), 178.

2   *ST* I–II, q.107, a.2, ad.1. With regard to Thomas' assumption that the New is not new at all, but is entirely and substantially in the Old, see also *ST* I–II, q.107, a.3, ad.2: "*Sed quantum ad ipsm substantiam praeceptorum Novi Testamenti, monia continentur in Veteri Testamento ...*" (as to the substance itself of the precepts of the New Testament, they are all contained in the Old).

3   Ernst's Introduction to *Summa Theologiae, Vol. 30 (Ia2ae. 106-114)*, xxiii.

4   *ST* I–II, q.106, a.1, co.

109–14.[5] But to make it right, this chapter will go through a sequence of four groups that Thomas considered in his treatise on grace: the necessity of grace (q.109), the essence of grace (q.110), the division of grace (q.111), and the cause and effects of grace (qq.112–4).

The Necessity of Grace (q.109)

One could probably say that the need for grace can be thought of in relation to human nature. For Thomas in q.109, this idea is self-evident. That self-evident idea, however, comes with a fairly complex and sophisticated argument from Thomas. In particular, the argument encompasses an analysis of a variety of aspects of the human condition, from knowledge to action, salvation, and perseverance. Below are ten articles (or sub-questions) that Thomas has considered in his first question about the need for grace:

1. Knowledge: whether without grace man can know any truth;

2. Moral action: whether man can will to do any good without grace;

3. Loving God above all things: whether man can love God above all things without grace, by His merely natural power;

4. Observance of the precepts of natural law: whether man, without grace, by his natural powers, can fulfill the precepts of the natural law;

5. Merit for eternal life: whether man can merit eternal life without grace;

6. Preparation for grace: whether man can prepare himself for grace by himself without the exterior help of grace;

7. Liberation from the consequences of sin: whether man can rise from sin without the help of grace;

5   A similar assessment of whether the actual starting point of Thomas' *ex professo* analysis of grace in the *Prima Secundae* is q.106 can be found in Joseph P. Wawrykow, "Grace," in Rik Van Niewenhove and Joseph P. Wawrykow, eds., *The Theology of Thomas Aquinas* (Notre Dame: University of Notre Dame Press, 2005), 192.

8. Avoidance from (mortal and venial) sins: whether without grace man can avoid sin;

9. Good works (conducive to salvation): whether the just man can perform good works and avoid sin without actual grace;

10. Perseverance: whether man in the state of grace requires the help of grace to persevere.[6]

Each of these articles (or sub-questions) unfolds in the method of *quaestiones disputatae*, and its main role is to prove the need for grace in various aspects of human nature from authority (such as Holy Scripture, early fathers, and theological reasoning/argument). But not all of them need to be discussed one by one here.[7] For one to grasp Thomas' teachings on the topic, it would suffice to consider what Joseph P. Wawrykow calls "three main distinctions": (1) the difference between natural and supernatural orders; (2) the difference between the pre- and post-Fall states; and (3) the difference between the two kinds of grace, habitual and actual.[8] Indeed, this threefold division appears in q.109 as an organizing principle that Thomas uses to discern and affirm the necessity of grace for humanity. Let us, then, proceed from the first division to the last.

First of all, Thomas assumes that what is natural lies within the powers of a being.[9] Therefore, it is natural for a person to think or will, for he or she is endowed with the capability for such thinking or willing. As embodied intellect, a person can know certain natural truths. More specifically, we humans can come to know anything that presents itself to the "senses,"[10] and on the basis of that evidence (given to the senses), the intellect is capable of forming a concept (or judgment) proportionate to our natural order.

---

6   *ST* I–II, q.109, aa.1–10.

7   For a more detailed summary and discussion of these ten articles (or sub-questions) in *ST* I–II.109, see Reginald Garrigou-Lagrange, *Grace: Commentary on the Summa Theologica of St. Thomas, Ia IIae, q. 109–114*, trans. Dominican Nuns of Corpus Christi Monastery (St. Louis, MO: B. Herder, 1952), 41–109.

8   Wawrykow, "Grace," 193.

9   *ST* I–II, q.109, a.2, co: "Man by his natural endowments could wish and do the good proportionate to his nature."

10   Ibid., q.109, a.1., co: "And thus the human understanding has a form, viz. intelligible light, which of itself is sufficient for knowing certain intelligible things, viz. those we can come to know through the senses."

However, non-rational creatures like lilies in the field or birds in the sky lack the ability to think and will. They simply sense and act upon instinct. If, then, one were to ask those lilies or birds to follow and even contribute to some form of intellectual reasoning/argument, it would be to ask of them what surpasses their natural powers. One is here provided with what can be termed an illustrative analogy to the "supernatural" that Thomas has assumed in q.109. Some knowledge is considered supernatural when it lies beyond or above the natural powers of a being. Of course, when he puts a sharp wedge between the natural and the supernatural, Thomas is concerned with humans in relation to God and especially human nature in relation to divine grace. Then, is the human capacity for knowledge something natural to us, or is it actually a divine attribute that surpasses the natural order? This very question is asked by Thomas in the first article of q.109 and is answered as follows: "We are enlightened to see what pertains to natural knowledge; and for this there is required no further knowledge, but only for such things as surpass natural knowledge."[11]

The first distinction in q.109 now goes beyond the question of knowledge and leads to the exploration of many other aspects of human nature. Roughly speaking, articles 2 to 4 deal with whether or not humans can do good, and articles 5 to 10 deal with whether grace is necessary for salvation.[12] Again, Thomas' answer to that question appears fairly easy and straightforward. If a certain specific action is natural to the human race, then grace will not be necessary, for intrinsic human power alone is sufficient. In other words, Thomas saw that human nature could do utilitarian goods, even after the Fall.[13] But if one's action is supernatural or oriented

---

11   Ibid., q.109, a.1, ad.2.
12   Garrigou-Lagrange, *Grace*, 41.
13   *ST* I–II, q.109, a.2, co: "Yet because human nature is not altogether corrupted by sin, so as to be shorn of every natural good, even in the state of corrupted nature it can, by virtue of its natural endowments, work some particular good, as to build dwellings, plant vineyards, and the like." As for the question of loving God above all things, Thomas has opened up one's natural possibility for loving God as such. Hence he writes: "Now to love God above all things is natural to man ... And the reason of this is that it is natural to all to seek and love things according as they are naturally fit (to be sought and loved) since 'all things act according as they are naturally fit' as stated in Phys. ii, 8." *ST* I–II, q.109, a.3, co. A similar view recurs in

to God as by God, then grace is necessary. This is especially evident when he deals with the matter of salvation:

> Hence man, by his natural endowments, cannot produce meritorious works proportionate to everlasting life; and for this a higher force is needed, viz. the force of grace. And thus without grace man cannot merit everlasting life; yet he can perform works conducing to a good which is natural to man, as "to toil in the fields, to drink, to eat, or to have friends."[14]

The problem arises, however, as Thomas considers all of these problems more closely and dynamically. Here, of course, no change or compromise appears in his general view of grace as necessary. He is only developing a theological argument to further support it, and what he employs for this is the second distinction: prelapsarian and postlapsarian states. From this second one, one can elicit a more complex reading of Thomas that undergirds the need for grace in the ambit of humanity.

In each and every article of q.109, Thomas relates his discussion of grace to the catastrophic effects of sin.[15] This is particularly evident in article 7, in which Thomas describes three elements of corruption and shows how in each case grace is needed to overcome sin:

> Man incurs *a triple loss* by sinning, as was clearly shown above (I–II:85:1; I–II:86:1; I–II:87:1), viz. *stain, corruption of natural good*, and *debt of punishment* ... None of these three can be restored except by God. For since the lustre of grace springs from the shedding of Divine light, this lustre cannot be brought back, except God sheds His light anew: hence a habitual gift is necessary, and this is the light of grace. Likewise, the order of nature can only be restored, i.e. man's will can only be subject to God when God draws man's will to Himself, as stated above (Article 6). So, too, the guilt of eternal punishment can be remitted by God alone, against Whom the

his *ST* I, q.60, a.5 and *ST* II, q.26, a.3. However, as Garrigou-Lagrange has noted well, the question of love is divided into *natural* and *supernatural*. The former can then be conceived in Thomas without any consideration of grace, while the latter is not. The same logic continues in Article 4: There, Thomas divides the possibility of our natural observance of divine law in two layers, *natural* and *supernatural*, and argues that grace is required in the latter (and even in the former, to some extent). Garrigou-Lagrange, *Grace*, 56; 61–2; and 67–8.

14   Ibid., q.109, a.5, co.
15   Garrigou-Lagrange, *Grace*, 41–109.

offense was committed and Who is man's Judge. And thus in order that man rise from sin there is required the help of grace, both as regards a habitual gift, and as regards the internal motion of God.[16]

Having stated so strongly the essential role of grace in the state of fallen humanity, Thomas continues in a later article (a.8) to talk of the role of saving grace in a person's sinful life. Here the basis of his argument lies in the fact that after the Fall humanity is in a state of mortal sin: Man is disoriented from his ultimate end, God, and thereby inclined toward some mortal sins. If we were to avoid all mortal sins and overcome all temptations, we must be helped by grace.[17] In a word, it can be said that there is no doubt within Thomas that grace is absolutely necessary for fallen humanity.

However, Thomas' mature understanding of sin provides us with a deeper insight than that simple fact that grace is needed. This insight not only informs us why he typologically understands grace, but also shows how grace is needed differently in the twofold state of nature: the prelapsarian state and the postlapsarian state. In order to appreciate it properly, it is necessary to recall for a moment the discussion of sin and nature in Chapter 4.

In the preceding chapter, Thomas' mature understanding of sin was stated as fundamentally disrupting human nature and its capacity. More specifically, sin ensures that the lower level of our human self is at war with its higher rational level. In addition, it also causes our human self to reject or rebel against the will of God, at which point a person arrives at a state of so-called *privation* that requires grace in relation to what is naturally and supernaturally good. Note here that this change caused by sin is not related to any corruption or total destruction of human nature itself. It simply represents a state of deficiency, and in this sense, there is an integral coherence between the prelapsarian and post-lapsarian natures of humanity. To clarify this point, Thomas writes in his *Terita Pars*: "Man's nature is the same before and after sin, but the state of his nature is not the same."[18] Then what does the change mean for Thomas? As we have already

---

16   *ST* I–II, q.109, a.7, co.
17   Ibid., q.109, a.8.
18   *ST* III, q.61, a.2, ad.2.

explained in the previous chapter, it refers to humanity's teleological character. One could describe it as the introduction of a moral gap, following Wawrykow's words:

> There is also a moral gap, established by human sin. By sin, both original and actual, human beings differ radically from the God who is utterly and wholly good; and by sin, humans are most unworthy of eternal life. God addresses human need ... in grace. In God's love for humans, God offers the grace that can bridge ... the moral gap.[19]

Grace, therefore, has one function in sinful man: to heal and (re)orient to God. By that grace, the sinful person is then restored to correct order to God, and in the self, the disruption (in a moral or teleological sense) is overcome. However, this recovery is not complete in this life. Full healing awaits the next life, when the person is in the immediate presence of God. Hence, for as long as we live in this world, we will need more grace. This further grace is called *auxilium* in Thomas' terms. Since a detailed discussion of this particular type of grace will take place in the subsequent discussion of q.111, here I will just point out that the *gratia auxilium* is God's operative and cooperative contribution to the natural and supernatural behavior required of us to attain God as our end.

It is now clear that Thomas is viewing that the sinful person needs grace. Thomas however also insists that man needs grace even in the prelapsarian state. In other words, mature Thomas observes a twofold need: one with respect to postlapsarian and the other with respect to prelapsarian. In the postlapsarian state, humans need healing grace. But in the state before the Fall, humans need not be healed. Neither do they require special added grace for morally good works commensurate with nature; their natural capacities alone sufficed.[20] For doing *supernatural* works or for observing the whole natural law, they need grace: "Not that we are sufficient in ourselves

---

19   Joseph P. Wawrykow, "Aquinas and Barth on Grace," in Bruce L. McCormack and Thomas Joseph White, O.P., eds., *Thomas Aquinas and Karl Barth: An Unofficial Catholic-Protestant Dialogue* (Grand Rapids, MI: Eerdmans, 2013), 195.
20   Garrigou-Lagrange, *Grace*, 52–4.

to claim anything as coming from us, but our sufficiency is from God (II Cor. 3:5)."[21]

To support this argument, Thomas cites innumerable texts from St. Augustine. An example comes from the *Sed Contra* of article 2: "Augustine says (*De Corrept. et Gratia* ii) that 'without grace men do nothing good when they either think or wish or love or act.'"[22] From this excerpt, one can infer the Augustinian origin of his position, that every creature cannot exist or act of itself.[23] More importantly, one should read up on the later article, where Thomas takes it further to establish a theological foundation that explains why even an innocent person needs grace. Indeed, a more careful reading of *Prima Secundae* shows that Thomas does so in article 6 with the principle of finality. The corollary of this principle is the order of agents or movers corresponds to the order of ends; hence it is necessary that man be directed to his last end by the motion of the first mover, just as "the spirit of the soldier is bent towards seeking the victory by the motion of the leader of the army – and towards following the standard of a regiment by the motion of the standard-bearer."[24] Moreover, according to this principle, every disposition, whether natural or supernatural, should have a certain *proportio* to the *forma* for which it disposes.[25] At the same time, a merely natural *esse* or *operatio* has no proportion with the supernatural; it cannot, by its own powers, move itself to – or prepare itself for – something which exceeds all nature created or capable of being created. Hence, the theological foundation established in article 6 by Thomas seems to presuppose an ontological gap between God and man which is exactly how the order of grace and the order of nature appear to function. Wawrykow explains:

> Without God's revelation in love, humans would not know where they are to go or how they are to get there. This understanding of salvation shapes the *Summa*'s teaching on grace. Its treatise on grace begins with a consideration of the *need* for

---

21   *ST* I–II, q.109, a.1. See also *ST* I–II, q.109, a.5, ad.3, where Thomas discusses the distinction between final natural end and supernatural end, confirming that man cannot by his natural powers produce works meritorious of eternal life.

22   Ibid., q.109, a.2, sc.

23   Garrigou-Lagrange, *Grace*, 53.

24   *ST* I–II, q.109, a.6, co.

25   Ibid. See also *ST* I–II, q.112, a.3.

grace. Aquinas observes ... a need. The vision of God, the end of the human person determined by God, transcends human capacity. Acts must be proportioned to their end; the acts that might lead to eternal life thus lie beyond human powers, beyond the human as creature who falls short of the Creator who is end. There is, then, an *ontological gap* as it were, between the human and the God who is the end of the human, as set by God.[26]

In fact, one can see in the second half of q.109 that Thomas confirms the gap time and again. His main argument there is to delve into the topics of salvation (a.6), conversion (a.7), restoration (a.8), sin (a.9), and perseverance (a.10), making it clearer that even in a perfect state, man cannot elevate himself into a supernatural life of grace. It is not only morally impossible, but ontologically impossible as well. Hence, grace is always needed for all of humanity, but in the innocent state of man it plays yet another function: to move and elevate.

The next (and final) distinction is between two kinds of grace. One is *gratia habitualis* and the other is *auxilium*. In Thomas' account, the former is concerned with the two obstacles between God and man: the moral and the ontological. Hence it has a twofold function, of healing and of elevating:

> In order to live righteously a man needs ... a *habitual* gift whereby corrupted human nature is *healed*, and after being healed is *lifted up* so as to work deeds meritoriously of everlasting life, which exceed the capability of nature.[27]

Neither seems for Thomas to take precedence. He considers both with equal seriousness in q.109. Of course, the moral need for grace comes to greater prominence, as Thomas proceeds to q.110 where the main inquiry goes to the link between *gratia habitualis* and theological virtue (faith, hope, and charity).[28] In terms of the need for grace, nothing has changed in Thomas. Both needs are of equal importance to man: To put it another way, for Thomas humans always need habitual grace, whether their nature is considered as apart from or under sin: "The act of the intellect or of any

---

26   Wawrykow, "Aquinas and Barth on Grace," 195.
27   *ST* I–II, q.109, a.9, co.
28   Ibid., q.110, aa.3–4.

created being whatsoever depends upon God ... for it is from Him that it has the form whereby it acts."[29]

The latter (*auxilium*) in Thomas relates to the Aristotelian framework of potency-action.[30] The outline of this framework in the treatise on grace is: Habitual grace refers to a potency added to the soul. This potency makes the person capable of, and inclined to, supernatural life or action, but it does not reduce itself to act. The potency is actualized only by *auxilium*, by God assisting people to act in accord with the empowerment of *gratia habitualis*.[31] From this framework, Thomas affirms that even a person healed and elevated by habitual grace still needs more grace: "Beyond this [two-fold qualification of habitual grace], man needs the Divine help, that he may be moved to act well."[32]

Summing up the discussion of q.109, one can therefore say: Thomas' discussion of the need for grace receives a threefold qualification, teaching that (1) humanity cannot exceed the natural order without the supernatural aid of grace, (2) humanity needs grace, either for moral or ontological needs, and (3) humanity needs grace in terms of healing or elevating, but insofar as he or she cannot, by his or her own natural powers, actualize – or reduce into action – the potency graciously added to the soul, humanity also needs grace in terms of actualizing or leading to.

29 Ibid., q.109, a.1., co.
30 For a brief summary of how Thomas has used that Aristotelian framework in conceptualizing the relationship between divine grace and human action, see Bernhard Blankenhorn, *The Mystery of Union with God: Dionysian Mysticism in Albert the Great and Thomas Aquinas* (Washington, DC: Catholic University of America Press, 2015), 259–62.
31 *ST* I–II, q.109, a.9, co: "Man needs the help of grace in order to be moved by God to act."
32 Ibid., q.109, a.2, co. See also *ST* I–II, q.109, aa.6–9.

The Essence of Grace (q.110)

The dynamics of sin is an important point of departure when dealing with the doctrine of grace in Western theology (particularly in the Augustinian tradition). But this is not the case for Thomas, in whose thought sin or evil does not occupy such a central place. Of course, Thomas thoroughly discusses sin and its effect on nature in the *Prima Secundae* (*ST* I–II, qq.71–89): The first man was created in the state of *naturae integrae*, but he fell from this state of perfection.[33] So one would be able to identify Thomas as an Augustinian, at least if he or she understood him in this respect. But, as Paul O'Callaghan has well noted in "'Created Grace' in the Medieval Period," Thomas explores the fundamental nature of grace independently of the problem of sin or evil.[34] This is because Augustine treats grace and sin in a kind of concrete and historical way, whereas Thomas treats it in a highly nuanced metaphysical way, using Aristotle's intrinsic and unaltering substantial forms – the import of these forms is that the nature of all creatures remain stable, even if either fallen or graced.[35] One example of this difference comes from *ST* I–II.110. Here Thomas is dealing with grace itself, and his main method is to deductively infer its essence from the effects of grace, not from its relationship to sin or evil. Thus, the review of this section on q.110 brings one further to Thomas' own idea of grace, especially the essence of grace metaphysically conceptualized in his theology.

The essence of grace, which Thomas has inferred in q.110, falls into four categories: (1) Grace is "*aliquid* [something]"[36] in the soul; (2) Grace is

---

33   For sin or evil in Thomas, see Chapter 4 of this book. But for more information, one can refer to O. Magrath, "St. Thomas' Theory of Original Sin," *Thomist* (1953): 161–89; P. De Letter, "Hereditary Guilt," *Irish Theological Quarterly* 20 (1953): 350–65 and "The Transmission of Original Sin," *Irish Theological Quarterly* 24 (1957): 339–45.

34   O'Callaghan, *Children of God in the World*, 179–80.

35   Blankenhorn, *The Mystery of Union with God*, 216–7. See also O'Callaghan, *Children of God in the World*, 180.

36   *ST* I–II, q.110, a.1, co: "*Gratia ponit aliquid in anima.*"

given into the soul as a quality – or "*nitor animae* [beauty or splendor]"[37] – of the soul[38]; (3) Grace is not identical with virtue[39]; (4) Grace is not in the powers of the soul as virtue is.[40] In the first category, Thomas discusses grace in terms of its effect on humanity. The point in this discussion is that grace is a gift caused by God's love, and this gift is identified as a divine *aliquid* or *being* in creation: *gratia ponit aliquid in anima*.[41] It should be noted here that the grace of God in creation – that is, created grace[42] – is not treated by Thomas as distinct from its origin – that is, uncreated grace.[43] He even argues that the former may also be understood as a quality of God himself, as divine love:

> Accordingly, when a man is said to have the grace of God, there is signified something bestowed on man by God. Nevertheless, the grace of God sometimes signifies God's eternal love.[44]

Then how does created grace relate to uncreated grace? Thomas' answer to this question is clear: Every created grace is "not co-eternal with the eternal love" of uncreated grace.[45] It is a "consequence and a manifestation of the possession of this uncreated grace."[46] In a word, Thomas rejects the

---

37 Ibid., q.110, a.2, sc. See also *DV*, q.27, a.1, sc: "*Gratia est nitor animae.*"

38 Ibid.

39 Ibid., q.110, a.3, sc.

40 Ibid., q.110, a.4, sc.

41 Ibid., q.110, a.1, sc.

42 Ibid., q.110, a.1, co. See also *ST* I–II, q.110, a.2, ad.3: "Grace is said to be created inasmuch as men are created with reference to it, that is, are given a new being out of nothing, that is, not from merits, according to Ephesians 2:10, 'created in Jesus Christ in good works.'"

43 In concluding the first article of q.110, Thomas observes that grace sometimes denotes the very eternal, uncreated love of God. For it is said from the Ephesians (1:5): "He hath predestinated us into the adoption of children ... unto the praise of the glory of His grace, in which He hath graced us in His beloved Son," that is, unto the manifestation of the beauty and splendor of His uncreated grace, by which we are made "pleasing to God." *ST* I–II, q.110, a.1, co; and *ST* I–II, q.110, a.1, ad.1.

44 *ST* I–II, q.110, a.1, co.

45 Ibid.

46 Gilbert Meilaender, *The Freedom of a Christian: Grace, Vocation, and the Meaning of Our Humanity* (Grand Rapids, MI: Brazos Press, 2006), 67.

equivalence between created grace and uncreated grace to preserve the transcendence of the latter.

However, it is also evident in q.110 that Thomas does not use the term grace so as to distinguish it from divine being itself, shared with creatures.[47] Thus, some Thomists like Anna Ngaire Williams or Melissa Eitenmiller have avoided concluding that Thomas is positing in q.110 any fundamental difference between created grace and uncreated grace. They rather suggest looking at it in terms of *mode* or *participation*.[48] The gist of their suggestion lies in making a comprehensive but somewhat problematic interpretation of the opposing principle that Thomas affirms in his treatise on grace: the transcendence of uncreated grace and its created presence in the soul. According to this interpretation, God's grace is not another being in competition with – or separation from – finite being. It is an *aliquid in anima* that communicates the whole of its essential content to us in a kind of analogical manner considered in terms of *mode* or *participation*.[49] Given what Thomas argues in *Commentary on the Sentences of Peter Lombard* or elsewhere in *Summa*, such an interpretation (by Williams or Eitenmiller) seems to do justice to the first article in q.110: He says in the former "[*gratia* is present in the soul] *prout res est in sua similitudine* [as something is present *in what is similar to it*]," [50] and in the latter "the

---

47   Anna Ngaire Williams, *The Ground of Union: Deification in Aquinas and Palamas* (New York: Oxford University Press, 1999), 84.

48   More specifically, Williams takes the former (mode), saying that the difference Thomas is pointing to lies not in any essential distinction, but in the difference between two modes of the same grace that exist in God and in us. Eitenmiller then takes the latter (participation), saying that for Thomas creatures do not share being in a univocal way with God, nor in a completely equivocal manner; in this respect the created grace is related to the uncreated grace in a participatory or transcendental-analogous manner. See Williams, *The Ground of Union*, 84–5 and Melissa Eitenmiller, "Grace as Participation according to St. Thomas Aquinas," *New Blackfriars* (2016): 689–708, at 691–5

49   Williams, *The Ground of Union*, 84; and Eitenmiller, "Grace as Participation according to St. Thomas Aquinas," 694.

50   *I Sent.*, d. 15, q.4, a.1, co: "*Unde sicut Spiritus Sanctus invisibiliter procedit in mentem per donum amoris, ita Filius per donum sapientiae; in quo est manifestatio ipsius Patris, qui est ultimum ad quod recurrimus. Et quia secundum receptionem horum duorum efficitur in nobis similitudo ad propria personarum; ideo secundum novum*

divine person is fittingly sent in the sense that *He exists newly in any one*; and He is given as possessed by anyone; and neither of these is otherwise than *by sanctifying grace*."[51]

After explaining that *gratia ponit aliquid in anima*, Thomas moves on to the second article in q.110, where he deals with the second category of grace, using the Aristotelian term *accidentia*.[52] The question set in this article concerns whether grace should be portrayed as a "*qualitas animae*" (quality of the soul) – or, more precisely, a "habitual gift ... infused by God into the soul."[53] In his reply to the second objection, Thomas answers: "*Id enim quod substantialiter est in Deo, accidentaliter fit in anima participante divinam bonitatem*" (Now what is *substantially* in God – that is, uncreated grace – becomes *accidental* in the soul participating the Divine goodness).[54] As is evident in this passage, Thomas sees grace in terms of an "accident," and what it means by "accident" here is Aristotelian: "Properly speaking, no accident comes into being or is corrupted, but is said to come into being and to be corrupted inasmuch as its subject begins or ceases to be in act with this accident."[55] His point is therefore obvious: Since we cannot be saved by something "created," as that would be neo-Arian, grace is not

---

modum essendi, prout res est in sua similitudine, dicuntur personae divinae in nobis esse, secundum quod novo modo eis assimilamur; et secundum hoc utraque processio dicitur missio." For a simple yet useful translation of – and commentary on – this excerpt from *I Sent.*, see O'Callaghan, *Children of God in the World*, 284.

51   *ST* I, q.43, a.3, co. See also *ST* I, q.8, a.3, ad.4 and *ST* III, q.7, a.13, co.

52   In his *Metaphysics*, Aristotle identifies ten categories of predication in the mode of being: substance, quantity, relation, place, time, position, condition, action, passion, and quality. But, as James Mittelstadt puts it well, Aristotle puts them back together into two fundamental categories. The first is substance and the second is the category of accidents. In his philosophical system, an accident means something that cannot exist in and of itself, but exists only in or through another thing. A substance, on the contrary, means something that exists by itself. James Mittelstadt, *Path to Wisdom: Introducing Western Philosophy* (Partridge Publishing Singapore, 2014), 61.

53   *ST* I–II, q.110, a.2, co.

54   Ibid., q.110, a.2, ad.2.

55   Ibid., q.110, a.2, ad.3.

created, but "a new mode of being on the part of the soul."[56] To unpack it a little further, grace does not change us into something entirely new. Nor does it produce "a metamorphosis of [our] human nature."[57] It qualifies us only in an accidental way, so when we are moved to the eternal good with grace, that grace does not go against our nature, but in accordance with its natural order.

This point, however, does not imply that Thomas speaks of grace as something secondary or of little importance. As we have already seen in q.109, Thomas presupposes the gap between the order of grace and the order of nature and is perfectly aware that it is only by means of grace that humans can reach their final end. Hence, grace is of unparalleled importance to Thomas, and what Thomas is trying to claim in using Aristotelian language is only a dynamically relational interpretation of grace; more precisely, he is trying to develop an intrinsic view of the life of grace in which *gratia* is seen in parallel with *natura* as an accidental, not a substantial, form or quality of the soul.[58] To confirm the logical validity or exegetical soundness of this point, we should consider Thomas' replies to the first and second objections, where the corollary of his argument is that one should not consider grace only in the order of effective causality[59] or as a completely living substance extrinsic to the soul.[60]

---

56   Matthew Levering, *Paul in the Summa Theologiae* (Washington, DC: Catholic University of America Press, 2014), 174.

57   O'Callaghan, *Children of God in the World*, 179.

58   *ST* I–II, q.110, a.2., ad.2. A similar reading is found in the comments by Paul O'Callaghan and Matthew Levering on the *ST* I–II, q.110. According to Paul O'Callaghan: "In using Aristotelian language here, Aquinas intends to present the doctrine of grace in parallel with that of nature. With grace, humans are moved gently and promptly (*suaviter et prompte*), in accordance with nature, to obtain the eternal good." With a similar sentiment, Levering writes: "In the second article of q.110, Aquinas argues that grace qualifies the soul. In this regard Aquinas cites Ephesians 2:10, where Paul states that we have been 'created in Christ Jesus for good works.' To be created a new in this way is to have our souls given a new quality or accidental form by grace, so that it becomes easy or (supernaturally) natural for us to move toward our supernatural good, eternal life." O'Callaghan, *Children of God in the World*, 290; and Levering, *Paul in the Summa Theologiae*, 176.

59   Ibid., q.110, a.2, ad.1.

60   Ibid., q.110, a.2, ad.2.

If grace is some form or quality in the soul, is this form or quality there as a virtue? It would seem so, since grace disposes (or perfects) our being to behave well in line with its supreme end, as virtues enable it to act more perfectly.[61] Thomas does not equate grace and virtue in his third category of *essentia gratiam*. According to Thomas, virtue is a "disposition of what is perfect."[62] And what he calls "perfect" here means something "disposed according to nature."[63] Grace is, on the other hand, a new nature upon which our virtues rely in order to produce actions befitting divinity.[64] The two are also explained in terms of causality, where Thomas says that grace is prevenient as a cause or principle of virtue, and virtue is the sheer effect of grace.[65] In a word, Thomas understands virtue as Aristotle defines it in his *Physics* (*Physics* VII, texts 17): Virtue always presupposes some nature, so the former is different from and depend on the latter.[66] Indeed, the same definition serves to clarify the distinction between grace and virtue in the third article of q.110:

> And thus, even as the natural light of reason is something besides the acquired virtues, which are ordained to this natural light, so also the light of grace which is a participation of the Divine Nature is something besides the infused virtues which are derived from and are ordained to this light.[67]

One question arises at this juncture: Why did Thomas rule out the equation between grace and virtue? The answer comes from his final category of the essence of grace. There – or, more precisely, in his *Respondeo* – Thomas says: Grace relates to the very essence of the soul, not just to one particular faculty or power thereof.[68] In other words, grace has a different

---

61 *ST* I, q.1, a.8, ad.2: "*Gratia non tollit naturam sed perficit*" (Grace does not remove nature, but perfects it).
62 *ST* I–II, q.110, a.3, co.
63 Ibid.
64 Ibid., q.110, a.3, ad.3.
65 Ibid.
66 Justin M. Anderson, *Virtue and Grace in the Theology of Thomas Aquinas* (Cambridge: Cambridge University Press, 2020), 117.
67 *ST* I–II, q.110, a.3, co.
68 Ibid., q.110, a.4, co.

subject than that which virtue has as its own: Or, to use his logic from the second book of *Super Sent.*, "grace is the perfection of the essence of the soul, while virtue is the perfection of the soul's powers."[69] This of course is not to say that *gratiam Dei* leaves our faculties or powers unaffected. To the contrary, it "perfects the intellect by the gift of wisdom" and "softens the affections by the fire of charity."[70] Nothing of what is human – regardless of whether it is material or spiritual, temporary or immortal, ontological or phenomenological – is excluded from the life of grace. Hence Thomas affirms:

> For as man in his intellective powers participates in the Divine knowledge through the virtue of faith, and in his power of will participates in the Divine love through the virtue of charity, so also in the nature of the soul does he participate in the Divine Nature, after the manner of a likeness, through a certain regeneration or re-creation.[71]

Nonetheless, as long as the subject of grace is the essence of our human soul, it must be distinguished from virtue, from that which has our natural faculty or power as its subject.[72] And it is even more so in that the inclination to grace befits divinity, while the inclination to virtue befits humanity.[73] Perhaps the Roman catechism is one of the best texts summarizing these principle elements of *essentia gratiam* discussed by Thomas: There, grace is defined as "a divine quality that inheres in the soul, a kind of splendor and light, which takes away all the stains of the soul and makes it more beautiful and luminous."[74]

---

69 Anderson, *Virtue and Grace in the Theology of Thomas Aquinas*, 115. For Thomas' own proposition that grace and virtue differ in essence, see *Super Sent.*, d.26, q.1, a.4, co.

70 *ST* I–II. q.79, a.3 co.

71 Ibid., q.110, a.4, co.

72 Ibid., q.110, a.4, ad.3.

73 Ibid., q.85, a.1, co.

74 *Roman Catechism* II, 2, 50.

The Division of Grace (q.111)

Thomas describes grace in various terms, giving one the impression that grace can somehow be divisible. For this reason, a prefatory caveat is essential: For Thomas, grace is one; a distinction cannot "divide grace in its essence, but only in its effects."[75] Like its divine source, grace is always to be regarded as an essential unity with myriad effects. In other words, grace is "a single pure-white light that is refracted into a rainbow of colors by a prism," and the various terms we can append to grace are but our expressions of what the entire being of the human person has experienced through that "single pure-white light."[76]

With this caveat in mind, we can then discuss the different ways in which grace has an effect on humanity. Thomas covers this topic in q.111 of the *Prima Secundae*, where grace is put into a fourfold division on the basis of the Pauline texts of 1 Corinthians 12:7–13:13.[77] First the division is drawn between *gratia gratum faciens* and *gratia gratis data*, then comes the second division: *gratia habitualis* and *gratia actualis/auxilium*. From this second division, Thomas develops a third: *gratia operans* and *gratia cooperans*. The fourth and final division is *gratia praeveniens* and *gratia subsequens*. We now turn to Thomas' first division of grace.

Gratia Gratum Faciens and Gratia Gratis Data

Thomas' first division of grace stems from the fact that the believer is both an individual and a member of the Church. God first gives to the believer a grace called *gratum faciens*. According to O'Callaghan, the term was first used by the thirteenth-century theologian Alexander of Hales and then appended to grace to provide a description of what divine grace achieves in relation to the individual.[78] In the treatise on grace (*ST* I–II.109–14),

---

75 *ST* I–II, q.111, a.3, ad.2.
76 O'Callaghan, *Children of God in the World*, 294.
77 *ST* I–II, q.111, aa.1–5.
78 O'Callaghan, *Children of God in the World*, 295–6.

Thomas takes this approach and uses it to describe the sanctification of a subject who has received divine grace from the Father, through the Son, in the Holy Spirit. So *gratia gratum faciens* is often defined in Thomas as "sanctifying grace," a grace that actually "makes man pleasing [*gratus*] to God"[79] or "*per quam ipse homo Deo coniungitur*" (by which man himself is united with God).[80]

The believer can at the same time receive a grace from God called *gratis data*. The term is derived from the end of Matthew 10:8, translated in the Vulgate as "*Gratis accepistis, gratis date*" (Freely you received, freely give).[81] The beginning of this Gospel passage consists of Matthew's discourse about the mission of Jesus' twelve apostles. Central to the discourse, however, is Matthew's testimony to the special gifts – or ecclesial charisms – Jesus gave to those disciples to facilitate their apostolic mission.[82] According to Thomas, *gratia gratis data* refers to that special gift, that ecclesial charism "*per quam unus homo cooperatur alteri ad hoc quod ad Deum reducatur*" (by means of which man cooperates with another in leading him to God).[83] In other words, grace as *gratis data* is not something that we receive for our own benefit. Rather, it is what we receive for the benefit of others: More specifically, the believer is favored by God not only as a recipient, but also as a mediator, that is, as a member of the Church called to the apostolic mission, that "heal the sick, raise the dead, cleanse lepers, cast out demons (Matthew 10:8)." Hence the grace called *gratis data* has the same divine source as all other graces, yet it is distinguishable from *gratia gratum faciens*, from that which *immediately* leads to union with God.

In any case, the implication of this distinction is that all are called to holiness, but not all are supposed to carry out the apostolic mission of the Church. In other words, there are different aspects or vocations in religious life, so not everyone receives the same charismatic gift in the same way.

---

79   *ST* I–II, q.iii, a.i, ad.3.

80   Ibid., q.iii, a.i, co.

81   O'Callaghan, *Children of God in the World*, 296.

82   See Augustin George and Pierre Grelot, "Charisms," in Xavier Leon-Dufour, ed., *Dictionary of Biblical Theology* (London: Geoffrey Chapman, 1978), 68–71.

83   *ST* I–II, q.iii, a.i, co.

The same discussion appears later in qq.183–9 of the *Secunda Secundae*.[84] There, Thomas speaks of the various "duties and states of life," from which one can colloquially describe a believer with *gratia gratis data* as a person extraordinarily *gifted* in addition to being *graced*.

Another implication is that the fact that certain Christians in the Church has received any gift or ecclesial charism does not make them "automatically holier at a personal level than those who have not received them."[85] *Gratia gratis data* is given only for the Church and for the efficacy of her mission. As they carry out their apostolic tasks or missions, of course, some believers may well thrive in holiness. But it can only be conceived *indirectly* because such gifts are nothing other than that which, by way of a mediation, leads to another's potential relationship with God: "Gratuitous grace ... is bestowed on a man, not to justify him, but rather that he may cooperate in the justification of another."[86] In this respect, Thomas recasts *gratia gratum faciens* and *gratia gratis data* in a hierarchical order: "Sanctifying grace is nobler than gratuitous grace."[87] That is to say, there is a difference between the two forms of grace in terms of proximity or distance: The former is to *attain* a goal, while the latter is to *anticipate* that goal. For this reason, Thomas puts more emphasis on *gratia gratum faciens* than *gratia gratis data* when discussing the nature, dynamics, or effects of grace in the treatise on grace.

Gratia Habitualis and Gratia Actualis/Auxilium

In the category of *gratia gratum faciens*, Thomas distinguishes between *gratia habitualis* (habitual grace) and *gratia actualis/auxilium* (actual grace). This second division in Thomas corresponds to the fact that in humans it is possible to distinguish between their essence and the concrete, transitory potency (or movement) of their will and intellect.[88]

---

84 See *ST* II–II, qq.183–9.
85 O'Callaghan, *Children of God in the World*, 296.
86 *ST* I–II, q.111, a.1, co.
87 See ibid., q.111, a.5, co.
88 O'Callaghan, *Children of God in the World*, 297.

Here *gratia habitualis* relates to the former (essence) and *gratia actualis/ auxilium* to the latter (potencies).

First with respect to *gratia habitualis* as the first species (or quasi-species) of *gratia gratum faciens*, Thomas describes it as a "*habituale donum nobis divinitus inditum*" (a habitual gift divinely bestowed on us).[89] How this grace is *habituale* can be understood in two ways in his doctrine of grace.[90] First it can be viewed by the subject itself: *gratia habitualis* means in this case the grace received as an "entitative" habit.[91] The term "entitative" here does not refer to the production of human effort or the result of any virtuous repetition of human behavior. It rather refers to that which is stably infused into the soul.[92] For a more specific definition of it, one probably needs to avert to an old Thomistic distinction: entitative vs. operative habit.[93] An entitative habit, on one hand, is a supernatural quality infused into the essence of the soul, which enables a participation in the very nature of God. An operative habit, on the other hand, accidentally qualifies a power of the soul to operate as a theological virtue (faith, hope, or charity) – or as a moral virtue (prudence, justice, fortitude, or temperance). The operative habit therefore does not reside in the essence as does the habit called entitative.[94] According to Jacobus M. Ramirez, grace, called habitual by Thomas, refers to the former in this division and has a temporally prior status to the latter (operative habit): "Operative supernatural or infused habits necessarily presuppose an entitatively supernatural infused

---

89   *ST* I–II, q.111, a.2, co.
90   The theological validity or suitability of this twofold approach is well argued by John M. Meinert in his "*Donum Habituale*: Grace and the Gifts of the Holy Spirit in St. Thomas Aquinas," according to which Thomas' concept of habitual grace can best be approached by the subject itself and by the effects it has on the soul. John M. Meinert, "*Donum Habituale*: Grace and the Gifts of the Holy Spirit in St. Thomas Aquinas" (PhD diss., The Catholic University of America, 2015), 55.
91   Meinert, "*Donum Habituale*," 51. See also O'Callaghan, *Children of God in the World*, 297.
92   O'Callaghan, *Children of God in the World*, 297–8.
93   Meinert, "*Donum Habituale*," 51–2.
94   O'Callaghan, *Children of God in the World*, 297.

form."[95] Hence the entitative habit is seen as equivalent to the state of grace in human nature – from which the gifts of the Holy Spirit and the virtues infused into the soul arise: That is to say, *gratia habitualis* is not a transitory gift, but a stable principle of supernatural life, an abiding gift present in humans that sanctifies them and makes them holy, children of God.

Next is another approach to *gratia habitualis*. One can divide it diversely by effects into *gratia operans* and *gratia cooperans*, and *gratia praeveniens* and *gratia subsequens*. However, since these two divisions will be addressed in the third and fourth discussions that follow, it will suffice here to state only the general effects of gratia *habitualis*. According to Thomas, habitual grace has two effects: healing and elevating.[96] In relation to the former, habitual grace is said to heal the soul, restoring the right order in the soul and before God. In relation to the latter, habitual grace is said to elevate the soul to a supernatural level, justifying and sanctifying the soul in its being. Hence, habitual grace is called sanctifying grace: It causes the healing and elevating of our fallen nature. But this of course does not mean that man has been confirmed in grace in this life: "*Homo non habet cor suum firmatum in Deo*" (man's heart is not so fixed on God).[97] Only in heaven will man be able to love God forever without sinning.

This imperfection of man in this life requires the help of another grace. Thomas explains this need with the notion of *gratia actualis*. Humans need actual grace not only to avoid sin, but to seek divine help in willing and doing good. In other words, they cannot persevere in Christian life without divine grace: "[By *gratia actualis*] God moves us to will and to act ... and helps [us] to the end intended."[98] The primary purpose of actual grace is therefore to elicit a supernaturally "sanctifying" act that allows the graced person to overcome temptation and continue on the path to God as end.[99]

---

95 Jacobus M. Ramirez, *Opera Omnia Tomus IX: De Gratia Dei in I-II Summa Theologiae Divi Thomae Expositio* (Salamanca: Editorial San Esteban, 1992), 611; quoted from Meinert, "*Donum Habituale*," 51–2.

96 *ST* I–II, q.111, a.2, co.

97 Ibid., q.109, a.8, co.

98 Ibid., q 111, a.2, co and ad.3. See also ibid., q.109, a.2, co: "[In any case] man needs the Divine help, that he may be moved to act well."

99 Ibid., q.109, aa.9–10; q.114, a.9.

The need for actual grace, however, is also discussed in Thomas when considering the movement of a person lacking grace into a state of grace – that is, into the reception of habitual grace. To put it another way, *gratia actualis* also heals and elevates in our pre-conversion journey to God – and, like the grace called *habitualis*, it is further divided into *operatio* and *cooperatio*. In his treatise on grace, Thomas makes this point clear in terms of form and matter:

> [E]very preparation in man must be by the help of God moving the soul to good. And thus even the good movement of the free-will, whereby anyone is prepared for receiving the [habitual] gift of grace is an act of the free-will moved by God. And thus man is said to prepare himself, according to Proverbs 16:1: "It is the part of man to prepare the soul"; yet it is principally from God, Who moves the free-will. Hence it is said that man's will is prepared by God, and that man's steps are guided by God.[100]

As shown in this excerpt from q.112, Thomas believes that matter always is geared toward the form. In other words, humans before grace do not have a habitual form yet, so they simply have matter as their being and must be oriented toward a state of grace, a state of *gratia habitualis* that corresponds to their formal perfection. In *ST* I–II.109.6; 112.2–3; 113(entire); and 114.5–6, Thomas regards this process as a kind of conversion achieved by the grace – *auxilium* – not by a further infused habit (*gratia habitualis*)[101] or a species of human work or effort (or, more precisely, free will unrelated to divine action).[102] Thus, his argument against *gratia actualis* not only suggests the way in which the latter differs from *gratia habitualis*, but also Thomas' own opposition to all forms of Pelagianism, who taught that the *initium fidei* was the fruit of human action.[103]

---

100   Ibid., q.112, a.2, co.
101   Ibid., q.109, a.9, co: "Now with regard to the first kind of help, man does not need a further help of grace, e.g. a further infused habit."
102   Ibid., q.112, a.2, co.
103   Flick and Alszeghy, *Il vangelo della grazia*, §§ 36–41; quoted from O'Callaghan, *Children of God in the World*, 387.

Gratia Operans and Gratia Cooperans

Each of these two graces – *gratia habitualis* and *gratia actualis* – is further distinguished into *operans* and *cooperans*. Here the terms "operans" and "cooperans" come from Augustine, especially from his work *De Natura et Libero Arbitrio*: "God by his cooperation perfects in us what by his operation he begins."[104] In q.111 of the *Prima Secundae*, Thomas uses these two terms to distinguish between *grace working in us* and *grace working with us*:

> [When] God is the sole mover, the operation is attributed to God, and it is with reference to this that we speak of "operating grace." But ... [when] the operation is not only attributed to God, but also to the soul; and it is with reference to this that we speak of "cooperating grace."[105]

As is evident from this passage above, any effect is attributed to the agent that causes (or activates) it. So if an effect is attributed only to God without any action on our part, it refers to "operative," the grace of God working in us. However, if we are incited to act not only by God, but also by ourselves, then we are talking about the effects attributed to both God and ourselves, so it refers to "cooperative," the grace of God working with us – not against us, as in Calvin.

Having set in place these two divisions of grace, Thomas now explains what each of them means when applied to *gratia habitualis* and *gratia auxilium*. First, when used of habitual grace, "operative" refers to what the divine alone causes immediately: It covers all the effects of habitual grace in its own production except free will.[106] In the second article of q.111, Thomas relates these effects to "being": By operative habitual grace, the being of a person, both morally and ontologically, is enhanced and the person is made pleasing to God.[107] To put it simply, the *gratia habitualis*, called operative,

---

104   *De Natura et Libero Arbitrio*. *PL*.44.247–90. This particular passage of Augustine
        is quoted by Thomas in *ST* I–II, q.111, a.2, co. There he rephrases it as "He operates
        that we may will; and when we will, He cooperates that we may perfect." *ST* I–II,
        q.111, a.2, co.
105   *ST* I–II, q.111, a.2, co.
106   Wawrykow, "Grace," 197.
107   *ST* I–II, q.111, a.2, co.

means in Thomas that God alone causes the renewal of our nature, and God alone elevate our nature to a supernatural end.

"Cooperative," on the other hand, refers to the disposition that Thomas also calls "operation" in the second article: By cooperative habitual grace, we are inclined to cooperate with the grace that works in us.[108] In the process of this cooperation, we are not simply passive agents. We are rather active agents participating in God's primal agency, with the habits that *gratia habitualis* operatively infuses into the depths of our souls. Hence, the *gratia habitualis*, called cooperative, means in Thomas that God works through and with our meritorious actions to complete our journey to God.[109]

The discussion of operative and cooperative *gratia auxilium* in *ST* I–II is somewhat more complicated, raising an interpretive debate about whether Thomas thinks of a person as requiring God's help after conversion. First when used of actual grace, "operative" means that God is the "mover" and the person is the "moved"[110] – or, to put it more specifically,

---

108 Ibid.: "if grace is taken for the habitual gift, then again there is a double effect of grace, even as of every other form; the first of which is 'being,' and the second, 'operation'; thus ... habitual grace, inasmuch as it heals and justifies the soul, or makes it pleasing to God, is called operating grace; but inasmuch as it is the principle of meritorious works, which spring from the free-will, it is called cooperating grace."

109 This cooperative relationship between divine grace and human action can also be explained in terms of primary and secondary causality: According to Thomas, although God is the primary cause, God works through created secondary causes that we can study and learn to manipulate (*SCG* 3, c.77). These are patterns embedded by God in creation, about which Thomas affirms that "just as the divine providence does not altogether banish evil from the world, so neither does it exclude contingency, nor impose necessity on things" (*SCG* 3, c.72). For Thomas, the perfection of divine providence therefore requires contingency, "intermediary causes" that God expects us to learn about and to work with, and as such the consummation of our salvation, ordained by God's providence (or grace), is not an immediate result of God's free choice, but rather is mediated by the patterns of causality (primary and secondary) that God has placed in the created world (*SCG* 3, c.77).

110 *ST* I–II, q.111, a.2, co: "Est autem in nobis duplex actus. Primus quidem, interior voluntatis. Et quantum ad istum actum, voluntas se habet et mota. Deus autem ut movens: et praesertim cum voluntas incipit bonum velle quae prious malum volebat" (But there is a double act in us. First there is an interior act of the will.

operative actual grace is God's motion [*motus*] on a passive soul,[111] that which (1) forgives sin,[112] (2) inaugurates the soul's conversion,[113] (3) moves the soul to receive *gratia habitualis*, and (4) keep the soul moving to God as end.[114] According to Garrigou-Lagrange, there are four ways by which God moves (*movet*) us operatively. First, God moves us by an operative motion to desire the good. Second, God moves us in our natural realm by a special inspiration (e.g., "poetic, philosophical, or strategic"). Third, God moves us to conversion toward God: God turns a person from sin and draws the person to Himself. Fourth, God moves us by a special empowerment of the Holy Spirit – to which we are habitually disposed. Strictly speaking, the first two are operative motions, not operative graces, while the last two are operative graces – but of the last two, Garrigou-Lagrange refers to the one that comes first – God moves us to conversion toward God – as operative *gratia auxilium*.[115] What is worth noting in this detailed account of operative grace is that Garrigou-Lagrange describes operative *gratia auxilium* in the context of conversion. Such a description corresponds exactly to Thomas, who presents conversion as a "*praesertim* [special]" example of such grace in qq.109 and 111.[116] Not only that, it also gains some theological sympathy from some Thomists who interpret that Thomas has seen conversion as the *only* example of operative *gratia auxilium*.[117] However, it is

And in regard to that act, the will is a thing moved, and God is the mover; and especially when the will begins to will good which before had willed evil).

111   Ramirez, *De Gratia*, 694; quoted from Meinert, "*Donum Habituale*," 29. See also Garrigou-Lagrange, *Grace*, 169: "The major is clear with regard to an inanimate thing that is moved as the cart is moved by the horse, but if the thing moved is a living thing and the operation is a vita act, it is elicited, indeed, from it." As is evident from this excerpt, Garrigou-Lagrange also views such grace as a motion in the person which elicits a vital act of the will and "operates on the will prior to its own activity 'producing the act of human salvation.'" Meinert, "*Donum Habituale*," 29.

112   *ST* I–II, q.113, a.2. In this second article of q.113, Thomas identifies the "remission of sin" with "justification."

113   Ibid., q.109, a.6.

114   Ibid., q.109, aa.9–10.

115   Joseph P. Wawrykow, *God's Grace and Human Action: Merit in the Theology of St. Thomas Aquinas* (Notre Dame, IN: University of Notre Dame Press, 1996), 170.

116   *ST* I–II, q 111, a.2, co and ad.3. See also *ST* I–II, q.109, a.2, co.

117   Wawrykow, "Grace," 197.

important to keep in mind that "special" does not mean "only"[118] – that is to say, Thomas does not restrict *gratia auxilium* to an initial or singular movement by God.

Indeed, he proposes in his treatise on grace another context in which operative *gratia auxilium* can be found. A clear example of this may be said to come from the last article of *ST* I–II.109, where Thomas writes, "We always need God's help [*divino auxilio*] for every thought, inasmuch as He moves the understanding to act; for actually to understand anything is to think, as is clear from Augustine (*De Trin.* xiv, 7)." Besides his notion of perseverance is not "an act of the person, but is worked in the person by God, in accordance with God's will for the person to reach eternal life."[119] To summarize, God moves us both before and after conversion. According to Thomas, God's help (or supernatural motion) – the *gratia auxilium* – means that human beings are passive when moved, but God is active, disposing us for the infusion of habitual grace (conversion) and the perseverance in habitual grace (perseverance).

For its part in the category of *gratia auxilium*, "cooperative" also relates to God's motion moving the soul. But here the moving [*movet*] implies that the soul also moves him or herself: "Our mind both moves and is moved, [and it is with reference to this that] the operation is not only attributed to God, but also to the soul."[120] In other words, actual grace does not drive (or act) of itself. It works with *liberum arbitrium*[121] – or, more precisely, it "is conferred for good works in which our will is not only moved, but moves itself."[122] *Gratia auxilium* is therefore not simply operative but also cooperative.

---

118   Shawn M. Colberg, "Aquinas and the Grace of *Auxilium*," *Modern Theology* 32, no. 2 (2016): 187–210, at 197.

119   Wawrykow, "Grace," 197. For a more detailed discussion of Thomas exploring the indispensability of actual grace in the matter of perseverance, see Colberg, "Aquinas and the Grace of *Auxilium*," 195–6.

120   *ST* I II, q.111, a.2, co.

121   Bernard Lonergan, *Grace and Freedom: Operative Grace in the Thought of St Thomas Aquinas*, ed. Frederick E. Crowe and Robert M. Doran (Toronto: University of Toronto Press, 2000), 130: operative gratia auxilium and cooperative gratia auxilium are "one and the same grace," but it "produces some effects by itself and others in conjunction with free will."

122   Ramirez, *De Gratia*, 694; quoted from Meinert, "*Donum Habituale*," 31.

Here one can readily expect that Thomas sees humans as not merely passive, but also active when this *divino auxilio* cooperates with them in doing what God requires of them for good.[123] One may wonder exactly how Thomas relates such grace to human acting, or to the three parts of the human act that he had outlined in *Prima Secundae*. In qq.8–17 of *ST* I–II, Thomas divides our human act into three main parts or segments, which, in Wawrykow's words, are as follows: (1) the "willing of the end, or intention"; (2) the "choice of the means"; and (3) the "performance of the act, implementing the chosen means to reach the intended end."[124] In q.111 of *ST* I–II, it is relatively easy for us to note that the first part of human act – which Thomas rephrases as the "interior act of the will" (a.2) – corresponds to operative *gratia auxilium* and the third – which Thomas rephrases as the "exterior act of the will" (a.2) – to cooperative *gratia auxilium*.[125] The difficulty lies in the middle; *how* is it that actual grace relates to our choice of the means? To put it differently, what is the scope of our human merit? To what extent can we contribute to the working out of our own salvation?

To address these questions, one needs to look at *ST* I–II.114. In the ten articles of q.114, Thomas examines whether merit should be treated as the effect of *gratia cooperans*, stating that the *gratia auxilium* – by which God has operatively moved the soul to the end – cooperates with the will in choice of the means and bodily execution.[126] To be more specific, when

---

123   *ST* I–II, q.111, a.2, co: "And because God assists us in this act [of willing *bonum*], both by strengthening our will interiorly so as to attain to the act, and by granting outwardly the capability of operating, it is with respect to this that we speak of cooperating grace."

124   Wawrykow, "Grace," 198.

125   *ST* I–II, q.111, a.2, co: "Now there is a double act in us. First, there is the interior act of the will, and with regard to this act the will is a thing moved, and God is the mover; and especially when the will, which hitherto willed evil, begins to will good. And hence, inasmuch as God moves the human mind to this act, we speak of operating grace. But there is another, exterior act; and since it is commanded by the will, as was shown above (I–II:17:9) the operation of this act is attributed to the will. And because God assists us in this act, both by strengthening our will interiorly so as to attain to the act, and by granting outwardly the capability of operating, it is with respect to this that we speak of cooperating grace."

126   *ST* I–II, q.114, aa.1–10. See also Wawrykow, "Grace," 198.

our will is oriented correctly toward the end (God), such willing is due to operative *gratia auxilium*. However, when we choose the right means to that end and actually do the act to attain that end, such acting is due to cooperative *gratia auxilium*. The question of how *gratia auxilium* relates to human acting can then be answered in the following way: In the first part, which is the principle of every human act, God alone moves us, but in the second and third parts of that act, God intervenes in such a way that we move ourselves. In this respect, it can be said that cooperative *gratia auxilium* is a constant movement of what is already in motion to move the soul's will – by which cooperation is effected in the moved soul.

Gratia Praeveniens and Gratia Subsequens

The last division of grace – *gratia praeveniens* and *gratia subsequens* – is perhaps the most straightforward in Thomas' divisions of grace. Like the third division above, this one proceeds according to the effects it produces, of which Thomas names five: "*sanatio animae, bonum velle, bonum efficaciter operare, in bono perseverare, ad gloriam pervenire*" (healing the soul, willing the good, doing the good efficaciously, persevering in the good, and reaching glory).[127] The order of these effects is essential to understanding what Thomas means by prevenient and subsequent. According to Thomas, one can say that a first/former effect that grace causes in us is prevenient with respect to a second/later effect. Alternatively, one can say that the second is subsequent with respect to the first, the third with respect to the second, and so on. Here Thomas reaffirms his fundamental premise: Grace is still one and simple in essence, insofar as it derives from God.[128] The temporal distinction therefore does not mean

---

127   Ibid., q.111, a.3, co1 "As grace is divided into operating and cooperating, with regard to its diverse effects, so also is it divided into prevenient and subsequent, howsoever we consider grace. Now there are five effects of grace in us: of these, the first is, to heal the soul; the second, to desire good; the third, to carry into effect the good proposed; the fourth, to persevere in good; the fifth, to reach glory."

128   Ibid., q.111, a.3, ad.2: "For subsequent grace, inasmuch as it pertains to glory, is not numerically distinct from prevenient grace whereby we are at present justified."

in Thomas that grace is essentially divisible, nor does it mean that grace is distinguished as prevenient or subsequent according to a plurality of phenomena. It simply means that grace is not merely passive, achieved once and for all, or static – as is the case with "the Logos or Demiurge typical of Platonic and Stoic cosmogonies"[129] – but active, enduring, and dynamic in the temporal cadence of human life; it does not destroy nature, but perfects it to the extent that the soul is healed and finally aims at the gracious attainment of glory in heaven.[130] Thus, the corollary of *gratia praeveniens* and *gratia subsequens* is the unveiling of a Thomistic abbreviation of *via salutis*, which corresponds to what Thomas has implied in his *ST* I–II.111.3 ad 2: that the Christian life in grace is seen as a present journey (*in via*) to our future heavenly homeland (*in patria*).[131]

The Cause and Effects of Grace (qq.112–4)

It is now clear that Thomas holds that God is the cause of grace. Without grace we are able neither to prepare ourselves for grace, nor to do the gracious acts that would be productive of gracious *habitus* (*ST* I–II.109.6). However, he reinforces this conclusion in q.112. "It is impossible," he says, "that any creature should cause grace."[132] We are the recipients of God's grace. Even if we somehow prepare ourselves for grace (especially for *gratia habitualis*) or reorient ourselves to God,[133] the degree to which

129 O'Callaghan, *Children of God in the World*, 218.

130 *ST* I–II, q.111, a.3.

131 Gregory P. Van Buskirk, "Iconic Dignity: Nature, Grace, and Virtue in the Theologies of John Wesley and Thomas Aquinas" (PhD diss., Boston University School of Theology, 2019), 277. For Thomas' explicit mention of *in via* and *in patria*, see *ST* I–II, q.111, a.3, ad.2: "*Sicut enim caritas viae non evacuatur, sed perficitur in patria, ita etiam et de lumine gratiae est dicendum, quia neutrum in sui ratione imperfectionem importat.*"

132 *ST* I–II, q.112, a.1, co.

133 Ibid., q.112, aa.2–3. As already stated earlier (*ST* I–II.111.2), grace is taken in two ways: first as a habitual gift of God, and secondly as an *auxilium* from God. If we speak of grace as it means an *auxilium* from God, no preparation is needed on

we are graced depends on God's will.[134] In other words, the gift of grace does not come after every preparation of human power, but precedes and excites it: "The gift of grace surpasses every capability of created nature, since it is nothing short of a partaking of the Divine Nature, which exceeds every other nature."[135]

Is there any role then for the human will? Thomas' emphasis on God as the cause of grace seems to suggest that grace overrides *liberum arbitrium*, and some people think that Thomas is committed exactly to this conclusion.[136] But he does not see it that way. As already said in Chapter 4, Thomas holds that grace is not a threat to *liberum arbitrium*, but rather a source and perfector of it. Thomas does not claim that God imposes necessity on things. Similarly, he does not deny the need for a right disposition of the human will (even if this is a result of grace).[137] Grace thus empowers humans to freely desire and act accordingly, instead of making them unfree or deprived of being voluntary in their actions.[138]

After establishing the cause of grace as God, Thomas moves onto the effects of grace, focusing on the grace of justification and the doctrine of merit. Regarding the first effect, justification, Thomas speaks of it more than simply a matter of God forgiving our sins (*remissio culpae*): "By His

man's part. But Thomas says in q.112 that if grace is taken in the first sense, some preparation is needed for it since "a form can only be in disposed matter." Ibid., q.112, a.2, co.

134   Ibid., q.113, a.4, co.

135   Ibid., q.113, a.1, co.

136   For a suitable critique of this immature reading of Thomas, see Brian Davis, *Thomas Aquinas's Summa Theologiae: A Guide and Commentary* (Oxford: Oxford University Press, 2014), 226.

137   *ST* I–II, q.112, a.2, co.

138   Ibid., q.112, aa.2–3. See also *ST* I, q.83, a.1, ad.3: God is the cause of all being, truth, goodness, motion, and the like. "And just as by moving natural causes [God] does not prevent their acts being natural, so by moving voluntary causes [God] does not deprive their actions of being voluntary: but rather [God] is the cause of this very thing in them; for [God] operates in each thing according to its own nature." This position is further confirmed in the third article of q.113 with a concise but firm conclusion that "no one comes to the Father by grace without the movement of free will." *ST* I–II, q.113, a.3, sc.

grace … sin is remitted to us, [and] God is at peace with us."[139] As can be seen in the third and fifth articles of q.113 in *ST* I–II, he takes it as a matter of us acting/moving in harmony with God's will.[140] In other words, justification entails both forgiveness (*remissio*) and conversion (*conversio*). That Thomas should hold this view is, in fact, not surprising given his position on how God's action relates to its effects. Thomas sees the agent's action as being in the patient.[141] More specifically, it is impossible for Thomas to dissociate "being forgiven by God" and "striving to act in accordance with God's will."[142] Furthermore, his theological notion of God as eternal and immutable prevents Thomas from seeing justification as an event in God.[143] In his view, to be forgiven involves one converting to *bonum* while repenting from *malum*.[144] So he thinks that we are forgiven by God as we repent and convert unto God (*conversio ad Deum*).[145] In other words, justification

---

139 Ibid., q.113, a.2, co.

140 Ibid., q.113, a.3, co: "[By] the gift of justifying grace … man is moved to it [*bonum*] by a movement of the will which is a movement of free-will." See also ibid., q.113, a.5, co: "the justification of the ungodly is a certain movement whereby the human mind is moved by God from the state of sin to the state of justice."

141 Michael J. Dodds, *The One Creator God in Thomas Aquinas and Contemporary Theology* (Washington, DC: Catholic University of America Press, 2020), 98. In *Disputatae de Potentia*, Thomas holds that God is substantially present as God acts on or in a creature: "The natural mover or agent moves and acts by an intermediary movement or action that is between the mover and the thing moved, between the agent and the patient: wherefore at least in this intermediary, agent and patient, mover and thing moved must come together. Wherefore the agent as such is not outside the genus of the patient as such: and consequently, each has a real relation to the other, especially seeing that this intermediary action is a perfection proper to the agent so that the term of that action is a perfection of the agent. This does not apply to God." *De pot.* q.7, a.10, ad.1. For a similar view that in God's action God is more intimately present to the creature, see also *ST* I, q.8, a.1, co and q.105, a.2, ad.1.

142 Davis, *Thomas Aquinas's Summa Theologiae*, 227.

143 *ST* I, q.10, a.2, co: "The idea of eternity follows immutability, as the idea of time follows movement … Hence, as God is supremely immutable, it supremely belongs to him to be eternal."

144 *ST* I–II, q.113, a.2. See also O'Callaghan, *Children of God in the World*, 343–4.

145 Ibid., q.113, a.4.

refers to being holy in us, not being taken to be holy in God even if one is not. In this sense, Thomas takes justification to be a living process in the patient, that is, an actual and ongoing movement of the individual acting in agreement with the grace-filled action of God.

To further explore this process (or movement), Thomas devotes most of his treatise to a study of justification (*ST* I–II.113.3–8). Here he describes the process of justification in terms of four different stages: (1) the granting of grace, (2) the movement of free will toward God, (3) the movement of free will against sin, and (4) the consummation of justification.[146] These four stages imply what we have confirmed earlier in speaking of *gratia operans* and *gratia cooperans*, that grace is not only operative, but also cooperative with the voluntary participation of human will. In other words, (1) corresponds to the movement of the Mover, and (2) and (3) to the movement of the moved. The former moves the will toward God and against sin preveniently, while the latter does so subsequently. As a result, our human will is incapable of achieving (4) on its own, but this does not imply that God completes justification on His own, nor that God would be incapable of achieving it on His own. The reality is that He simply does not do so without a "*motus liberi arbitrii*" (movement of free will) on our part, without the free and responsive consent of our souls to His gracious

146   Ibid., q.113, a.6, co: "There are four things which are accounted to be necessary for the justification of the ungodly, viz. the infusion of grace, the movement of the free-will towards God by faith, the movement of the free-will towards sin, and the remission of sins. The reason for this is that, as stated above (Article 1), the justification of the ungodly is a movement whereby the soul is moved by God from a state of sin to a state of justice. Now in the movement whereby one thing is moved by another, three things are required: first, the motion of the mover; secondly, the movement of the moved; thirdly, the consummation of the movement, or the attainment of the end. On the part of the Divine motion, there is the infusion of grace; on the part of the free-will which is moved, there are two movements – of departure from the term 'whence,' and of approach to the term 'whereto'; but the consummation of the movement or the attainment of the end of the movement is implied in the remission of sins; for in this is the justification of the ungodly completed."

will.[147] In this respect, Thomas concludes that the effective consummation of justification requires both divine action and human autonomy.[148]

However, Thomas mentions three further issues when examining the topic of justification. First of all, he says in the seventh article of q.113 that justification is an instantaneous process because it is a work of grace from God who "knows no tardy efforts."[149] This means that the process of justification is not the fruit of an extended preparation of the will; rather, it is the outcome of a *gratia Dei* that "can suddenly dispose any matter whatsoever to its form."[150] In this respect, Thomas concludes that the infusion of grace is the substance of justification, and the time or deliberation that the will requires for its reduction to action is "*non est de substantia iustificationis, sed via in iustificationem.*"[151]

After having drawn this distinction, Thomas compares justification with creation in terms of *terminus a quo* and *terminus ad quem*.[152] First, he teaches that in terms of *terminus a quo*, justification is less great than creation, because unlike the former, the latter has ontological nothingness as its starting point. Then, in terms of *terminus ad quem*, Thomas teaches that justification is greater than creation, because, unlike the latter, the former has the divinization of being as its point of arrival.[153] Thomas appreciates justification not only in relation to creation, but also to glorification – where the focus is to make it clear that justification is a greater divine work than the other two, since it is the consummation in the natural realm of creation and the natural incarnation of glorification.[154] In a word,

---

147   Ibid.: "God's motion to justice does not take place without a movement of the free-will."
148   Ibid., q.113, a.3, sc.
149   Ibid., q.113, a.7, sc.
150   Ibid., q.113, a.7, co.
151   Ibid., q.113, a.7, ad.1: "The movement of the free-will, which concurs in the justification of the ungodly, is a consent to detest sin, and to draw near to God; and this consent takes place suddenly. Sometimes, indeed, it happens that deliberation precedes, yet this is not of the substance of justification, but a way of justification; as local movement is a way of illumination, and alteration to generation."
152   Ibid., q.113, a.9.
153   Ibid., q.113, a.9, co.
154   O'Callaghan, *Children of God in the World*, 344–5.

in Thomas the notion of justification can be understood as giving priority to grace, yet affirming the full respect that grace has for human nature. To use Thomas' own words, "He moves man to justice according to the condition of his human nature."[155]

This understanding becomes more evident in his third teaching on justification. According to Thomas, justification is not a miraculous work; rather, it deifies the person while respecting the rules and laws of nature, which miraculous interventions may distort, or at best force to go beyond nature ("*supra naturam*").[156] Of course, miracles can occasion a powerful experience, and the visibility of that experience may produce some extraordinary manifestation or awe-inspiring admiration.[157] The purpose of such visible miracles, however, is to reveal an invisible justification, as Jesus explains in the Gospel: "But I want you to know that the Son of Man has authority on earth to forgive sins (Mt 9:6)." In a similar sense, Thomas briefly mentions the miracle that took place in Paul's conversion,[158] but the point of that mention is to teach that the visible miracle is exceptional and its purpose is one of preparing the path to conversion or of manifesting the work of justification. Thus one can confirm time and again that grace is taken in Thomas as being dynamically related to nature.

Regarding the second effect (merit), Thomas speaks of it in the context of grace. In other words, his doctrine of merit is not talking about something earned, something owed to a person, nor about the right of a person to his or her earnings, to what is owed him or her. He thinks that no one can claim a reward from God, because human beings are not equal to God[159] or, more precisely, because human beings cannot claim a right

---

155   *ST* I–II, q.113, a.3, co.
156   Ibid., q.113, a.10, sc: "Miraculous works are beyond natural power. Now the justification of the ungodly is not beyond natural power; for Augustine says (*De Praed. Sanct. v*) that 'to be capable of having faith and to be capable of having charity belongs to man's nature; but to have faith and charity belongs to the grace of the faithful.' Therefore the justification of the ungodly is not miraculous."
157   O'Callaghan, *Children of God in the World*, 345.
158   *ST* I–II, q.113, a.10, co.
159   Ibid., q.114, a.1, co: "Now justice is a kind of equality, as is clear from the Philosopher (*Ethic.* v, 3), and hence justice is simply between those that are simply equal; but where there is no absolute equality between them, neither is there absolute justice ... Now it is clear that between God and man there is the greatest inequality: for

toward God and demands by the law of justice that they be paid for anything they have done. God, however, is pleased to allow us what we do not deserve, or what we cannot achieve of ourselves. In other words, God has decided that by our work or labor we are to obtain from God as a sort of recompense (*pretium*).[160] Thus, Thomas argues in q.114 of *ST* I–II that merit should not be thought of in relation to the notion of desert, but in relation to this blessed situation (that we are now capable of meriting by the effect of God's cooperative grace).

So, what exactly does Thomas mean by merit? And in terms of grace, what can we merit and what can we not? To answer this question, one needs to first look at what Thomas says typologically about merit in the final question of his treatise on grace. There are two types of merit: merit *de condigno* (condign) and merit *de congruo* (congruous).[161] According to Thomas, the first type, condign merit, corresponds to what one can merit in terms of justice,[162] whereas the second type, congruous merit, corresponds to what seems appropriate or reasonable.[163] In the former case, God's gracious motion, which makes our works *absolutely* meritorious, is at stake, but in the latter case, God's liberality and magnanimity to the *liberum arbitrium*, which makes our works *only proportionally* meritorious. No one (except those in the life of grace), says Thomas, can claim in justice a right to what he or she cannot achieve on his or her own.[164] Moreover, God has debts only with Himself, not with humans or any other creature: "*Inquantum debitum est ut sua ordinatio impleatur*" (He has the debt of fulfilling his own ordering).[165] One can speak of merit, therefore, *not* because God and I enter into a mutual agreement in terms of which it is agreed that if I do such and such, then God must reward me in a certain way, *but* only

---

they are infinitely apart, and all man's good is from God. Hence there can be no justice of absolute equality between man and God."

160   Ibid., q.114, a.1, co.
161   Ibid., q.114, aa.3, 6, 7.
162   For Thomas, justice is "a kind of equality." So, in his view, it holds "simply between those that are simply equal." Ibid., q.114, a.1, co.
163   Ibid., q.114, a.6, co.
164   Ibid., q.114, a.3, ad.3. See also *ST* I–II, q.114, a.6, co.
165   Ibid., q.114, a.1, ad.3.

because God is faithful to the words He has given: "There is a reward for thy work" (Jer. 31:16).[166] To sum up: For Thomas merit can be understood in two different types, each of which explains that God merits condignly, while man merits congruously – but if in grace, the man becomes capable of meriting condignly.[167]

Having set this twofold type of merit in place, Thomas now reveals what we are capable of meriting in or out of the life of grace. One can summarize this in five points. First, a graced person can merit two things condignly: (1) the glory of life everlasting[168] and (2) the increase of charity or grace.[169] Second, when a person does meritorious work that comes from both "free will" and "the grace of the Holy Spirit,"[170] that person's faith can congruously merit the salvation of another and the temporary benefits for oneself and one's neighbor.[171] Third, a person without grace cannot condignly merit the first point, but may congruously merit the second point (e.g., good work for the poor, seeking forgiveness in prayer, etc.). Fourth, when not in grace a person cannot merit a series of holy works that he or she might desire, for example, to repent of one's own grave sin or to merit condignly (and congruously) the first grace for oneself and others.[172] Lastly,

---

166   Ibid., q.114, a.1, sc.
167   Ibid., q.114, a.3, ad.3: "The grace of the Holy Ghost which we have at present, al-
         though unequal to glory in act, is equal to it virtually as the seed of a tree, wherein
         the whole tree is virtually. So likewise by grace of the Holy Ghost dwells in man;
         and He is a sufficient cause of life everlasting; hence, 2 Corinthians 1:22, He is
         called the 'pledge' of our inheritance."
168   Ibid., q.114, a.3, sc: "Man [with grace] merits everlasting life condignly."
169   Ibid., q.114, a,7, ad.3: "Hence it must be said that every act of charity merits eternal
         life absolutely."
170   Ibid., q.114, a.3, co. Here Thomas speaks of the bond between grace and nature and
         the Holy Spirit. This bond is the basis for forming in Thomas' moral theology the
         concept of *a general divine presence reserved in all creation, but accidentally aug-
         mented only by grace*. Such a concept is similar to and directly related to Wesley's
         notion of prevenient grace, as noted in fn. 119 of Chapter 3 above. This similarity
         suggests an important fact: for both theologians, the true meaning of our nature's
         role in salvation, including merit and virtue, can only be understood when it re-
         lates to the divine grace that indwells us through the Holy Spirit.
171   Ibid., q.114, a.6, ads.1 and 3.
172   Ibid., q.114, a.5.

no one but Christ can condignly merit the grace of final perseverance for oneself.[173] The main implication of these five points, according to Thomas, is that there is a dynamic cooperation between God and man in the making of merit, and our merit with God is freely and graciously disposed to associate with the work of grace. Therefore, Thomas' doctrine of merit is not a mere marginal add-on to the gospel of grace. It constitutes and confirms one of the most central aspects of his understanding of grace: the *synergeia* between God and humanity.

Conclusion

Thomas Aquinas develops one of the most comprehensive accounts of the notion of grace in the history of Christian theology. His work represents a synthesis of the Christian tradition with the resources and perspectives of Aristotelian philosophical thinking. It is, in a sense, also a qualified reconstruction of Augustine's doctrine of grace, which now assumes a specific Thomist character.

His brilliant theology of grace is well developed in *Prima Secundae*. A review of it then comes to the following conclusion. First, Thomas gives many nuanced divisions of grace (e.g., *gratia gratum faciens* and *gratia gratis data*, *gratia habitualis* and *gratia actualis/auxilium*, *gratia operans* and *gratia cooperans*, *gratia praeveniens* and *gratia subsequens*), but he never waivers from the essential unity of grace. Next, Thomas regards grace as a free gift and sanctifying motion of God, the acting out of His healing and elevating disposition in and for us. Here, the dynamics of grace and nature are confirmed from a collaborative point of view, and with it, Thomas makes the case for a blessed paradox: The soul may come to partake of the divine, and the wills of God and humanity will work together for unity in a *proportional*, rather than *inverse* ratio. Finally, Thomas concludes in his treatises on justification and merit that the life of grace is an instantaneous gift

---

173   Ibid., q.114, a.9.

from God, yet a process on the part of humans, a spontaneous movement of those who are moved toward the greatest possible perfection in God.

These different approaches to the notion of grace in Thomas can be further organized into a visual arrangement, as we did for Wesley's doctrine of grace in Chapter 3. This visual arrangement is shown in the diagram below, from which one can get more help in comparing Wesley's and Thomas' typologies of grace:

	Gratia Gratis Data	*Gratia Gratum Faciens*	
Praeveniens ↓	Gratuitous Grace (*Operans*): A heir of another's *gratia gratis data* may experience sanctifying grace.	Actual Grace (*Operans*): God forgives sin, inaugurates the soul's conversion, moves the soul to receive *gratia habitualis*, and keep the soul moving to God as end.	Habitual Grace (*Operans*): God heals and elevates the soul and makes its being (*esse*) pleasing (*gratus*) to God.
Subsequens	Gratuitous Grace (*Cooperans*): A gifted person's cooperation with God may bring others to conversion (and justification).	Actual Grace (*Cooperans*): God strengthens the will interiorly, empowers it to operate exteriorly, and moves the responsive soul to freely actualize the potency of his or her converted will.	Habitual Grace (*Cooperans*): God works through and with our meritorious actions to complete our journey to God.

CHAPTER 6

Grace and Nature in John Wesley and Thomas Aquinas

In the preceding chapters we argued that John Wesley and Thomas Aquinas avoided the tendency to either stress God's sovereignty alone or focus on human merit exclusively. We now turn to consider their teachings about grace and nature from a comparative point of view. This chapter will initially point out an impressive number of parallels between their positive appraisals of human nature, and then proceed to a clarification of the theological points of contacts we have already begun to notice between Wesley's and Thomas' teachings on grace. The purpose of this chapter is to argue for the theological comparability between Wesley's and Thomas' doctrines of grace and nature by pulling together the key elements discussed so far in this book.

Nature in Wesley and Thomas

Wesley and Thomas articulated their understanding of human nature with the following themes: (1) original sin and original justice, (2) free will (*liberum arbitrium*) and conscience (*synderesis*), and (3) outward sin (actual sin) and inward sin ("sin remaining" or "*fomes peccati*"). As we already discussed, each of these themes appears to constitute a common concern that exists in Wesley's and Thomas' theological anthropology: For both of them, sin does not totally destroy the image of God in us, nor does it leave our graced human nature totally depraved and without any natural capacity for our voluntary and doxological cooperation with God. To figure this out more clearly, let us turn first to the first theme – original sin and original justice – and then to the second and third, which Wesley and Thomas use to further emphasize their positive (compatible) vision of human nature.

Original Sin and Original Justice

Wesley's and Thomas' understanding of human nature is related to Augustine's teaching of original sin. In this respect, they all viewed Adam's fall as a historical narrative and affirmed the communication of original sin through carnal concupiscence (or the semen) by accepting Augustine's doctrine of communal guilt. In further examination of Wesley's and Thomas' teachings on original sin, however, we found that they did not stop at simply imitating Augustine. In a metaphysical context, they went further by linking original sin to its opposite doctrine, original justice. At the same time, they took a different path from Augustine – who had understood original sin positively and thus viewed nature as substantially unstable, either fallen or graced. In this way, they came to affirm the dynamic relationship of human nature to divine grace.

It was in his early sermon "The Image of God" that Wesley discussed original sin in relation to original justice (or what he had once called "ancient perfection"[1] in 1727). Here he argued that the image of God in us cumulatively results in our happiness, for all of our capacity is fully satisfied with God as its proper object.[2] From this point of view he then regarded original justice as a prelapsarian perfection that constitutes the full integrity of our natural powers and original sin as a privation or loss of this full integrity. As we have already seen, Wesley further exhibited this negative

---

1   Wesley, "On Mourning for the Dead," in *Works* 4, §5: "It was, indeed, of man's own, not of God's creation; who may permit, but never was the author of, evil. The same hour gave birth to grief and sin, as the same moment will deliver us from both. For neither did exist before human nature was corrupted, nor will it continue when that is restored to its *ancient perfection*."

2   Wesley, "Image of God," in *Works* 4, I.4.

(or privative) view of original sin in his 1746 sermon "The Way to the Kingdom": "Know that corruption of thy inmost nature, whereby thou art very far gone from *original righteousness*, whereby 'the flesh lusteth' always 'contrary to the Spirit,' through that 'carnal mind' which 'is enmity against God,' which 'is not subject to the law of God, neither indeed can be.'"[3] Yet the view was finally confirmed at a formal and ecclesial level when Wesley redacted the Thirty-Nine Articles for North American Methodists, where he entirely omitted Augustine's statement about concupiscence, leaving the second half of the article on the Anselmian tradition of original justice untouched.[4]

Thomas' account of original sin likewise turned out to be a discussion of original justice. In *Summa Contra Gentiles IV* and *Summa Theologiae I-II*, Thomas used the term to express the prelapsarian state of human nature. As already discussed, he saw that in the state of original justice, human nature was established with an internal harmony that holds "all the soul's parts together in one."[5] The harmony in nature was a threefold subjection: "The inferior powers were perfectly subject to reason, the reason to God, the body to the soul."[6] This was not a purely natural state, but a state

---

3　Wesley, "The Way to Kingdom," in *Works* 1, II.1. See also Wesley, "The Doctrine of Original Sin," in *Works* (Albany) 9, Pt.7, especially on page 500: "Adam, by his sin, became not only guilty, but; corrupt; and so transmits guilt and corruption to his posterity. By his sin he stripped himself of his original righteousness and corrupted himself. We were in him representatively, as our moral head; we were in him seminally, as our natural head. Hence we fell in him; 'by his disobedience' we 'were made sinners;' his first sin is imputed to us. And we are left without that original righteousness." Commenting on the Ninth Article of the Church of England, Wesley further clarifies: "Original sin – is the fault and corruption of the nature of every man, - whereby man is very far gone from original righteousness, and is of his own nature inclined to evil, so that the flesh lusteth always contrary to the spirit; and therefore in every person born into this world, it deserveth God's wrath and damnation." Wesley, *A Farther Appeal to Men of Reason and Religion*, in *Works* (Albany) 8, Pt.1. II.5.

4　For a comparison of Wesley's redaction to the original Thirty-Nine Articles, see Thomas C. Oden, *Doctrinal Standards in the Wesleyan Tradition: Revised Edition* (Nashville, TN: Abingdon Press, 2008), 130–48.

5　*ST* I–II, q.82, a.2, ad.3.

6　*SCG* 4, c.52. 6.

of grace: Original justice was a gift from God to the first man God created. Original sin, according to Thomas, is thus nothing but the privation of this very state of grace: "Original sin denotes the privation of original justice."[7]

One of Wesley's beliefs is, of course, the interpretation of original sin as a disease. Almost all Wesleyans acknowledge the presence of this theme, and many suggest its priority in his teachings on original sin.[8] Indeed, we have confirmed this biological view of original sin in several of his sermons: "Circumcision of the Heart," "One Thing Needful," "The Trouble and Rest of Good Man," and "Upon Our Lord's Sermon on the. Mount I." Interestingly, Thomas also understood original sin as a disease. It is this view that stands behind his *ST* I–II, q.81, a.1, wherein Thomas related original sin to what he called "infection of nature."[9] This parallel reading of Wesley and Thomas thus reveals that they all understood original sin as an infectious disease attached to our human nature.

How does original sin actually infect human nature? According to Wesley, the disease infects the intellect.[10] In this state, the will now goes unchecked and yields first to pride, then to self-will, and worldly loves.[11] Elsewhere, Wesley adds anger, truth-aversion, injustice, and cruelty to his nuanced description of original sin and teaches that the disease infects the

---

7   *ST* I–II, q.82, a.1, ad.1.
8   Wesley, "The Circumcision of the Hearth," in *Works* 1, I.5; "The One Thing Needful," in *Works* 4, I.4; "The Trouble and Rest of Good Man," in *Works* 3, Preamble §1; and "Upon Our Lord's Sermon on the Mount I," in *Works* 1, I.4.
9   *ST* I–II, q.81, a.1.
10 Wesley, "Original Sin," in *Works* 2, III.3.
11 Ibid., III.1 and 3: "the proper nature of religion ... is θεραπεία ψυχῆς, God's method of healing a soul which is *thus diseased*. Hereby the great Physician of souls applies medicine to heal this sickness; to restore human nature, *totally corrupted in all its [intellectual] faculties*. God heals all our atheism by the knowledge of himself, and of Jesus Christ whom he hath sent; by giving us faith, a divine evidence and conviction of God and of the things of God .... By repentance and lowliness of heart the deadly disease of *pride* is healed; that of *self-will* by resignation, a meek and thankful submission to the will of God. And for *the love of the world* in all its branches the love of God is the sovereign remedy. Now this is properly religion, 'faith thus working by love,' working the genuine, meek humility, entire deadness to the world, with a loving, thankful acquiescence in and conformity to the whole will and Word of God."

heart.[12] In other words, original sin does not infect the ontological part, but rather the moral – intellectual and affective – part of humanity, which had once existed in a state of original justice and worked integrally and perfectly toward its proper object, God.

Thomas, too, is explicit that original sin infects our rational and appetitive capacities. As we have already seen in Chapter 4, this view is based on the *ST* I–II, q.81, a.1; q.82, a.3; and q.83, aa.3–4, where the point Thomas sought to establish appears to be compatible with Wesley's: Adam's primal sin did not destroy our human nature itself. What was destroyed (or, as it turns out, taken away) was a gift from God – that is, the *justitia originalis* that may have enabled our human parts (soul and body) and moral powers (intellective, sensory, and appetitive) to function properly and optimally, in harmony with God. In other words, original sin for Thomas is not like the concept of *peccatum* claimed by Augustine as concupiscence. Rather than the incoming of concupiscence, original sin is the privation or absence of original justice. Therefore, concupiscence is not identical to original sin per se for Thomas, but an effect of original sin – with which "all the powers of the soul are ... lacking an order proper to them."[13]

We may thus conclude that for Wesley and Thomas, original sin is likened to a disease that attaches to our nature (especially to our rational soul and bodily appetites/desires). It disposes us from original justice, a gift from God that orders our natural capacities. In this sense, our post-lapsarian nature is best understood for them as a privation of order, or due harmony, in nature – instead of a broken reality in which evil has positive ontological status and our moral dignity (free will and conscience) disappears in a substantial sense.[14]

---

12   Wesley, "On the Education of Children," in *Works* 2, §§5–11.

13   *ST* I–II, q.85, a.3.

14   Wesley explicitly affirmed this Augustinian view that evil has no essence in his early Oxford sermon "On Mourning for the Dead (1727)": "It was, indeed, of man's own, not of God's creation; who may permit, but never was the author of, evil. The same hour gave birth to ... sin ... For neither did [it] exist before human nature was corrupted, nor will it continue when that is restored to its ancient perfection." Wesley, "On Mourning for the Dead," in *Works* 4, §5. Like Wesley, Thomas accepts Augustine and rejects the Manichaean idea of sin that we unwillingly sin, that is,

Free Will and Conscience

In the preceding chapters, Wesley's and Thomas' positive appraisal of humanity expanded into a deeper discussion of the *imago Dei*. In this discussion we have seen that both argue that the image of God was not destroyed after the Fall, but preserved in the form of either free will or conscience. First with regard to free will, Wesley wrote: "Men are as free in believing, or not believing, as if he [God] did not know it at all."[15] A similar view was made in his later sermon "What is Man?" as we had discussed in Chapter 2: "And although I have not an absolute power over my own mind, because of the corruption of my own nature; *yet*, through the grace of God assisting me, I have a power to choose and do good, as well as evil."[16] To be clear, Wesley did not exclude human volition, even if its freedom was limited. Furthermore, he even declared that through fellowship with God's grace, one's free will can return to its original state (perfection): "I only assert, that there is a measure of free-will supernaturally restored to every man, together with that supernatural light which "enlightens every man that cometh into the world."[17] According to Wesley's understanding of human nature, original sin weakens free will to such an

---

humans are compelled by the principle of evil, the independent reality against God. See *ST* I–II, 1.5, aa.1–3.

15 Wesley, "On Predestination," in *Works* 2, §5.

16 Wesley, "What Is Man?," in *Works* 3, §11.

17 Wesley, "Predestination Calmly Considered," in *Works* (Albany) 10, especially on page 229–30. As for the charge of Wesley being a Pelagian, who holds a measure of free will back to man without grace, Wesley defends himself from the accusations of Dr. Erskine, saying that "Why Dr. E. should quarrel with me concerning natural free-will, I cannot conceive, unless for quarrelling's sake. For it is certain, on this head, if no other, we are precisely of one mind. I believe that Adam, before his fall, had such freedom of will, that he might choose either good or evil, but that, since the fall, no child of man has a natural power to choose anything that is truly good. Yet I know (and who does not?) That man has still freedom of will in things of an indifferent nature." Wesley, "Some Remarks on A Defense of the Preface to the Edinburgh Edition of Aspasio Vindicated," in *The Works of the Rev. John Wesley*, Vol. 6: 127.

extent that no one thereafter can either love God as he or she ought, believe in God, or even do good for God's sake apart from a unique divine grace that alone can make us still free and responsible agents.

Thomas, too, had a compatibilist understanding of free will. He thus argued that an agent can still have free will while being caused or preveniently moved by divine grace, as we had noted in Chapter 4: "Forasmuch as man is rational it is necessary that man have a free will [i.e., *liberum arbitrium*]."[18] To be sure, "necessity" lies at the heart of what Thomas have to say about *liberum arbitrium*. Are human beings free, self-determining agents, or the pawns of fate? This is the underlying question that drives Thomas to his compatibilist position that we encountered at the second half of Chapter 4. One's will, moved necessarily, is, according to Thomas, an affront to the Scripture, the Christian tradition, the wisdom of moral philosophy, and so forth.[19] Necessity renders human nature *non*-human, and evacuate individual agency.[20] And if we are not agents, our actions can never be ours. It is only because of *liberum arbitrium*, our actions are truly genitive of our nature (i.e., "ours") and really genuine to our nature (i.e., "really ours"). Thus, even though he does not treat the will as a separate faculty of the soul that can act upon the intellectual nature or rational appetite of human beings at a practical level that Thomas affirms a positive reading of fallen humans; even in the *status corruptionis* we still possess a measure of *liberum arbitrium*.

What we see in Wesley's free will and Thomas' *liberum arbitrium* is a common concern regarding nature: Humanity is not exempt from his or her moral agency in sin. However, as this concern pertains to our moral life and dignity without necessity, it is worth paying attention to another emerging notion – "choice" – that we have discussed in previous chapters regarding this matter of necessity. In Question 83 of the *ST* I, Thomas argues that the proper act of *liberum arbitrium* is "choice" – that is, to "take one thing while refusing another."[21] In almost the same sense, Wesley likewise states that the proper act of free will is choice, "a capacity of choosing the

18   *ST* I, q.83, a.1, co.
19   *QDM*, q.6, co.
20   Ibid., q.6. See also *ST* I, q.83, aa.3–4.
21   *ST* I, q.83, a.3, co.

one and refusing the other."[22] He then ties our appetitive power of choice to "reason"[23] – to what he defined earlier in his *Earnest Appeal to Men of Reason and Religion* as a faculty of our mind that apprehends an object and presents it dialectically to the affective will.[24] For Wesley, free will is thus an appetitive power of *electio* (choice) that proceeds from the judgment of reason, just as *liberum arbitrium* is for Thomas. It is thus possible to argue that, while their terms for *electio* are not identical and may be arranged differently from a theoretical perspective, Wesley and Thomas can converge on a practical level; in particular, they both agree that, even in the postlapsarian state, we are not devoid of moral purpose, but, with the help of God's grace, we are still capable of free choices.

Wesley and Thomas also converge in their views on conscience. For Wesley, conscience is a moral habit. This habit refers to the faculty constitutive of human nature in his theology, or, more clearly, to any natural propensity to good in our graced nature.[25] Thomas likewise sees conscience (or *synderesis* in his words) as a moral habit or ability.[26] For him, the conscience as a moral habit is a self-evident part of human nature, which helps the soul discern what is good and orders it toward good.[27]

These two theologians, however, root their notion of conscience or *synderesis* on its supernatural basis (*imago Dei*). In other words, the notion

---

22 Wesley, "The Original, Nature, Properties, and Use of the Law," in *Works* 2, I.1.

23 Ibid.

24 In his *Earnest Appeal to Men of Reason and Religion*, Wesley establishes a dynamic relationship between cognition and appetite within his epistemological system. For Wesley, reason is a faculty of our intellectual and affective will that operates in a three-fold way: (1) apprehension, that is "barely conceiving a thing in the mind, the first and most simple act of understanding," (2) judgment, "the determining that the things before conceived either agree with or differ from each other," and (3) discourse, which is "the motion of progress of the mind from one judgment to another." Wesley, "The Case of Reason Impartially Considered," in *Works* 2, especially on page 590.

25 Wesley, "The Original, Nature, Properties, and Use of the Law," in *Works* 2, II.6, III.10; "The Law Established through Faith," in *Works* 2, III.5; and "On Working Out Our Own Salvation," in *Works* 3, III.4.

26 *DV*, q.16, a.1, co.

27 Ibid.

of conscience or *synderesis* has its origin from something divine, not entirely natural to man in their theology. Wesley thus often unfastens conscience from nature and ties it to prevenient grace.[28] As we have already confirmed in Chapter 2, his argument for conscience, however, pertains not only to prevenient grace, but also to the image of God. As a result, Wesley comes to correlating conscience to "a copy of the eternal mind" or "a transcript of the divine nature" inscribed in both our pre- and post-lapsarian natures.[29] Then he further complicates it into the natural image of God enduring in our souls, as a manifestation of our moral life and dignity, which is still preserved in man after the Fall.[30] Such a way of paralleling *synderesis* to the *imago Dei* is evident in Thomas as well. As we have already discussed in Chapter 4, Thomas regards *synderesis* in his *De Veritate* as a kind of enduring natural image of God. He then argues that if we make good use of this image, *bonum* will be done and *malum* can be avoided. Thomas's understanding of *synderesis* has nothing to do with atheistic humanism, but rather, it points to a theologically nuanced positive vision of human nature: Our moral life and dignity are still present (if not perfect) after the Fall and are not "taken even from the damned."[31] For these reasons, the correlation of Thomas' *synderesis* with Wesley's conscience seems to be evident, which then provides us with more evidence confirming that a strictly prohibitive and totally depraved tone of our natural abilities is hardly perceptible in Wesley's and Thomas' theology.

28 Wesley, "On Working Out Our Own Salvation," in *Works* 3, II.1 and III.4.
29 Wesley, "The Original, Nature, Properties, and Use of the Law," in *Works* 2, II.6 and III.10.
30 See fn. 72 in Chapter 2.
31 *DV*, q.16, a.3, ad.5.

Actual Sin and Original Sin as "Sin Remaining (*Fomes Peccati*)"

Another striking similarity between Wesley and Thomas stems from their deeper understanding of sin. Both avoid the strict Augustinian claim – that original sin is an act caused by inordinate desire, or some kind of active concupiscence, and that it is this positive (not privative) disorder that Adam conveys in the act of generation. As opposed to original sin, actual sin (or "outward sin"[32] in Wesley's terms), reasons Wesley, is *in actu*: It entails the concurrence of the will in the commission of sin.[33] Similarly, Thomas distinguishes actual sin from original sin: In Thomas the former stresses action, not mere inclination.[34] In addition, the former is the result of an act of willing *malum*, whereas the latter is a habit of inordinate disposition into which Adam was cast as a result of his actual sin.

With the idea of sin understood by this logic, Thomas now concludes that each individual can be praised or blamed for what he or she performs (actual sin), not for what he or she is born with (original sin).[35] The same conclusion is made in Wesley, specifically in his sermon "Salvation By Faith," as we so confirmed in Chapter 2: Since one's natural weakness (original sin) has no concurrence of his or her will, such deviations – whether in act, word, or thought – are not "properly" sins; in other words, our moral and personal responsibility does not come from Adam's guilt, but from actual sin, from the actualization of what comes from original sin by either habit, will, or desire.[36] Of particular note here, however, is not this mere

---

32   Wesley, "The Great Privilege of Those that are Born of God," in *Works* 1, II.2: "By sin, I here understand outward sin, according to the plain, common acceptation of the word; an actual, voluntary transgression of the law; of the revealed, written law of God; of any commandment of God, acknowledged to be such at the time that it is transgressed."

33   Wesley, "Christian Perfection," in *Works* 2, II.4, 7, 20. See also Wesley, "The Great Privilege of Those that are Born of God," in *Works* 1, II.7, 9.

34   *ST* I–II, q.71.5.

35   *SCG* 4, c.52.6.

36   Wesley, "Salvation By Faith," in *Works* 1, II.6.

distinction; rather, we should focus on their term for "original sin": the "sin remaining" for Wesley, and the *"fomes peccati"* for Thomas. Using this term, Wesley and Thomas draw a positive outlook on human nature, saying that no part or power of the soul was totally destroyed by sin, but preserved in terms of human dignity, authentic human autonomy, or moral responsibility. First with regard to the "sin remaining," Wesley speaks of it as an inward sin that lies deep within human nature. He then makes it explicitly refer to any sinful temper, passion, or affection – or, more precisely, to an abiding "desire" for sin which human nature has been plunged into by its fall from original righteousness.[37]

Insofar as the notion of "sin remaining" means an abiding inclination or desire for sin, one can possibly correlates it with a similar conception of original sin by Thomas: *fomes peccati*. The term *fomes peccati* derives from Peter Lombard's 2 *Sent.* 30.8(2): *"Originale peccatum dicitur fomes peccati, scilicet concupiscentia vel concupiscibilitas, quae dicitur lex membrorum, sive languor naturae, sive tyrannus qui est in membris nostris, sive lex carnis."* In *SCG* 4, Thomas uses this Lombardian term to overcome Augustine's biological model of original sin and move on to a discussion of actual sin.[38] His point here is the same as that of Wesley: Original sin does not exhaust our biological nature. The result of original sin is the absence of an extra gift bestowed out of God's generosity (original justice or "ancient perfection" in Wesley's peculiar term). As we have already seen, this privative model of original sin pertains to some kind of habitual (not ontological) damage in both Wesley and Thomas: Neither of them sees our human nature as fundamentally altered or totally destroyed after the Fall. It is this very fact that stands behind Wesley's "sin remaining" and Thomas' *"fomes peccati."* One can thus affirm considerable similarity in their understanding of original sin, which in turn gives us more evidence of the commonality of

---

37 Wesley, "Christian Perfection," in *Works* 2, II.21, 24; and "The Scripture Way of Salvation," in *Works* 2, I.4. Insofar as the notion of "sin remaining" points to an abiding inclination or desire for sin, one may recast it into Augustine's *desiderium peccati*. See Andrew J. Cheatle, *W. E. Sangster: Herald of Holiness – A Critical Analysis of the Doctrines of Sanctification and Perfection in the Thought of W.E. Sangster* (Eugene, OR: Wipf and Stock), 124.

38 *SCG* 4, c.52.16.

their optimistic vision for humanity: Human nature is mystery; it is not a closed entity but like a pole from a dialectical relation that communicates with another pole; in this communication it becomes true to itself by exceeding itself.

Grace in Wesley and Thomas

From Chapters 3 and 5 we have already begun to notice some of the dynamics of grace in Wesley and Thomas – for instance, the notion of divine initiative and human response, or grace as both operative and cooperative. In this small section, our focus is therefore on making this dynamic more evident by paralleling the teachings of grace unfolded in each theologian's work: the *Sermons* for Wesley, and the *ST I–II* for Thomas. This current work of paralleling these two theologians will then proceed by examining the following questions in turn: What is their primary concern for grace? How do they relate grace to nature? What does it mean for us to grow in grace? How does this relate to our good/virtuous acts? The answers to these questions will be made by retracement of what has been covered in the preceding chapters, which in turn will clarify the point of contact between Wesley and Thomas regarding the doctrine of grace.

Let us begin by discussing the subject – grace – in light of what Wesley and Thomas have claimed regarding grace. Having provided an abbreviated version of his *via salutis* (way of salvation), Wesley wrote:

> For, first, God works; therefore you can work. Secondly ... God worketh in you; therefore you must work: you must be "workers together with him" (they are the very words of the Apostle); otherwise he will cease working.[39]

In a mere 37 words, Wesley summed up what he believed about grace. God's initial grace is demonstrative of the divine initiative in salvation, and it stands as the cause of our response. Without it, our fallen nature

39   Wesley, "On Working Out Our Own Salvation," in *Works* 3, III.2, 7.

can neither will nor do what is pleasing to God. With it, however, we are able to work out our own salvation. It is important to note here that Wesley was not saying in the sermon that perseverance in grace (salvation) is automatically achieved by a singular infusion of God's prevenient grace. One's fall from grace is possible for Wesley; and our cooperative task is required if we are to sojourn along the way of salvation.

Like Wesley, Thomas argues for the absolute necessity of grace in salvation. He also believes that although human nature can perform good works even after the Fall,[40] God's initiating grace is absolutely necessary if man's actions are supernatural or oriented to God as by God. This is especially evident when he deals with the matter of salvation in the *Prima Secundae* of *Summa Theologiae*:

> Hence man, by his natural endowments, cannot produce meritorious works proportionate to everlasting life; and for this a higher force is needed, viz. the force of grace. And thus without grace man cannot merit everlasting life; yet he can perform works conducing to a good which is natural to man, as "to toil in the fields, to drink, to eat, or to have friends."[41]

A shift of emphasis arises, however, when Thomas considers the idea of grace as *auxilium*. In his treatise on grace (*ST* I–II. 109–14), Thomas notably emphasizes this idea, arguing that the question of salvation is not a unilateral verdict or predestination by the grace of God. As we have identified earlier in Chapter 5, it is rather a mystery to Thomas in which grace and nature work together cooperatively to compose a unity. In other words, Thomas acknowledges the primacy of a divine initiative in the matter of salvation, while providing a theological argument for how it works specifically in and with humans. The corollary of this argument is that God's grace does not move the human soul in a coercive manner. For Thomas, God cooperates with the human soul (now healed and elevated by what he calls *gratia habitualis*) as He works in us through His grace. What is at stake for Thomas' doctrine of grace thus implies a common concern that is also primary and theologically evident in Wesley's

---

40   *ST* I–II, q.109, a.2, co.
41   Ibid., q.109, a.5, co.

doctrine of grace: "The greater the presence of divine grace, the greater human freedom and response."

At the heart of this very concern for grace lies the dynamic relationship of grace to nature. Thomas' view of this dynamic is evident in *ST* I, q.1, a.8, ad.2, as we have seen in the previous chapter: "*Gratia non tollit naturam sed perficit*" (Grace does not remove nature, but perfects it).[42] He even says that grace presupposes nature, seeing it as a testament to the eternal value of human nature that constitutes the moral agency and dignity of our souls.[43] Perhaps one could further elaborate this sentiment in the words of Thomas Gilby, who well summarized in Thomas the relationship between grace and nature: "The supernatural [grace] does not derogate from the natural [nature], but witnesses to our human dignity, for if impotent of ourselves to scale the heights, our impulse is towards them. It is this nobility that grace takes, and makes capable of glory."[44]

Wesley gives a similar view on the relationship between grace and nature. As we confirmed earlier in Chapter 2, Wesley retains a softened version of the strict Calvinist anthropology that presupposes the total depravity of man. His idea of prevenient grace plays a crucial role in the formation of that distinctive anthropological vision. According to his sermon "On Working Out Our Own Salvation," prevenient grace does not cancel, or simply remain indifferent to, a certain dignity of humanity; it restores to our nature the ability to respond positively to God's grace, to God's work of salvation.

Of course, Wesley sometimes describes grace and nature as two opposing principles. An example comes from his sermon "Original Sin," III.5: "By nature ye are wholly corrupted," he declares, but "by grace ye shall be wholly renewed."[45] As can be seen from this short excerpt, there is clearly a wedge in Wesley between grace and nature. It is worth noting, however,

---

42   *ST* I, q.1, a.8, ad.2.

43   Ibid., q.2, a.2, ad.1: "for faith presupposes natural knowledge, [thus] grace presupposes nature, and perfection supposes something that can be perfected."

44   Thomas Gilby, "Appendix 8: Natural and Supernatural," in Thomas Gilby, ed., *Summa Theologiae, Vol.1: Christian Theology (Ia. 1)* (Cambridge: Blackfriars, 1964), 101.

45   Wesley, "Original Sin," in *Works*, III.5.

that the wedge is unlikely to overturn what was previously confirmed in Chapter 2 as we go through his vocabulary on sin – for example, guilt, power, outward, inward, habitual, commission (committing), infirmity, voluntary, involuntary, willful, and etc. Essential to this vocabulary was to surface a positive assessment of human will, which in turn helped the middle Wesley to understand man as a moral agent assisted by grace or as a graced partner of grace in the journey of salvation. Moreover, the idea of total depravity pertains to what he calls "the natural man," that is, to an ungraced person – yet, as Wesley claims, no such "natural man" can actually exist.[46] According to Wesley, the very notion of separating grace from nature needs to be carefully nuanced. On the one hand, such separation may be construed as reflecting the ontological difference between God and man, or the absolute necessity of grace for salvation (as Thomas so discussed in *ST* I–II. 109). On the other hand, it should give way to some kind of additional conditioning when interpreted in relation to the question of how grace *cooperatively* relates to nature. In other words, Wesley is unwilling to position himself on the Calvinistic position in which nature is left without any natural capacity for virtue and goodness. Rather, he would try to approximate the Thomistic axiom – *gratia non tollit naturam sed perficit* – as Wesley himself put it on the subject: Grace does not destroy, but empowers nature,[47] so when the soul receives grace it does not cancel "but balances the [intellect and] affections, which the God of nature never designed should be rooted out by grace, but only brought and kept under due regulations."[48]

Since grace does not destroy nature, but rather completes it, Wesley and Thomas are equally involved in the dynamics of grace. The result is a moral conception of grace; "growing in grace" is not only possible, but is required in our journey to God. A careful review of Wesley in Chapter 3 shows that this claim is implicit in his view of grace as operative and cooperative. For Wesley, grace itself is singular, but the effects of it are manifold. Wesley first divides grace into "preventing," "accompanying," "following," and

46 Kenneth J. Collins, *The Theology of John Wesley: Holy Love and the Shape of Grace* (Nashville, TN: Abingdon Press, 2007), 73–4.

47 Wesley, "The General Spread of the Gospel," in *Works* 2, §11.

48 Wesley, "Upon Our Lord's Sermon on the Mount, II," in *Works* 1, I.3.

"convincing." His focus is, however, mainly on the first of these four types of grace, and by this grace he says that God directly favors a person. Of particular note here is that Wesley regarded God's salvific work as a linear process culminating in perfection, not a judicial or forensic moment in time.[49] In other words, Wesley saw that God's work by prevenient grace occurs according to a historical context, "time." There is, of course, another important notion – "agency" – which we discussed earlier in relation to the "convincing" grace. Applying these two contexts thereto, Wesley's prevenient grace can thus be understood as follows: From the point of view of "time," prevenient grace precedes justification; but since it already begins to infuse in human nature the potency toward *bonum*, the prevenient grace is not essentially separate from "justifying" grace, but presupposes and dynamically aims to win it. From the point of view of "agency," prevenient grace does not move the soul operatively, but works cooperatively with it: The former does not destroy the latter, but it enlightens, strengthens, and invigorates its faculties and their intellectual and affective functioning. For these reasons, Wesley even says that "growing in grace" is not simply possible, but is required as a clear responsibility of those who are graced by God: "[No matter how much grace] any man has attained, or in how high a degree soever he is perfect, he hath still need to 'grow in grace.'"[50] From such a dynamic point of view, one could possibly rephrase that for Wesley grace entails a moral imperative to "work out our own salvation" in cooperation with God's graciously empowering work.

As he continues to expound on this theme, Wesley comes to speak as to what this synergistic cooperation in the life of grace will ultimately include:

> How exactly did Macarius, fourteen hundred years ago, describe the present experience of the children of God? "The unskillful," or unexperienced, "when grace operates, presently imagine they have no more sin. Whereas they that have discretion cannot deny, that even we who have the grace of God may be molested again ... For we have often had instances of some among the brethren, who have experienced such

49   In his sermon dated from 1760, "The New Birth," Wesley first distinguishes between justification and sanctification. He then defines salvation as "a progressive work carried on in the soul by slow degrees from the time of our first turning to God." Wesley, "The New Birth," in *Works* 2, IV.3.

50   Wesley, "On Working Out Our Own Salvation," in *Works* 3, I.9.

grace as to affirm that they had no sin in them; and yet, after all, when they thought themselves entirely freed from it, the corruption that lurked within was stirred up anew, and they were well-nigh burned up."[51]

It appears from this passage that Wesley frames his view of "growing in grace" (or what he would prefer to call "perfection") within the spiritual battle against the darkness of man's nature; in a similar way, the Pseudo-Macarius denotes his view of spiritual progress in terms of "thoughts against thoughts, mind against mind, soul against soul, spirit against spirit."[52] In this ongoing battle or inner struggle, Wesley is confident that those who cry unto the Lord will not only find in the heart the disclosure of the kingdom of God, but will also gain the three characteristics of "growing in grace" within the Holy Spirit: righteousness, joy, and peace.[53] But this act of seeking comfort and growth in God's grace must not fall into the conclusion that human endeavor ultimately is all in vain. In contrast, Wesley emphasizes that in response to the work of the Holy Spirit, a person must orient to the practice of virtues, such as the pure in heart, love for one's neighbors, victory over evil passions, and obedience to God's commands.[54] In the mid-1750s, Wesley discussed the matter in his sermon "Self-Denial." He taught here that if man does not continue to practice any virtue, including self-denial, the probability of a "shipwreck of the faith" will rise sharply, and that man will not reach perfection: "He is not, as once, hungering and thirsting after righteousness, panting after the whole image and full enjoyment of God, as the hart after the waterbrook. Rather he is weary and faint in his mind, and as it were hovering between life and death. And why is he thus, but because he hath forgotten the word of God, 'By works is faith made perfect'? He does not use all diligence in working the works of God."[55] For Wesley, a person is never totally depraved, and the nature of that person does not conflict with grace

---

51   Wesley, "The Scripture Way of Salvation," in *Works* 2, I.7.
52   Pseudo-Macarius, *The Fifty Spiritual Homilies and The Great Letter*, trans. George A. Maloney (New York, NY: Paulist Press, 1992), 200.
53   Wesley, "A Plain Account of Christian Perfection," in *Works* (Albany) 11, §25, especially on page 503.
54   Wesley, "The Marks of the New Birth," in *Works* 1, I.1–IV.5.
55   Wesley, "Self-Denial," in *Works* 2, II.6.

but is in a dynamic relationship with it. The person must therefore draw out a dynamically relational life of growing in grace and live according to divine virtues – for example, Christ-like humility, repentance, good works, and abandonment of self-will to God.[56]

Likewise, the growth of grace is important to Thomas, and its relevance to our good/virtuous works is as clear as it appears in Wesley's case. From previous chapters one may have already begun to notice this similarity, but to clarify that here we want to bring some relevant points from Chapter 5. First, Thomas links growth in grace (*augmentum gratiae*) to a moral understanding of grace. In other words, the notion relates to his view of grace: For Thomas, grace is one and simple in essence,[57] but it is distinguished as prevenient or subsequent according to a plurality of phenomena. The distinction here means that for Thomas, as in Wesley, grace is not merely passive, achieved once and for all, or static. Rather, it is active, enduring, and dynamic in the temporal framework of human life; it does not destroy nature, but cooperates with it to the extent that the soul is healed and elevated.

Of particular note regarding the parallels of Wesley and Thomas on "growing in grace" is, however, the *gratia habitualis*, a type of grace taken by Thomas as a *habitus* of the soul. Thomas' *gratia habitualis*, although

56   In his sermon dated from 1734, "The One Thing Needful," Wesley appeals to 2 Peter 1:4 and draws out a soteriological implication of participating in the divine nature; that one who becomes a partaker of the divine nature will be saved from all sin, whether sins of omission or commission. He then goes on to speak of an ethical counterpart of that soteriological implication: the conformity of the divine and human wills procured by the work of the Holy Spirit, in whom growth in grace is both possible and providential. Albert C. Outler's comments on this 1734 sermon are noteworthy. According to Outler, Wesley was heavily influenced by the Cambridge Platonists such as Malebranche, John Norris, and William Law. This influence enabled Wesley to elaborate in this sermon the Neoplatonic vision of the *imago Dei* – created, defaced, restored – as the dynamic essence of human nature. For Wesley's sermon "The One Thing Needful" with Outler's comments, see Albert C. Outler, *John Wesley's Sermons: An Anthology* (Nashville, TN: Abingdon Press, 1991), 33–8.

57   *ST* I–II, q.111, a.3, ad.2: "For subsequent grace, inasmuch as it pertains to glory, is not numerically distinct from prevenient grace whereby we are at present justified."

not lexically identifiable with Wesley's prevenient grace, retains a common meaning: Grace as habitual refers to a potency added to the soul, and this potency makes the person capable of, and inclined to, supernatural life or action. The potency, however, does not reduce itself to act, for it to be realized the person needs *gratia auxilium*.[58] Thomas then goes on to speak of the goal of God's gracious *habitus* in us. Since God's infusion of gracious *habitus* does not contradict our human nature, the *habitus* so infused in us, says Thomas, can be increased and strengthened by way of suitable actions, which means we can grow in grace.[59] In other words, grace may be present in individuals with different grades or intensities, even though the critical factor in *augmentum gratiae*, according to Thomas, is the gift of God.[60] This variety refers, of course, not to fundamental aspect of God's salvific plan for humanity, but rather to the grade or intensity with which this dynamic of grace is confided by God to each person and carried out by that person. In the case of *augmentum gratiae*, we can see thus that for Thomas human beings are not irredeemably enslaved (*servum arbitrium*). Through fellowship with God's empowering grace, they are enabled to embark on a progressive spiritual journey toward perfection, as well as to attain participation in the life and virtues of God. Accordingly, a life of grace always aims at continuation and growth, and it is God's *auxilium* that works with us to bring us to further growth in grace – unto eternal life.[61]

In exploring the idea of *augmentum gratiae*, Thomas emphasizes the moral, rather than the ontological dimension of our growing in grace. Thus,

---

58   The same goes for Wesley, especially for "convincing" grace: Since we are incapable of realizing what is infused into our souls, we need more grace, or, more precisely, "convincing grace," whereby God reduces us to gracious action. See Wesley, "On Working Out Our Own Salvation," in *Works* 3, II.1.

59   *ST* I–II, q.51, a.4, ad.2: "That God works in all according to their mode, does not hinder God from doing what nature cannot do: but it follows from this that He does nothing contrary to that which is suitable to nature." See also *ST* I–II, q.51, a.4, ad.3: "Acts produced by an infused habit, do not cause a habit, but strengthen the already existing habit; just as the remedies of medicine given to a man who is naturally health, do not cause a kind of health, but give new strength to the health he had before."

60   Ibid., q.112, a.4, co.

61   Ibid., q.114, a.8.

for Thomas the idea was not so much that one becomes divine in nature as that one is continuously at work in order to grow in virtues and overcome vices. In the last question of his treatise on grace, Thomas clearly articulates this ethical conception of *augmentum gratiae* that when in "grace upon grace," a person does not remain a passive agent but can merit a series of holy works: For instance, to repent of one's own grave sin or to merit condignly (and congruously) the increase of charity for oneself and others.[62] Growth in grace by means of doing good with God's *auxilium* is thus another point of convergence between Wesley and Thomas.

Regarding the idea of *augmentum gratiae*, we finally need to bring into conversation Wesley's and Thomas' teaching on merit. Wesley explains his idea of merit in terms of perfection, where one grows in love by grace. The idea comes first from the August 2, 1745 Conference Minutes. In these early Minutes, Wesley refuses to label the pious works of Cornelius (Acts 10) as "splendid sins," since they were not done antecedently, but posteriorly to – and in tandem with – the "grace of Christ."[63] He then carefully cracks a window open to the value of merits in the *ordo salutis*. One would probably find a similar sentiment in the Conference Minutes of 1770, where he says:

> We have received it as a maxim, that "a man is to do nothing in order to justification." Nothing can be more false. Whoever desire to find favor with God, should "cease from evil, and learn to do well." So God himself teaches by the Prophet Isaiah. Whoever repents, should "do works meet for repentance." And if this is not in order to find favor, what does he do them for.[64]

Of course, there is no doubt that Wesley has repudiated any strict concept of merit in salvation: "[T]here is no merit, taking the word strictly, but in the blood of Christ; that salvation is not by the merit of works; and that there is nothing we are, or have, or do, which can, strictly speaking, deserve the least thing at God's hand."[65] He argues, however, that merit can

---

62   Ibid., q.114, a.5.
63   Wesley, "Conversation 2" on August 2, 1745 in *Works* (Albany) 8, qq.1–25, especially on page 305.
64   Wesley, "Minutes of Several Conversations," in *Works* (Albany) 8, q.77, a.3, especially on page 374.
65   Wesley, "Of Merit," in *Works* (Albany) 10, IX, §33, especially on page 466.

be taken in both "proper" and "improper" senses, defining it in "a looser sense" as nearly equivalent to Thomas' merit *de congruo* (congruous):

> I do not mean that it [one's human work] merits or deserves a reward in the proper sense of the word. Instances of the word taken in [an] improper sense [however] occurs all over the Bible ... [So I] grant that ... [you may] take it in an improper [sense] as nearly equivalent with rewardable.[66]

Perhaps the doctrine of merit may sound quite paradoxical to many Wesleyans – mostly because of their fear of the notion of merit as Pelagian. Indeed, Stephen Gunter notes that Wesley's positive account of merit differs from that of Wesley's early sermons or publications. Gunter thus tends to dismiss Wesley's voice of merit: "[T]hese statements inclined more in the direction of moralism than anything Wesley had ever preached or published."[67] Kenneth Collins also expresses his negative attitude toward the doctrine of merit, saying that "[it is unfair] to read Wesley's soteriological thought through the interpretive lens of Trent.[68]

However, we should note that Wesley's primary context in dealing with the doctrine of merit is growth in grace (or perfection). Besides, Wesley himself made it clear in his 1765 sermon "The Lord Our Righteousness" that the language of *imputation* should relate only to justification, to forgiveness and acceptance, and not to sanctification itself.[69] He then implies in the same sermon that his understanding of merit takes into account a twofold purpose of this doctrine: First, the teaching of merit shows that God's grace does not place any and all goodness beyond the reach of human nature but invites us into the cooperative dynamic of grace working in us, for us, and with us. Second, the teaching reveals the moral dignity and increasing perfection of a graced person who merits in holy life. Thus, contrary to Gunter's and Collins' arguments against those two minutes of 1745 and 1770, Wesley shows that his understanding of merit constitutes

---

66   Ibid.
67   Stephen Gunter, *The Limits of Love Divine: John Wesley's Response to Antinomianism and Enthusiasm* (Nashville, TN: Abingdon Press, 1989), 252.
68   Kenneth Collins, *The Scripture Way of Salvation: The Heart of John Wesley's Theology* (Nashville, TN: Abingdon Press, 1997), 204.
69   Wesley, "The Lord Our Righteousness," in *Works* 1, II.20.

and confirms one of the most important aspects of grace: the *synergeia* between God and humanity.

Thomas also links his understanding of merit to the idea of "growing in grace." Since this is not the place to unfold the content of his doctrine of merit, we simply point out what Thomas carefully affirms in addressing the doctrine of merit: Man cannot merit salvation. Our human work cannot thus be regarded as merits in a proper sense[70]; it does so only in an improper sense (or, in Thomas' words, only in the sense of merit *de congruo*).[71] In other words, grace is a free gift from God for Thomas, just as it is for Wesley.[72] And since this gratuitous gift invites man as a moral agent to the *via salutis*, Thomas sees that man can merit a series of holy works in grace by grace (e.g., good work for the poor, seeking forgiveness in prayer, etc.). Thus, Thomas' teaching of merit seems to be very close to that of Wesley, which then provides us with more evidence confirming that both in Wesley's and in Thomas' theology, in virtue of grace, our attainment of "growing in grace" is made more perfect with merit than without it.

Grace, Nature, and the Holy Spirit in Wesley and Thomas

Wesley's and Thomas' way of linking grace with nature is pneumatological.[73] Although not giving a specific account of grace and nature, Kenneth M. Loyer examines these two theologians' understanding of grace and nature with a special focus on *pneumatology* in the broader context of the triune God's economy of salvation.[74] As Loyer well points

70   *ST* I–II, q.114, aa.3, 6, 7.
71   Ibid., q.114, a.6, co.
72   Wesley, "Free Grace," in *Works* 3, §14.
73   See fn. 119 in Chapter 3 and fn. 170 in Chapter 5 above.
74   Kenneth M. Loyer, *God's Love through the Spirit: The Holy Spirit in Thomas Aquinas and John Wesley* (Washington, DC: Catholic University Press of America, 2014), 197: "[I]t is now widely claimed that the problem of insufficient attention to the doctrine of the Holy Spirit has left a significant lacuna in modern Western theology, and even in Western theology as a whole. Indeed, allegations of a pneumatological

out, Thomas introduces his richly pneumatological soteriology in *ST* I–I, q.38, in which the Christian life as a whole is itself considered a gift of the Holy Spirit.[75] Human power on its own avails nothing for participation in God; rather the human being's participation in God must be freely given from above. The Christian life, therefore, is rightly identified as a gift, and indeed the gift of the Holy Spirit.[76] Even in his commentary on Romans 5:5, Thomas draws a very clear connection between the Holy spirit and the Christian life: "The Holy Spirit, who is the love of the Father and the Son, is given to us in order to bring us to participate in the love who is the Holy Spirit. By this participation we are made lovers of God."[77] As the two examples above suggest, the Spirit is the gift of the Father and the Son, the giver of life, and the cause of all holiness whose effects in creation and renewal bring about the Father's redemptive purposes in and with the Son. It can therefore be said that the Holy Spirit's gift to human beings of their participation in God is the theological context in which Thomas discusses grace and nature.

Looking at his conception of *caritas*, one can further discern the way in which Thomas views the relationship between grace and nature through a pneumatological lens. *Caritas* is essential for examining the subject of the Spirit's gift in the economy of salvation, and three features of it stand out in *ST* II–II, qq.23–4: First, what might be named its essence[78]; second, its effect[79]; and third, its object.[80] Regarding the first feature (essence), Thomas defines *caritas* in terms of friendship. It is, he says, a certain *amicitia* (friendship) between God and man.[81] Although this is a friendship between

---

deficiency afflicting modern Western theology are made on the same grounds of overly concentrated christological formulations that leave nothing to be attributed to the Spirit, and those sweeping criticisms of Western theology across the ages are often fueled by this precise worry that the tradition accounts for the acts of the triune God without giving the Spirit anything to do."

75 Ibid., 178.
76 *ST* I–I, q.38, a.1c.
77 *Epistolam ad Romanos*, 5, lect. 1, n. 392.
78 *ST* II–II, q.23, a.1c.
79 Ibid., q.24, a.2c.
80 Ibid., q.23, a.4 ad 2.
81 Ibid., q.23, a.1c.

un- or non-equals, it is nothing less than true friendship, established by God. Friendship is between friend and friend and requires a certain mutual love based on some kind of communication. Hence the love of *caritas*, as *amicitia*, presupposes "communication between God and man," a communication of "His happiness to us."[82] The Father communicates with us by calling us into the fellowship of His Son, through the power of the Holy Spirit (cf. 1 Cor 1:9).[83] The love which is based on this communication is *caritas*: Wherefore it is evident that *caritas* is our friendship with God, which is made possible by the way in which God has chosen to relate to us.[84]

Then, with respect to the second feature (effect), Thomas argues that *caritas* does not merely exceed human nature in a supernatural way, but is reserved in us as some habitual form "superadded to the natural power, inclining that power to the act of *caritas*, and causing it to act willingly and delightfully."[85] Or, as Loyer well quotes from Thomas' *De caritate*, the Holy Spirit "moves the human will to the act of love by providing the form and power whereby the human will is inclined to that to which the Holy Spirit moves it, so that the will tends to the act of love not in any coerced way but rather on its own free accord" (*De caritate*, a. 1c).[86] *Caritas* therefore unites us to God by means of the power of the indwelling Spirit, who makes possible and inclines us toward our voluntary act of love.

Finally, with respect to the third feature (object), Thomas explains the object of *caritas* in terms of the last end of human life, viz. everlasting happiness in God.[87] God is loved out of *caritas* for God's own sake. More precisely, *caritas* regards principally but "one aspect of lovableness, namely God's goodness, which is His substance, according to Psalm 105:1: 'Give glory to the Lord for He is good.'"[88] Every act of *caritas* is performed therefore in respect to God as the object of *caritas*. As these three features (essence, effect, object) show well, Thomas uses the concept of *caritas* to identify

---

82   Ibid.
83   Ibid.
84   Ibid.
85   Ibid., q.23, a.2c.
86   Loyer, *God's Love through the Spirit*, 150.
87   *ST* II–II, q.23, a.4 ad 2.
88   Ibid., q.23, a.5 ad 2.

the person and work of the Holy Spirit. But more important (for the purposes of this book) is that he identifies a close and profound relationship between God and man (or between grace and nature) through his pneumatological renderings of *caritas*. *Caritas* is "a matter of friendship with God that is established through the Spirit, union with the inimitable object and end of human life."[89] In an important sense, then, Thomas' account of *caritas* is an *ad extra* economy of the triune God's salvation that affirms the pnumatological nature of the indwelling bond of grace with the soul, or human nature.

The subject of *our participation in God's life through the Holy Spirit* is also prominent in Wesley's writings. In his sermon "The New Birth," for example, Wesley explains his understanding of the spiritual senses and how they enable Christians to participate in God. Spiritually reborn to new life in Christ, the person "feels, is inwardly sensible of, the graces which the Spirit of God works in his heart."[90] As a result, the person's spiritual senses are augmented so as to discern the power and presence of the indwelling Spirit. Through the use of these senses, it is possible for the spiritually newborn person, eye now opened and heart full of love, to increase daily in the knowledge of God and to grow in grace through a sharing in God's own life. Wesley equates this state of being with true and abundant life, for now may this person

> properly be said to live: God having quickened him by his Spirit [cf. 1 Pt 3:18], he is alive to God through Jesus Christ [Rom 6:11]. He lives a life which the world knows not of, a "life" which "is hidden with Christ in God" [Col 3:3]. God is continually breathing, as it were, upon his soul, and his soul is breathing unto God. Grace is descending into his heart, and prayer and praise ascending to heaven. And by this intercourse between God and man, this fellowship with the Father and the Son [1 Jn 1:3], as by a kind of spiritual respiration, the life of God in the soul is sustained: and the child of God grows up, till he comes to "the full measure of the stature of Christ" [Eph 4:13].[91]

89   Loyer, *God's Love through the Spirit*, 151.
90   Wesley, "The New Birth," in *Works* 2, II.4.
91   Ibid.

As can be seen from the passage above, the theme of communication with God is as emphasized in Wesley as it is in Thomas. But this time it was couched in terms of a spiritual sensorium that sustains the life of God in the soul all the way to the point of maturity in Christ through the Spirit. Through the grace of the Holy Spirit indwelling in the hearts of Christian believers, they come into fellowship with the triune God. Awakened to God by virtue of the Spirit's influence on and through the spiritual senses, the human soul is thereby drawn evermore deeply into God's triune life of communion (or, in Thomas' terms, the friendship with God that *caritas* is).

Wesley was also interested in using the term *love* to describe the sanctification of our hearts and lives in and by the Holy Spirit.[92] But above all else, it is when Wesley develops his own terms for grace, especially prevenient grace, when the dynamic relationship of grace, nature, and the Holy Spirit comes into prominence. As discussed earlier in Chapter 2, Wesley argues that the fallen human being has lost the image of God. While this loss does not imply total depravity as the Calvinists claim, it is nothing less than a privation of divine influence. But Wesley ties the motif of loss in the fallen nature with the divine presence. Strictly speaking, for Wesley, the image of God after the Fall is the indwelling of the Holy Spirit, interpreted in terms of prevenient grace. This pneumatological rendering of *imago Dei* provides Wesley with a moral theological tool for solving the problem of moral agency. But on the other hand, it unearths a place for the Holy Spirit in Wesley's soteriology, enabling pneumatological support for the claim that God and humanity (or grace and nature) ever work together in the process of salvation.

All of the above examples demonstrate that Wesley presupposes and affirms the Holy Spirit as the indwelling cause of all love and holiness in those who believe (or, to borrow Thomas' term, the *vinculum amoris*

92   Wesley's understanding of love has a theologically characteristic focus and finds practical expression in the life of faith. It deals specifically with the twofold love of which Christ himself speaks, love of God and neighbor (Mt 22:36–40). According to Wesley, perfection in love is not a static state or isolated momentary event but rather an active, dynamic holiness of heart since it can only be made possible by the gift of God's love continually filling the heart through the Spirit.

between God and the believer).[93] It is the Holy Spirit who makes union and communion with God possible in the Christian life and heart. Through the sanctifying power of the indwelling Spirit, the Christian comes by grace to know and love God, to the end that the Christian life expresses something of God's own love and holiness. This pneumatological dimension of soteriology finds its most beautiful expression in a hymn on Pentecost, published by Wesley with his brother Charles:

> Granted is the Saviour's prayer,
>
> Sent the gracious Comforter;
>
> Promise of our parting Lord,
>
> Jesus to his heav'n restored.

> Christ, who now gone up on high
>
> Captive leads captivity,
>
> While his foes from him receive
>
> Grace, that God with man may live.

> God, the everlasting God,
>
> Makes with mortals His abode;
>
> Whom the heavens cannot contain,
>
> He vouchsafes to dwell in man.

> Never will he thence depart,
>
> Inmate of an humble heart;
>
> Carrying on his work within,
>
> Striving till he cast out sin.

> There he helps our feeble moans,
>
> Deepens our imperfect groans;

---

93   *ST* I–I, q.37, a.1.

Intercedes in silence there,

Sighs th' unutterable prayer.

Come, divine and peaceful guest,

Enter our devoted breast;

Holy Ghost, our hearts inspire,

Kindle there the gospel-fire.

Crown the agonizing strife,

Principle, and Lord of life;

Life divine in us renew,

Thou the gift and giver too!

Now descend and shake the earth,

Wake us into second birth;

Now thy quick'ning influence give,

Blow – and these dry bones shall live!

Brood thou o'er our nature's night,

Darkness kindles into light;

Spread thy over-shadowing wings,

Order from confusion springs.

Pain and sin, and sorrow cease,

Thee we taste, and all is peace;

Joy divine in thee we prove,

Light of truth, and fire of love.[94]

---

94   John Wesley and Charles Wesley, *Hymns and Sacred Poems* (London: William
     Strahan, 1739), "Hymn for Whitsunday," 213–4.

For Wesley, the Holy Spirit is the Third Person of the Triune God who fulfills Christ's promise of a Comforter or Advocate who will establish and confirm his followers in God's life (cf. Jn 14:15–31). In this mystery of grace, the Holy Spirit comes to dwell in the human heart and caresses the night of our nature, causing darkness to pass away and light to come, and chaos to recede and order to spring up.

Even with their own nuances and expressions, Thomas and Wesley are therefore compatible in that they see the life of grace through a pneumatological lens. Thomas links the Holy Spirit and the Christian life with a participatory motif. In particular, by establishing a relationship between God and believers, characterized by *caritas*, with the Spirit who makes us friends of God and guides us to live as such, he stresses a soteriology that pneumatologically underpins the communion of grace and nature. Wesley, for his part, emphasizes the importance of an experiential knowledge of God through the spiritual senses and attributes to the Holy Spirit the renewal of the *imago Dei* in believers as manifested in love for God and neighbor even unto perfection. In each case, the gift of the Holy Spirit, which unites grace with nature, is of great importance, as seen in the previous quotations from Thomas' *Emitte Spiritum* and Wesley's hymn on Pentecost. Yes, the Spirit is the one who ties God and humanity here, thus implying a certain connection between grace and nature, but this connection need not lead to an overshadowing of the Trinity by the Spirit since in God the three we speak of are also one. For both Thomas and Wesley, the Holy Spirit indwells human persons, restoring them to the image of God and uniting their human nature with grace to a point of participation and communion with the Holy Trinity.

Conclusion

Wesley's and Thomas' doctrines of grace and nature are not altogether identical. A side-by-side review of these doctrines has shown, however, a strong compatibility between Wesley and Thomas. To recap, Wesley and Thomas describe the doctrine of nature in a very similar sense. Before the

Fall, Adam possessed a supernatural order of nature – original justice – pre-established by God and common to all humans, but his tragedy is that after the Fall he was deprived of this order. Original sin is thus a loss – or a disease resulting from such absence – which limits, but does not totally destroy, the image of God in human nature. Original sin is simply a dis-order that limits freedom and conscience (Wesley) – *liberum arbitrium* and *synderesis* (Thomas) – by rendering the natural capacity of humanity play at variance with its prelapsarian order. This conception of sin has led to a reasonably optimistic model of human nature that gives value to the moral life and dignity of our souls – not to an ontological model that re-gards sin as constitutive of our biological nature (or genetic make-up) and the image of God in us as radically altered or totally destroyed.

Wesley and Thomas express the dynamics of grace in an analogous way, but each resorts to a distinctive armory of terms and concepts: the "prevenient (with the efficacy of justifying grace)," "accompanying," "con-vincing," and "following" grace for Wesley, and the "operative habitual," "cooperative habitual," "operative actual," and "cooperative actual" grace for Thomas. Wesley exhibits an anti-Calvinist concern in maintaining an active and participatory role of the will alongside the efficacy of grace; he draws a sharp distinction between grace and nature, but also emphasizes grace's cooperative role in perfecting human nature. For his part, Thomas famously claims that *gratia non tollit naturam sed perficit*. Finally, both theologians stress the ethical dimension of grace, as a reality that elicits and empowers our true human response, rather than unilaterally effecting and determining its free and conscientious functioning. In other words, grace undergirds not only our *being* and *acting*, but also our *becoming* and *growing*. We can thus conclude that for both Wesley and Thomas the orders of grace and nature are dynamically (or more precisely, pneumatologically) interrelated, and are not merely juxtaposed or opposed to each other.

Conclusion

As a Wesleyan pastor, I sympathize with the ecumenical vision that John Wesley demonstrates in his sermons "Catholic Spirit (1771)" and "On Zeal (1781)," and I also respect its intrinsic significance by teaching my local congregation the richness of our shared patrimony with Catholics in faith, mission, and sacramental life. This genuine affection for ecumenism in my pastoral vocation has been inspired by the 53 years of ongoing bilateral dialogue between Wesleyans and Catholics.[1]

If one reviews a total of ten joint Methodist-Catholic reports that have sought a number of bilateral exchanges over the past 53 years with a view to deepening the ecumenical unity and communion between Wesleyans and Catholics, one will see the lack of a thorough, meaningful study of grace and nature between Wesleyan and Catholic traditions.[2] The relationship

1   In 2010, the Joint International Commission for Dialogue between the World Methodist Council (WMC) and the Roman Catholic Church synthesized the work done up to that point. The synthesis begins with a recognition of the ongoing WMC-Catholic dialogue's goals and challenges: "From the beginning of the dialogue, without any glossing over of difficulties, members of the Joint Commission have increasingly discovered the richness of the certain, though sadly as yet imperfect, communion that Methodists and Catholics already share. The ultimate goal of our dialogue is full ecclesial communion – 'full communion in faith, mission and sacramental life.' As we move in that direction, we acknowledge the vital elements in the partial communion we already enjoy, while also recognizing the remaining differences on which further work needs to be done." A way forward emerged in 2016, when the joint commission suggested future engagement based on mutually recognizing each tradition's theology of grace. My book organically adopts this suggestion by providing a rich buttress for continued ecumenical exchange: an extended theological comparison of the theology of grace and nature in Wesleyan and Catholic traditions. The phrase in quotation marks comes from *Synthesis: Together in Holiness – 40 Years of Methodist and Roman Catholic Dialogue* (Lake Junaluska, NC: The World Methodist Council, 2010), §3.

2   The ecumenical dialogue between Wesleyans and Catholics took place in 1967 after World War II. The ecumenical dialogue, which marks its 53rd anniversary in

between grace and nature, however, is a crucial issue that serves as organizing principle for the totality of Christian theology – especially anthropology and soteriology. For instance, it addresses the axial problem underlying God's reality and human's reality and covers its *theo*-logical and *anthropo*-logical *loci*: for example, the mystery of being human, the fall and its effect upon humankind and creation, the grace of God in Jesus Christ, the grace of God through the Holy Spirit, the fullness of the Christian life in love and holiness, the grace of God and the merit of good works, and etc.

But in the past 53 years of ongoing bilateral dialogue between Wesleyans and Catholics, Wesleyan theologians have not given much attention to the relationship between grace and nature.[3] Although many of them still pay lip-service to the Wesleyan notion of prevenient grace, which is often used to distinguish Methodism from Calvinism within a larger body of Protestantism, the rhetoric, language, and symbols of grace and nature and the theological jargons, technical terms, and practical experiences that beget them are alien to many Wesleyans.[4]

2020 this year, has set up a joint agenda every five years and conducted a series of comparative studies on it. The cumulative effect of this study is to document a set of differentiated convergences drawn by both parties on the agenda in the form of a report. The full text of these reports can be seen and downloaded from the following link: <https://worldmethodistcouncil.org/resources/ecumenical-dialogues/>.

3   For the past 53 years, the WMC-Catholic dialogue has documented a total of ten reports: (1) Denver Report (1971); (2) Dublin Report (1976); (3) Honolulu Report (1981); (4) Nairobi Report (1986); (5) Singapore Report (1991); (6) Rio Report (1996); (7) Brighton Report (2001); (8) Seoul Report (2006); (9) Durban Report (2011); and (10) Houston Report (2016). Briefly speaking, the first two reports list preliminary studies needed to register broad agreement on a range of topics. Succeeding reports have addressed core Christian doctrines, ecclesial issues of episcopal/pastoral order and authority, and the different ways in which Methodists and Catholics actually teach and hand on the apostolic tradition. Unfortunately, none of these reports have led to an in-depth involvement in the theology of grace and nature. For a brief summary of these reports showing the lack of such involvement, William J. Abraham and James E. Kirby, eds., *The Oxford Handbook of Methodist Studies* (Oxford: Oxford University Press, 2009), 455–6.

4   See W. Brian Shelton, *Prevenient Grace: God's Provision for Fallen Humanity* (Anderson, IN: Francis Asbury, 2014). "Prevenient Grace," Jeff Paton, "n.d.," accessed April 21, 2020, <http://www.eternalsecurity.us/prevenient_grace.htm>.

The same is perhaps true of Catholics after the Second Vatican Council. The post-Vatican II Catholics do not find themselves to talk about this problem easy – and very often. There was, of course, a time when Catholics were present and active in discussing the relationship between grace and nature. For example, many debates which mark the ground for theological inquiry in the counterreformation era – especially from the time of Michael Baius (whose teaching was condemned in 1567) to the time of Cornelius Jansen (whose teaching was condemned in 1653) – are ultimately debates about grace and nature.[5] Most of the debates that mark twentieth-century Catholic theology are also those of grace and nature taken up again by *nouvelle théologie* (French for "new theology"). However, this resurgence did not last long in its early glory. More specifically, as the Second Vatican Council allegedly validated the *sententia communis* of *nouvelle théologie* in *Gaudium et Spes*, without adequately addressing the concerns of its redoubtable opponents, the resurgence turned into a state of theological indifference.[6] Wesleyan theologians have been equally silent, except that

See also "Prevenient Grace," Pastor D. L. Hartman, "n.d.," accessed April 21, 2020, <http://www.imarc.cc/pregrace/hartpg.html>.

5   Michael Baius's view of grace and nature is very similar to that of Cornelius Jansen. Both stressed the total depravity of fallen human nature and thus the absolute necessity and exigency of grace. From their point of view, our voluntary volition has nothing to do with our human cooperation in and with divine grace. It simply refers to what we can achieve by exercising no resistance to grace. In short, Christian salvation and liberation have nothing to do with human free will. For a concise, yet more detailed explanation of Baius' and Jansen's doctrine of grace and nature, see Paul O'Callaghan, *Children of God in the World: An Introduction to Theological Anthropology* (Washington, DC: Catholic University of America Press, 2016), 205–10.

6   In its Pastoral Constitution on the Church in the Modern World, Vatican II solemnly taught: "For, since Christ died for all men, and since the ultimate vocation of man is in fact one, and that divine, we ought to believe that the Holy Spirit, in a manner known only to God, offers to every man the possibility of being associated with this paschal mystery." *Gaudium et Spes* §22, cited from *The Documents of Vatican II*, ed. Walter M. Abbott, S.J. (New York: America House Press, 1966), 221–2. See also Stephen J. Duffy, *The Graced Horizon: Nature and Grace in Modern Catholic Thought* (Collegeville, MN: Michael Glazier/Liturgical, 1992), 49; and Edward T. Oakes, S.J. "Scheeben the Reconciler: Resolving the Nature-Grace Debate," *Nova et Vetera* (English Edition) 11, no. 2: 435–53, 440–1.

they have recently produced in collaboration with Catholics a preliminary report – *The Call to Holiness: From Glory to Glory* (2016) – registering their broad agreements and divergent points with Catholics on matters of grace and nature.

Christian churches must once more address the problem of grace and nature. They must rather develop and transform it into the subject of a rigorous and thorough theological inquiry that enables deeper fellowship, visible unity, and profound dialogue between them.

Thus, in response, I conducted a comparative study of John Wesley's and Thomas Aquinas' theology of grace and nature. By way of comparison, I note the following in this book: (1) Both hold that original sin is a loss – or a disease resulting from such absence – which limits, not totally destroys, the image of God in human nature; (2) both see the twofold capacity of nature – freedom and conscience (Wesley) and *liberum arbitrium* and *synderesis* (Thomas) – as an extension of the integrity of the *imago Dei*; (3) both distinguish between original sin and actual sin – "sin remaining" and "sin reigning" (Wesley) and *fomes peccati* and *peccatum* (Thomas) – to ensure that their portrait of our post-lapsarian nature accommodates human agency and moral responsibility; (4) both attempt to maintain the efficacy of grace alongside the God-imaged liberty of human nature; (5) both believe that human nature can perform utilitarian goods even after the Fall, but they argue for the absolute necessity of grace in salvation; (6) both claim that grace does not destroy nature but enlightens, strengthens, and invigorates its faculties and their intellectual and affective functioning; and (7) both affirm that our life of grace always aims at continuation and growth, and it is God's *auxilium* that works with us to bring us to further growth in grace – unto eternal life.

These results are valuable for several reasons: (1) My work has shown the commensurability of the theologies of Wesley and Thomas in the areas I have chosen. Wesley and Thomas are not speaking entirely different languages and their concerns and conclusions are often remarkably similar; (2) my comparison of Wesley and Thomas has cast in high relief the lack of a thorough, meaningful study of grace and nature between Wesleyans and Catholics – and Wesley and Thomas in particular; and (3) my demonstration that Wesley's vocabulary on the cooperative relationship between grace and nature corresponds to that of Thomas may not only give a fresh impetus to the resurgence, and the rethinking, of the grace-nature debate among Wesleyans and Catholics alike but also serve to make their 53-year ecumenical dialogue more conducive to moving forward with a further realistic and ecumenical vision of grace and nature.

My parallel reading of Wesley and Thomas has established a whole array of theological continuities between their theologies of grace and nature, and this leads us to the historical fact that the soteriological problem of grace and nature is the only problem that Wesleyans and Catholics have gone into their separate ways with little sharing of a common problem, criteria of judgment, or glossary of technical terms and abbreviations. Although a great many of the mysteries of the Christian faith that I deliberately excluded from my work remain unresolved in this book, I have yielded an abundance of surprising commonalities between Wesley and Thomas, and this may well provide a clue to solving that "only" problem between Wesleyans and Catholics.

My findings may be subject to further inquiry or criticism, and the entire content of this book can be viewed as quite conventional and explanatory rather than constructive and experimental. However, as my work maps out those findings in a dialogical mode, it shows that Wesleyans and Catholics can reach a mutual agreement on the supernatural nature of grace and humanity's ability to respond to it. Moreover, my deeper engagements with Wesley and Thomas can help the diverse bodies of both churches to overcome outdated views of each other – and give clarity to the Wesleyan and Catholic grace-nature conceptions. Both Wesleyans and Catholics may, therefore, benefit from this book to see farther, embrace more, and exchange deeper of what is paralleled in tension, or what is tensioned in parallelism, within the inter-relationship between Wesley and Thomas.

Hopefully, my comparative study can contribute to the rich body of Christian theology as an academic resource for understanding and developing the complex and subtle theological relationships between Methodism and Catholicism.

Bibliography

Primary Sources

Augustine of Hippo

Augustine. *Against Julian*. Translated by Matthew A. Schuhmacher. Washington, DC: The Catholic University of America Press, 2004.

____. *Saint Augustine: The Retractations*. Translated by Sister Mary Inez Bogan, Fathers of the Church 60. Washington, DC: Catholic University of America Press, 1968.

____. *Contra Faustum* (Reply to Faustus the Manichaean), *Nicene and Post-Nicene Fathers*, Series 1. Edited by Philip Schaff. Grand Rapids, MI: Christian Classics Ethereal Library, 2001; available online at the Christian Classics Ethereal Library <https://ccel.org/fathers>.

____. *Confessiones* (Confessions), *Nicene and Post-Nicene Fathers*, Series 1. Edited by Philip Schaff. Grand Rapids, MI: Christian Classics Ethereal Library, 2001; available online at the Christian Classics Ethereal Library <https://ccel.org/fathers>.

____. *Contra litteras Petiliani* (Answer to the Letters of Petilian, Bishop of Cirta), *Nicene and Post-Nicene Fathers*, Series 1. Edited by Philip Schaff. Grand Rapids, MI: Christian Classics Ethereal Library, 2001; available online at the Christian Classics Ethereal Library <https://ccel.org/fathers>.

____. *Contra mendacium* (Against Lying), *Nicene and Post-Nicene Fathers*, Series 1. Edited by Philip Schaff. Grand Rapids, MI: Christian Classics Ethereal Library, 2001; available online at the Christian Classics Ethereal Library <https://ccel.org/fathers>.

____. *De correptione et gratia* (On Rebuke and Grace), *Nicene and Post-Nicene Fathers*, Series 1. Edited by Philip Schaff. Grand Rapids, MI: Christian Classics Ethereal Library, 2001; available online at the Christian Classics Ethereal Library <https://ccel.org/fathers>.

_____. *De dono perseverantiae* (On the Gift of Perseverance), *Nicene and Post-Nicene Fathers*, Series 1. Edited by Philip Schaff. Grand Rapids, MI: Christian Classics Ethereal Library, 2001; available online at the Christian Classics Ethereal Library <https://ccel.org/fathers>.

_____. *De gestis Pelagii* (On the Proceedings of Pelagius), *Nicene and Post-Nicene Fathers*, Series 1. Edited by Philip Schaff. Grand Rapids, MI: Christian Classics Ethereal Library, 2001; available online at the Christian Classics Ethereal Library <https://ccel.org/fathers>.

_____. *De gratia et libero arbitrio* (On Grace and Free Will), *Nicene and Post-Nicene Fathers*, Series 1. Edited by Philip Schaff. Grand Rapids, MI: Christian Classics Ethereal Library, 2001; available online at the Christian Classics Ethereal Library <https://ccel.org/fathers>.

_____. *De libero arbitrio* (On Free Choice of The Will), *Nicene and Post-Nicene Fathers*, Series 1. Edited by Philip Schaff. Grand Rapids, MI: Christian Classics Ethereal Library, 2001; available online at the Christian Classics Ethereal Library <https://ccel.org/fathers>.

_____. *De natura et gratia* (On Nature and Grace), *Nicene and Post-Nicene Fathers*, Series 1. Edited by Philip Schaff. Grand Rapids, MI: Christian Classics Ethereal Library, 2001; available online at the Christian Classics Ethereal Library <https://ccel.org/fathers>.

_____. *De peccatorum meritis et remissione et de baptismo parvulorum* (On Merits and Remission of Sin, and Infant Baptism), *Nicene and Post-Nicene Fathers*, Series 1. Edited by Philip Schaff. Grand Rapids, MI: Christian Classics Ethereal Library, 2001; available online at the Christian Classics Ethereal Library <https://ccel.org/fathers>.

_____. *De perfectione iustitiae hominis* (On Man's Perfection in Righteousness), *Nicene and Post-Nicene Fathers*, Series 1. Edited by Philip Schaff. Grand Rapids, MI: Christian Classics Ethereal Library, 2001; available online at the Christian Classics Ethereal Library <https://ccel.org/fathers>.

_____. *De praedestinatione sanctorum* (On the Predestination of the Saints), *Nicene and Post-Nicene Fathers*, Series 1. Edited by Philip Schaff. Grand Rapids, MI: Christian Classics Ethereal Library, 2001; available online at the Christian Classics Ethereal Library <https://ccel.org/fathers>.

_____. *De spiritu et littera* (On the Spirit and the Letter), *Nicene and Post-Nicene Fathers*, Series 1. Edited by Philip Schaff. Grand Rapids, MI: Christian Classics Ethereal Library, 2001; available online at the Christian Classics Ethereal Library <https://ccel.org/fathers>.

_____. *De symbolo ad catechumenos* (On the Creed: A Sermon to Catechumens), *Nicene and Post-Nicene Fathers*, Series 1. Edited by Philip Schaff. Grand Rapids,

MI: Christian Classics Ethereal Library, 2001; available online at the Christian Classics Ethereal Library <https://ccel.org/fathers>.

____. *Enchiridion* (Enchiridion)*, Nicene and Post-Nicene Fathers,* Series 1. Edited by Philip Schaff. Grand Rapids, MI: Christian Classics Ethereal Library, 2001; available online at the Christian Classics Ethereal Library <https://ccel.org/fathers>.

John Wesley

Wesley, John. *The Bicentennial Edition of the Works of John Wesley*. Edited by Frank Baker, Richard P. Heitzenrater, and Randy L. Maddox. 35 vols. Nashville, TN: Abingdon Press, 1984–. [N.B.: Volumes 7, 11, 25, and 26 were first published as *The Oxford Edition of The Works of John Wesley*. Oxford: Oxford University Press, 1975–83.]

____. *Explanatory Notes Upon the New Testament*. 3rd edn. 2 vols. Bristol, UK: Graham & Pine, 1760–2. [Reprinted multiple times.]

____. *Explanatory Notes on the Old Testament*. 3 vols. Bristol, UK: Pine, 1765.

____. *John Wesley*. Edited by Albert C. Outler. New York: Oxford University Press, 1964.

____. *John Wesley: Containing Tracts and Letters on Various Subjects*. 10 vols. New York: J. & J. Harper Press, 1827.

____. *The Letters of the Rev. John Wesley, A.M.* Edited by John Telford. 8 vols. London: Epworth Press, 1931.

____. *The Sunday Service of the Methodists in North America*. London: Stranhan, 1784; reprint ed., Nashville, TN: United Methodist Publishing House, 1992.

____. *The Works of John Wesley*. 3rd edn. 14 vols. Albany, OR: Ages Software, 1997.

____. *The Works of the Rev. John Wesley, A.M.* 3rd edn. Edited by Thomas Jackson. 14 vols. London: J. Mason, 1829–31.

____. *The Works of John Wesley*, vol. 3. Edited by Albert C. Outler. Nashville, TN: Abingdon Press, 1984.

____. *The Works of John Wesley*, vol. 9. Edited by Rupert E. Davies. Nashville, TN: Abingdon Press, 1989.

____. *The Works of John Wesley*, vol. 11. Edited by Gerald B. Cragg. Nashville, TN: Abingdon Press, 1987.

Wesley, John and Charles Wesley. *Hymns and Sacred Poems*. London: William Strahan, 1739.

Thomas Aquinas

Thomas Aquinas. *Disputed Questions on Evil [De Malo].* Edited by Brian Davies. Translated by Richard Regan. Oxford: Oxford University Press, 2003.

_____. *Disputed Questions on Truth* [De Veritate]. 3 vols. Translated by Robert W. Mulligan (vol. 1), James V. McGlynn (vol. 2), and Robert W. Schmidt (vol. 3). Chicago: Henry Regnery Company, 1952–4.

_____. *Emitte Spiritum.* Translated by Jeremy Holmes and Peter Kwasniewski. *Faith and Reason* 30, nos. 1–2 (2005): 108–39.

_____. *Scriptum Super Sententiis: An Index of Authorities Cited.* Edited by Charles H. Lohr. Avebury, NY: Fordham University Press, 1980.

_____. *Summa Theologiae.* 5 vols. Translated by the Fathers of the English Dominican Province. New York: Benziger Brothers, 1947.

_____. *Summa Contra Gentiles.* 5 vols. Edited and translated by Anton C. Pegis (vol. 1), James F. Anderson (vol. 2), Vernon J. Bourke (vols. 3–4), and Charles J. O'Neil (vol. 5). Garden City, NY: Image Books, 1955–7.

Secondary Sources

Abbott, Walter M., S.J. ed. *The Documents of Vatican II.* New York: America House Press, 1966.

Abraham, William J. *Wesley for Armchair Theologians.* Louisville: Westminster John Knox, 2005.

Abraham, William J. and James E. Kirby. eds. *The Oxford Handbook of Methodist Studies.* Oxford: Oxford University Press, 2009.

Anderson, Justin M. *Virtue and Grace in the Theology of Thomas Aquinas.* Cambridge: Cambridge University Press, 2020.

Arminius, James. *The Works of James Arminius, Volume 2.* Translated by James Nichols. Auburn, NY: Derby & Miller, 1853.

Berkhof, Louis. *Systematic Theology.* Grand Rapids, MI: Eerdman's Publishing, 1996.

Blankenhorn, Bernhard. *The Mystery of Union with God. Dionysian Mysticism in Albert the Great and Thomas Aquinas.* Washington, DC: Catholic University of America Press, 2015.

Bobrinskoy, Boris. "The Adamic Heritage According to Fr John Meyendorff." *St Vladimir's Theological Quarterly* 42, no. 1 (1998): 33–44.

Bray, Gerald. *Documents of the English Reformation, 1526–1701.* Cambridge: James Clarke, 2004.

Brown, Peter. *Augustine of Hippo: A Biography.* Berkeley: University of California Press, 2000.

Bullen, Donald A. *A Man of One Book? John Wesley's Interpretation and Use of the Bible.* Eugene, OR: Wipf & Stock, 2007.

Burns, J. Patout. *The Development of Augustine's Doctrine of Operative Grace.* Paris: Études Augustiniennes, 1980.

Calvin, John. *The Institution of the Christian Religion: The Four Books – Complete and Unabridged.* Translated by Thomas Norton. San Bernardino, CA: Createspace Independent Publishing Platform, 2017.

Cannon, William Ragsdale. *The Theology of John Wesley: With Special Reference to the Doctrine of Justification.* New York: Abingdon-Cokesbury Press, 1946.

Castelo, Daniel. *Embodying Wesley's Catholic Spirit.* Eugene, OR: Pickwick, 2017.

Chapman, Mark. *Anglican Theology.* London: T&T Clark International, 2012.

Cheatle, Andrew J. *W. E. Sangster: Herald of Holiness—A Critical Analysis of the Doctrines of Sanctification and Perfection in the Thought of W.E. Sangster.* Eugene, OR: Wipf and Stock.

Chenu, M.-D., O.P. *Toward Understanding Saint Thomas.* Chicago: Henry Regnery Co., 1963.

Colberg, Shawn M. "Aquinas and the Grace of *Auxilium.*" *Modern Theology* 32, no. 2 (2016): 187–210.

Collins, Kenneth J. *John Wesley: A Theological Journey.* Nashville, TN: Abingdon Press, 2003.

____. *The Scripture Way of Salvation: The Heart of John Wesley's Theology.* Nashville, TN: Abingdon Press, 2010.

____. *The Theology of John Wesley: Holy Love and the Shape of Grace.* Nashville, TN: Abingdon Press, 2007.

Colón-Emeric, Edgardo. *Wesley, Aquinas, and Christian Perfection: An Ecumenical Dialogue.* Waco, TX: Baylor University Press, 2009.

Coppedge, Allan. *Shaping the Wesleyan Message: John Wesley in Theological Debate.* Nappanee, IN: Francis Asbury Press of Evangel Publishing House, 2003.

Couenhoven, Jesse. *Stricken by Sin, Cured by Christ: Agency, Necessity, and Culpability in Augustinian Theology.* New York: Oxford University Press, 2013.

Cox, Leo G. "Prevenient Grace – A Wesleyan View." *Journal of the Evangelical Theological Society* 12/3 (Summer 1969): 143–9.

Crofford, Gregory. *Streams of Mercy: Prevenient Grace in the Theology of John and Charles Wesley.* Lexington, KY: Emeth, 2010.

Davies, Brian. *Thomas Aquinas's Summa Contra Gentiles: A Guide and Commentary.* Oxford: Oxford University Press, 2016.

DeYoung, Rebecca Konyndyk, Colleen McCluskey, and Christina Van Dyke. *Aquinas's Ethics: Metaphysical Foundations, Moral Theory, and Theological Context*. Notre Dame, IN: University of Notre Dame Press, 2009.

Dodds, Michael J. *The One Creator God in Thomas Aquinas and Contemporary Theology*. Washington, DC: Catholic University of America Press, 2020.

Duffy, Stephen J. *The Graced Horizon: Nature and Grace in Modern Catholic Thought*. Collegeville, MN: Michael Glazier/Liturgical, 1992.

Dunning, H. Ray. *Grace, Faith, and Holiness: A Wesleyan Systematic Theology*. Kansas City, MO: Beacon Hill Press, 1988.

Eitenmiller, Melissa. "Grace as Participation according to St. Thomas Aquinas." *New Blackfriars* (2016): 689–708.

Ernst, Cornelius. "Introduction." In *Summa Theologiae, Vol. 30 (Ia2ae. 106-114): The Gospel of Grace*, edited by Cornelius Ernst, xv–xxvii. Cambridge: Cambridge University Press, 1972.

Fowler, Edward. *The Principles and Practices of Certain Moderate Divines of the Church of England (Greatly Mis-understood), Truly Represented and Defended*. London: Lodowick Lloyd, 1670.

Garrigou-Lagrange, Reginald. *Grace: Commentary on the Summa Theologica of St. Thomas, Ia IIae, q. 109–114*. Translated by Dominican Nuns of Corpus Christi Monastery. St. Louis, MO: B. Herder, 1952.

Gatiss, Lee. ed. *The Sermons of George Whitefield, Volume 1*. Wheaton, IL: Crossway, 2012.

———. *The Sermons of George Whitefield, Volume 2*. Wheaton, IL: Crossway, 2012.

George, Augustin and Pierre Grelot, "Charisms." In *Dictionary of Biblical Theology*, edited by Xavier Leon-Dufour, 68–71. London: Geoffrey Chapman, 1978.

Gibson, W., P. S. Forsaith, and M. Wellings. eds. *The Ashgate Research Companion to World Methodism*. Farnham, UK: Ashgate Publishing, 2013.

Gilby, Thomas. "Appendix 8: Natural and Supernatural." In *Summa Theologiae, Vol.1: Christian Theology (Ia. 1)*, edited by Thomas Gilby, 99–101. Cambridge: Blackfriars, 1964.

Gilman, Daniel Coit, Harry Thurston Peck, and Frank Moore Colby. eds. *The New International Encyclopaedia, Volume 2*. New York: Dodd, Mead and Company, 1902.

Gritsch, Eric W. and Robert W. Jenson. *Lutheranism: The Theological Movement and Its Confessional Writings*. Philadelphia, PA: Fortress Press, 1976.

Gunter, Stephen. *The Limits of Love Divine: John Wesley's Response to Antinomianism and Enthusiasm*. Nashville, TN: Abingdon Press, 1989.

Hannah, Vern A. "Original Sin and Sanctification: A Problem for Wesleyans." *Wesleyan Theological Journal* 18, no. 2 (Fall 1983): 47–53.

Harvey, Susan Ashbrook and David G. Hunter. eds. *The Oxford Handbook of Early Christian Studies*. Oxford: Oxford University Press, 2008.

Herbert, Thomas W. *John Wesley as Editor and Author*. Princeton, NJ: Princeton University Press, 1940.

Hillerbrand, Hans J. ed. *The Oxford Encyclopedia of the Reformation*, 4 vols. New York: Oxford University Press, 1996.

Hillerbrand, Hans J. and Robert Kolb. eds. *The Encyclopedia of Protestantism: D-K*. New York, London: Routledge, 2004.

Houck, Daniel W. *Aquinas, Original Sin, and the Challenge of Evolution*. Cambridge: Cambridge University Press, 2020.

____. "*Natura Humana Relicta est Christo*: Thomas Aquinas on the Effects of Original Sin." *Archa Verbi* 13 (2016): 68–102.

Houston, Joel. *Wesley, Whitefield and the 'Free Grace' Controversy: The Crucible of Methodism*. London and New York: Routledge, 2019.

Hughes, P. H. *The Theology of the English Reformers*. London: Hodder and Stoughton, 1965.

Hwang, Alexander Y. *Intrepid Lover of Perfect Grace: The Life and Thought of Prosper of Aquitaine*. Washington, DC: Catholic University of America Press, 2009.

Hynson, Leon O. "Original Sin as Privation: An Inquiry into a Theology of Sin and Sanctification." *Wesleyan Theological Journal* 22, no. 2 (Fall 1987): 65–83.

Ilić, Luka. *Theologian of Sin and Grace: The Process of Radicalization in the Theology of Matthias Flacius Illyricus*. Göttingen: Vandenhoeck & Ruprecht, 2014.

Johnson, Keith L. and David Lauber. eds. *T&T Clark Companion to the Doctrine of Sin*. London and New York: Bloomsbury T&T Clark, 2016.

Jones, Scott J. *John Wesley's Conception and Use of Scripture*. Nashville, TN: Kingswood Books, 1995.

Knell, Matthew. *Sin, Grace, and Free Will, Volume 1: A Historical Survey of Christian Thought*. Cambridge: James Clarke, 2017.

Knight III, Henry H. "Love and Freedom 'by Grace Alone' in Wesley's Soteriology: A Proposal for Evangelicals." *PNEUMA: The Journal of the Society for Pentecostal Studies* 24, no. 1 (Spring 2002): 57–67.

Kurtz, Johann Heinrich. *Church History, Volume 2*. Translated by John MacPherson. New York: Funk and Wagnalls Company, 1889.

____. *History of the Christian Church: From the Reformation to the Present Time*. London: T. & T. Clark, 1864.

Lancaster, Sarah H. "Current Debates over Wesley's Legacy among His Progeny." In *The Cambridge Companion to John Wesley*, edited by Randy L. Maddox and Jason E. Vickers, 298–316. New York: Cambridge University Press, 2010.

Lee, Umphrey. *John Wesley and Modern Religion*. Nashville, TN: Cokesbury Press, 1936.

Letter, P. De. "Hereditary Guilt." *Irish Theological Quarterly* 20 (1953): 350–65.

____. "The Transmission of Original Sin." *Irish Theological Quarterly* 24 (1957): 339–45.

Levering, Matthew. *Paul in the Summa Theologiae*. Washington, DC: Catholic University of America Press, 2014.

Livingston, Neil R. *A Calvinistic Concept of Prevenient Grace* [Master's Thesis, Dallas Theological Seminary]. Proquest Dissertations and Theses Global, 1961.

Locke, Kenneth A. *The Church in Anglican Theology: An Historical, Theological and Ecumenical Exploration*. Aldershot: Ashgate, 2009.

Lombardo, Nicholas E., O.P. "Evil, Suffering, and Original Sin." In *The Oxford Handbook of Catholic Theology*, edited by Lewis Ayres and Medi Ann Volpe, 138–50. Oxford: Oxford University Press, 2019.

Lonergan, Bernard. *Grace and Freedom: Operative Grace in the Thought of St Thomas Aquinas*. Edited by Frederick M. Crowe and Robert E. Doran. Toronto: University of Toronto Press, 2000.

Long, D. Stephen. *John Wesley's Moral Theology: The Quest for God and Goodness*. Nashville, TN: Kingswood Books, 2005.

Loyer, Kenneth M. *God's Love through the Spirit: The Holy Spirit in Thomas Aquinas and John Wesley*. Washington, DC: Catholic University Press of America, 2014.

Lukken, G. M. *Original Sin in the Roman Liturgy: Research into the Theology of Original Sin in the Roman Sacramentaria and the Early Baptismal Liturgy*. Leiden: Brill, 1973.

Luther, Martin. *On the Bondage of the Will Luther and Erasmus: Free Will and Salvation*. Translated by E. Gordon Rupp. Louisville: Westminster John Knox, 2006.

Maddox, Randy L. "Be Ye Perfect?" *Christian History* 69 (2001): 32–4.

____. "John Wesley and Eastern Orthodoxy: Influences, Convergences and Differences." *The Asbury Theological Journal* 45, no. 2 (1990): 29–53.

____. *Responsible Grace: John Wesley's Practical Theology*. Nashville, TN: Abingdon Press, 1994.

____. ed. *Rethinking Wesley's Theology for Contemporary Methodism*. Nashville, TN: Kingswood Books, 1998.

Magrath, O. "St. Thomas' Theory of Original Sin." *Thomist* (1953): 161–89.

Malony, Jr. H. Newton. *The Amazing John Wesley: An Unusual Look at an Uncommon Life*. Downers Grove, IL: InterVarsity Press, 2012.

Marin-Sola, Francisco, O.P. *Do not Resist the Spirit's Call*. Washington, DC: Catholic University of America Press, 2013.

Marshall, John. "The Ecclesiology of the Latitude-men, 1660–1689: Stillingfleet, Tillotson and 'Hobbism.'" *Journal of Ecclesiastical History* 36 (1985): 407–27.

Matthaei, Sondra Higgins. *Making Disciples: Faith Formation in the Wesleyan Tradition*. Nashville, TN: Abingdon Press, 2000.

Matthews, Rex D. "John Wesley's Idea of Christian Perfection Reconsidered." *Wesleyan Theological Journal* 50, no. 2 (2015): 25–67.

Maximus the Confessor. *On the Cosmic Mystery of Jesus Christ: Selected Writings from St. Maximus the Confessor*. Crestwood, NY: St. Vladimir's Seminary Press, 2003.

____. "The Four Hundred Chapters on Love." In *Maximus the Confessor: Selected Writings*, translated by George C. Berthold, 33–98. Mahwah, NJ: Paulist, 1985.

McDonald, Jr. Paul A. "*Original Justice, Original Sin and the Free-Will Defense.*" *The Thomist* 74 (2010): 105–41.

McGonigle, Herbert Boyd. *Sufficient Saving Grace: John Wesley's Evangelical Arminianism*. Carlisle, UK: Paternoster Press, 2001.

McGrath, Alister E. *Christian Theology: An Introduction*. Chichester, UK: Wiley Blackwell, 2011.

____. *Iustitia Dei: A History of the Christian Doctrine of Justification, Second Edition*. Cambridge: Cambridge University Press, 1998.

Meilaender, Gilbert. *The Freedom of a Christian: Grace, Vocation, and the Meaning of Our Humanity*. Grand Rapids, MI: Brazos Press, 2006.

Meinert, John M. *Donum Habituale: Grace and the Gifts of the Holy Spirit in St. Thomas Aquinas* [Doctoral dissertation, The Catholic University of America]. Proquest Dissertations and Theses Global, 2015.

Meyendorff, John. *Christ in Eastern Christian Thought*. St Vladimir's Seminary Press, 1975.

Miller, Rev. Joseph B. D. *The Thirty-Nine Articles of the Church of England: The Ninth Article, Hamartiology*. London: Simpkin, Marshall, & Co., 1885.

Mittelstadt, James. *Path to Wisdom: Introducing Western Philosophy*. Singapore: Partridge Publishing, 2014.

Murphy, Tim. "Natural Law and Natural Justice: A Thomistic Perspective." In *Research Handbook on Natural Law Theory*, edited by Jonathan Crowe and Constance Youngwon Lee, 304–25. Cheltenham, UK: Edward Elgar Publishing, 2019.

Newman, John Henry. *The Via Media of the Anglican Church Illustrated in Lectures, Letters and Tracts Written between 1830 and 1841*. London: Longmans, 1901.

Noia, J. A. Di, O.P. "Not 'Born Bad': The Catholic Truth about Original Sin in a Thomistic Perspective." *The Thomist* 81 (2017): 345–59.

O'Callaghan, Paul. *Children of God in the World: An Introduction to Theological Anthropology*. Washington, DC: Catholic University of America Press, 2016.

Oakes, Edward T., S.J. "Scheeben the Reconciler: Resolving the Nature-Grace Debate." *Nova et Vetera* (English Edition) 11, no. 2 (2013): 435–53.

Oden, Thomas C. *Doctrinal Standards in the Wesleyan Tradition: Revised Edition.* Nashville, TN: Abingdon Press, 2008.

_____. *John Wesley's Scriptural Christianity: A Plain Exposition of His Teaching on Christian Doctrine.* Grand Rapids, MI: Zondervan, 1994.

_____. *The Transforming Power of Grace.* Nashville, TN: Abingdon Press, 1993.

Ogliari, Donato. *Gratia Et Certamen: The Relationship between Grace and Free Will in the Discussion of Augustine with the So-called Semipelagians.* Leuven, Belgium: Peeters, 2003.

Olson, Mark K. "John Wesley's Doctrine of Sin Revisited." *Wesleyan Theological Journal* 47, no. 2 (Fall 2012): 53–71.

_____. *John Wesley's 'A Plain Account of Christian Perfection': The Annotated Edition.* Fenwick: Alethea In Heart, 2005.

Outler, Albert C. *Theology in the Wesleyan Spirit.* Nashville, TN: Tidings, 1975.

Parry, Ken. ed. *The Wiley Blackwell Companion to Patristics.* Chichester, UK: Wiley Blackwell, 2019.

Pseudo-Macarius. *The Fifty Spiritual Homilies and The Great Letter.* Translated by George A. Maloney. New York, NY: Paulist Press, 1992.

Ramirez, Jacobus M. *Opera Omnia Tomus IX: De Gratia Dei in I-II Summa Theologiae Divi Thomae Expositio.* Salamanca: Editorial San Esteban, 1992.

Rogers, Charles A. *The Concept of Prevenient Grace in the Theology of John Wesley* [Doctoral dissertation, Duke University, 1967]. Proquest Dissertations and Theses Global, 1967.

_____. "John Wesley and William Tilly." *Proceedings of the Wesleyan Historical Society* 35 (June 1966): 137–41.

Runyon, Theodore. *The New Creation: John Wesley's Theology Today.* Nashville, TN: Abingdon Press, 1998.

Russell, Robert P. "Introduction." In *The Teacher; The Free Choice of the Will; Grace and Free Will*, translated by Robert P. Russell, 3–6. Washington, DC: Catholic University of America Press, 2010.

Sammons, Peter. *Reprobation: From Augustine to the Synod of Dort: The Historical Development of the Reformed Doctrine of Reprobation.* Göttingen: Vandenhoeck & Ruprecht, 2020.

Sanders, Fred. *Wesley on the Christian Life: The Heart Renewed in Love.* Wheaton, IL: Crossway, 2013.

Schreiner, Thomas S. "Does Scripture Teach Prevenient Grace in the Wesleyan Sense?" In *The Grace of God, the Bondage of the Will, Volume 2: Historical and Theological Perspectives on Calvinism*, edited by Thomas R. Schreiner and Bruce A. Ware, 365–83. Grand Rapids, MI: Baker Pub Group, 1995.

Shelton, W. Brian. *Prevenient Grace: God's Provision for Fallen Humanity.* Anderson, IN: Francis Asbury, 2014.

Shipley, David C. "Wesley and Some Calvinistic Controversies." *The Drew Gateway* XXV (1955): 195–210.

Sloyan, Gerard S. *Religions of the Book*. Lanham, MD: University Press of America, 1996.

Stucco, Guido. *God's Eternal Gift: A History of the Catholic Doctrine of Predestination from Augustine to the Renaissance*. Bloomington, IN: Xlibris Corporation, 2009.

Stump, Eleonore. "Aquinas's Account of Freedom: Intellect and Will." *The Monist* 80, no. 4 (1997): 576–97.

Swafford, Andrew Dean. *Nature and Grace: A New Approach to Thomistic Ressourcement*. Eugene, OR: Pickwick Publications, 2015.

Teske, Roland J. "The Trouble at Hadrumetum." In *Answer to the Pelagians, IV: To the Monks of Hadrumetum and Providence*, 12–7. Hyde Park, NY: New City Press, 2003.

Ting, Moi Kieng. *Augustine's and Wesley's Concepts of Prevenient Grace: A Comparative Study*. Saarbrücken, Germany: LAP Lambert Academic Publishing, 2010.

Tyson, John R. *The Way of the Wesleys*. Grand Rapids, MI: William B. Eerdmans, 2014.

Van Buskirk, Gregory P. *Icon Dignity: Nature, Grace, and Virtue in the Theologies of John Wesley and Thomas Aquinas* [Doctoral dissertation, Boston University School of Theology]. Proquest Dissertations and Theses Global, 2019.

Vandervelde, G. *Original Sin: Two Major Trends in Contemporary Roman Catholic Reinterpretation*. Amsterdam: Rodopi N.V., 1975.

Wainwright, Geoffrey. "Speaking the Truth in Love." In *A Man of the Church: Honoring the Theology, Life, and Witness of Ralph Del Colle*, edited by Michel René Barnes, 88–95. Eugene, OR: Pickwick, 2012.

Wawrykow, Joseph P. "Aquinas and Barth on Grace." In *Thomas Aquinas and Karl Barth: An Unofficial Catholic-Protestant Dialogue*, edited by Bruce L. McCormack and Thomas Joseph White, O.P., 193–211. Grand Rapids, MI: Eerdmans, 2013.

——. *God's Grace and Human Action: Merit in the Theology of St. Thomas Aquinas*. Notre Dame, IN: University of Notre Dame Press, 1996.

——. "Grace." In *The Theology of Thomas Aquinas*, edited by Rik Van Niewenhove and Joseph P. Wawrykow, 192–221. Notre Dame, MI: University of Notre Dame Press, 2005.

Weaver, Rebecca Harden. *Divine Grace and Human Agency: A Study of the Semi-Pelagian Controversy*. Macon, GA: Mercer University Press, 1996.

Weinandy, Thomas, Daniel Keating, and John Yocum, eds. *Aquinas on Scripture: An Introduction to His Biblical Commentaries*. London: T&T Clark, 2005.

Wetzel, James. *Augustine and the Limits of Virtue*. Cambridge: Cambridge University Press, 1992.

Whaling, Frank. ed. *John and Charles Wesley: Selected Prayers, Hymns, Journal Notes, Sermons, Letters, and Treatises*, Classics in American Spirituality. New York: Paulist Press, 1981.

Williams, Anna Ngaire. *The Ground of Union: Deification in Aquinas and Palamas*. New York: Oxford University Press, 1999.

Williams, L. Bryan. "Introduction." In *Via Media Philosophy—Holiness unto Truth: Intersection between Wesleyan and Roman Catholic Voices*, edited by L. Bryan Williams, vii–xiv. Newcastle: Cambridge Scholars Publishing, 2009.

Wilson, Walter. *The History and Antiquities of Dissenting Churches and Meeting Houses, in London, Westminster, and Southwark, Volume 3*. London: W. Button & Son, 1808.

Winn, Christian T. Collins. ed. *From the Margins: A Celebration of the Theological Work of Donald W. Dayton*. Eugene, OR: Pickwick, 2007.

World Methodist Council. *Synthesis: Together in Holiness—40 Years of Methodist and Roman Catholic Dialogue*. Lake Junaluska, NC: The World Methodist Council, 2010.

Online Sources

"Prevenient Grace," Jeff Paton, "n.d.," accessed April 21, 2020, <http://www.eternalsecurity.us/prevenient_grace.htm>.

"Prevenient Grace," Pastor D. L. Hartman, "n.d.," accessed April 21, 2020, <http://www.imarc.cc/pregrace/hartpg.html>.

"Recent Dissertations in Wesley Studies: Randy L. Maddox [Last Updated: January 19, 2018] - PDF," accessed January 19, 2018, <http://religiondocbox.com/Christianity/70251723-Recent-dissertations-in-wesley-studies-randy-l-maddox-last-updated-january-19-2018.html>.

"The Call to Holiness: From Glory to Glory" – PDF," accessed December 20, 2019, <http://worldmethodistconference.com/wp-content/uploads/2016/01/The-Call-to-Holiness-Final-copy-28062016.pdf>.

"The Word of Life: A Statement on Revelation and Faith – PDF," accessed December 10, 2019, <http://www.vatican.va/roman_curia/pontifical_councils/chrstuni/meth-council-docs/rc_pc_chrstuni_doc_19951115_word-life-rio_en.html>.

Index

Printed by
CPI books GmbH, Leck